SAKHAROV SPEAKS

SAKHAROV

SPEAKS

ANDREI D. SAKHAROV

Edited and with a Foreword
by HARRISON E. SALISBURY

ALFRED A. KNOPF | NEW YORK | 1974

CONTENTS

v

SAKHAROV SPEAKS

FOREWORD

On June 22, 1941, a thin, tall, blond, shy young student named Andrei Dmitrivich Sakharov had just completed his third year in the physics faculty of Moscow University. At noon on that warm sunshiny day he—like all Russians—was stunned to hear on the radio the voice of Foreign Minister Molotov announcing that Russia was at war, that Germany had attacked before dawn that morning. The immediate impulse of the twenty-year-old Sakharov was to join his classmates in a rush to the colors, to sign up for service in the Soviet armed forces. But this was not to be. Sakharov was regarded as possibly the most brilliant physics student in the memory of the Moscow faculty. He was, in effect, declared a national asset, reserved from military duty. Graduating in 1942, he spent the rest of the war years as an engineer in a military fac-

3

tory. In 1947, at the age of twenty-six, he received a degree of Candidate of Doctor of Science. There is no precise American equivalent of this degree, but it is an academic achievement somewhat comparable to an American Ph.D.

Sakharov's degree was awarded for work in cosmic-ray theory at the famous Lebedev Institute of Physics of the Soviet Academy of Science, where he had joined the "Tamm group," an extraordinary constellation of young physicists who had gathered around the future Nobel laureate Dr. Igor E. Tamm.

The brilliance of young physicists is, of course, axiomatic. Not a few look back from the sturdy age of twenty-six or twenty-seven to say, "My best work was done at twenty-two." Sakharov's genius by no means peaked at twenty-two, but the vigor and creativity of his youthful mind were consistent with the tradition of physics scholarship.

Before he was twenty-seven Sakharov had appeared in the Soviet *Journal of Experimental and Theoretical Physics* with two papers, one on the generation of a hard component of cosmic rays (probably drawn from his doctoral thesis) and another, foreshadowing his new era of concentration, concerning the interaction of electrons and positrons. One more scientific paper under Sakharov's signature was published in 1948. It dealt with the "temperature of excitation in plasma of a gaseous discharge." From then on, silence. For nearly a decade the name of Sakharov vanished. No published research, no papers, no citations. Nothing. It was as though Russia's most promising young scientist had disappeared without a trace.

As we now know, Sakharov did not vanish. He, together with Tamm and others, had been put to work in deepest secrecy developing the principles of the H-bomb, and, indeed, by 1950 Sakharov and Tamm had perfected the method of an electrical discharge in a plasma, placed in a magnetic field, which produces a thermonuclear reaction, i.e., the H-bomb.

For these achievements and others connected with the theory and production of the hydrogen weapon Sakharov was to receive—in secret—the Stalin Prize, three Orders of Socialist Labor (the highest civilian honor in the Soviet Union), and an extraordinary salary fixed by the Kremlin of two thousand rubles a month, about twenty-seven thousand dollars a year at current exchange rates; every possible privilege in living comforts, special housing, chauffeurs, access to restricted consumer goods; and a twenty-four-hour-a-day bodyguard who accompanied him everywhere—even when he went swimming and skiing.

But no one outside a few scientists holding the highest security clearances, the principal officers of the Soviet government, and, of course, of the Ministry of Medium Machine Construction (as the Soviet Union called and still calls its atomic energy agency) knew of the existence of this still thin, still blond, still shy, still incredibly brilliant young man who would at the age of thirty-two be elected in 1953 a full member of the Soviet Academy of Sciences and named a Doctor of Science. He was the youngest man ever so honored, an honor underlined by the fact that in the same year in which he catapulted to full membership his remarkable colleague, Dr. Tamm, after *twenty years* as a corresponding member of the Academy, also was named a full member.

It is obvious that in speaking of Sakharov we are

speaking of one of the great intellects of our age—a man whose name flows easily and naturally into the rhythm of the list of those like Rutherford, Einstein, Bohr, Heisenberg, Kapitsa, and Oppenheimer, whose minds have changed the world.

There is clearly something about the discipline of physics that causes a great physicist to look beyond the formulas, the theorems, the infinitely intricate hypotheses by which he tests and determines the natural laws of the universe and into the seemingly simpler but actually much more complex phenomena of man's society. Or, perhaps, this is an illusion. Perhaps it is simply that with their finely tuned minds the physicists are able to penetrate more swiftly and more deeply the murk and bias with which human beings normally shroud their affairs.

Whatever the cause, it is a fact that after Einstein elaborated his great Theory of Relativity his mind began to struggle with questions of war and peace. Oppenheimer turned from the A-bomb to the deep humanistic implications of the role of a scientist in society. So have many others.

Thus it is not surprising that at the advanced age of thirty-seven Andrei Sakharov, still cloaked by the deepest of security classifications (although he had managed to publish an article on U-meson reaction in hydrogen in the *Journal of Experimental and Theoretical Physics* with his close collaborator Yakov Zeldovich in 1957), began to thrust his thoughts outward—from the intense, narrow world of applied physics and nuclear weapons production and away from the remote center where he and his colleagues conducted their research in monastic seclusion—to the more earthly problems of the society in which he lived.

That process, slowly gathering momentum and steadily broadening in scope, is still going on and, much more than his fathership of the Soviet H-bomb, is why the name Sakharov is today known throughout the world as the symbol of global humanitarianism.

The Russian society that formed and shaped Sakharov had undergone enormous changes even in the brief period of his life. Born in Moscow in 1921, when the flames of civil war and revolution were just flickering out, Sakharov was the son of a physicist, Dmitri Sakharov, well-known, respected, author of a familiar classroom physics text, and a professor at the Lenin Pedagogical Institute. Thus Sakharov was born into a well-known stratum of Russian society, the scientific intelligentsia, and it is this circumstance that has given to his life its characteristic content and luminosity. The Russian *intelligent* has no precise counterpart in other societies. He is not simply a university graduate or an individual given over to intellectual pursuits. He is not, for example, a white-collar man as opposed to a blue-collar man. In fact, it is not his academic or economic status that distinguishes the Russian *intelligent* but, rather, his moral and social outlook, his sense of dedication to principle, to the improvement of the lot of his fellow man, to the elimination of social evils, to selflessness, to the moral imperative of speaking the truth as he believes it, regardless of physical and material consequences. He is imbued, to some extent, by the traditional spirit of Russian universalism. He believes in the perfectability of man and in his own duty to put sacrifice above self. The ideals of the Russian *intelligent* were nourished during the long and bloody years of struggle against the backwardness and tyranny of the Czarist regime. They gave the revolutionary movement moral fervor and philosophical justification. And, as difficult as the Soviet period proved to be, with its police, its repressions, its purges, its propaganda, and its thought control, the unique spirit of the Russian *intelligent,* like a phoenix, has survived.

It was in this milieu of earnest, dedicated, passionately honest, fiercely principled scientists and thinkers, writers and philosophers, that Sakharov's early years were spent and in which, to be certain, he has continued to live during his adult life, even though the strict regulations of Soviet security (not to mention his own fierce concentration on nuclear and cosmic studies) tended to limit the range of his social and personal contacts.

It was probably inevitable that at a certain point a man of Sakharov's upbringing would begin to turn his attention to subjects outside the world of physics. He had been able to morally sustain his intense preoccupation with weapons research and theory in the belief, as he expressed it, that "I was working for peace." At the time he and Tamm began their research on the problem of the H-bomb the Soviet Union had just conducted her first successful A-bomb test (in October 1949). The crash program initiated by Stalin to match the American nuclear breakthrough of 1945 had paid off with startling swiftness under the forced draft of a research and production effort headed by Lavrenti P. Beria, Stalin's notorious chief of secret police. Production of the 1949 A-bomb left Russia far from parity with the huge American nuclear inventory steadily piled up in the years after the war, yet the Soviet A-bomb was a critically important achievement, which gave Russia at least the possibility of nuclear response to an American strike. But much more was needed if parity in deterrence was to be achieved—a long-range missile and rocket program (which ultimately gave the Soviets the ICBM and Sputnik) and a new generation of nuclear weapons, which physicists knew had to be the H-bomb. It was this achievement that was attained by Sakharov and Tamm. They had nothing to do with the A-bomb program or the rocket program, but in a breakneck race with American scientists the Russian team won. They produced an H-bomb before the Americans and for the first time gave the Kremlin a guarantee that Russia was now qualitatively ahead of the United States, even if still far behind quantitatively.

To Sakharov this undertaking was clearly in the cause of humanity. If, he reasoned, both the United States and the Soviet Union possessed this terrible nuclear capability, they would be compelled to draw the logical conclusions—to negotiate their differences rather than destroy each other and the world. Nourished by this conviction (which hardly differs from the convictions of many of the physicists who worked on the American A-bomb, such as Oppenheimer, Bethe, Szilard, and others), Sakharov seems to have had no moral problems with his H-bomb weapons work. In this it should be noted that he differed, as did Tamm, from the most famous of Russian physicists, Peter Kapitsa, who refused Stalin's request to work on the A-bomb and, in consequence, was held under house arrest for a number of years.

The watershed in Sakharov's evolution from brilliant weapons physicist to concerned Soviet and world citizen came in 1957–8. By this time Soviet security vis-à-vis the United States had been assured with the H-bomb and the ICBM. Soviet international prestige had been raised high by Sputnik and the Soviet space program, which the United States was now frantically attempting to match. The Chinese even felt that the balance of power had moved to the Communist side and Chairman Mao was confidently proclaiming that "the East Wind prevails over the West Wind." Khrushchev, not so sanguine, was actively preparing for the move toward détente, which was to flower in 1959 with his visit to the United States and the famous "spirit of Camp David."

It was an appropriate moment for thought-taking. In 1958, though still distant from Moscow in the secret Soviet nuclear weapons research center, Sakharov moved out of theory and theorems into the field of politics and policy. He did two things—one private and one public. Privately, for the first time in his career, he sought to influence a major Soviet policy decision. There had been a six-month interval in Soviet atmospheric tests and Sakharov, convinced that further testing in the air was not needed for scientific purposes and would only tend to aggravate the arms race and increase the dangers from fallout, sought to halt a scheduled series of Soviet weapons tests. He managed to convince Igor Kurchatov, then in charge of the program. Kurchatov sought permission from Khrushchev to cancel the sequence. But Khrushchev refused and the tests went on.

In this same year, 1958, Sakharov for the first time took a public stand on a major question of public policy. He and his associate, Zeldovich, wrote a letter raising basic questions about the Soviet educational system and setting forth the principles of a new program for especially gifted children.

It was a moment when the question of educational

reform was in the forefront of discussion. Khrushchev had launched a major drive to subject Soviet education to a strong infusion of what he called "practical" work, reducing the time spent on formal studies and sending youngsters into factories and out into the fields. The educational process would be interrupted at the age of fifteen or sixteen for two or three years of practical work. Khrushchev proposed to make this a mandatory across-the-board regulation except for a few artistic students, such as those in the Soviet ballet school.

Sakharov and Zeldovich took the view that training of talented youngsters in the fields of mathematics and physics should be accelerated rather than interrupted; there should be special programs in Soviet schools that would send these pupils into the universities and institutes at the age of sixteen or seventeen, two years earlier than normal and without any factory or farm work.

Their argument was that the most productive years in pure science were those of extreme youth; the ages of twenty-two to twenty-six were probably the most creative; and every effort should be made to equip the talented student to utilize the full powers of his intellect in this "golden interlude."

Sakharov and Zeldovich proposed a thorough shaking up of mathematics instruction, the abandonment of teaching of Euclidian geometry, less emphasis on algebraic problems and trigonometry, and concentration on probability theory, analytic geometry, calculus, and vector analysis. Their appeal won the day and special treatment of mathematics-physics students was decreed.

The more Sakharov began to think about social problems and particularly the social results of his work in the field of nuclear weaponry, the more concerned he became. As he was later to tell Hedrick Smith, the *New York Times* correspondent in Moscow:

"I gradually began to understand the criminal nature not only of nuclear tests but of the enterprise as a whole. I began to look on it and other world problems from a broader, human perspective."

It was the emergence of this philosophy that slowly but surely brought Sakharov into conflict with his government. He again unsuccessfully challenged Khrushchev, in September 1961, on the necessity of a series of large-scale nuclear tests. But he did not give up. He complained violently in 1962 about a third test series, which was held despite his objections.

"I could not," he told Hedrick Smith, "stop something I knew was wrong and unnecessary. It was terrible. I had an awful sense of powerlessness. After that I was a different man. I broke with my surroundings. It was a basic break."

Sakharov shifted his attention to the broader world of science and again he took the road of public protest. Soviet genetics, biology, botany, and agronomy had for years been poisoned by the dictatorship of a charlatan named Trofim D. Lysenko, who had won Stalin's confidence. Lysenko had employed his privileged position to destroy the foundations of Soviet genetics. He hounded the principal Soviet geneticist, N. I. Vavilov, into prison and death, drove many distinguished scientists from their posts, closed down some Soviet scientific institutes, and prostituted others to his own purposes. With Stalin's death Lysenko suffered a setback, but in the early 1960's he made a brief comeback under Khrushchev's auspices.

Sakharov joined forces with two Soviet agricultural specialists, V. P. Efroimson and F. D. Shchepotyev, to attack the persistence of Lysenkoism and to blame it for a criminal lag in Soviet genetics and biological theory. Although the president of the Soviet Agricultural Academy angrily rebuked Sakharov, the criticism struck home. Lysenko's comeback was halted and the Soviet government gave to biology and the life sciences the freedom from doctrinaire political interference that had already been won by the physical sciences.

When one of Lysenko's close associates, Nikolai Nuzhdin, was nominated for membership in the Academy of Sciences, Sakharov joined with many other Academicians in opposing Nuzhdin's candidacy, and it was rejected. Later, Sakharov was active in opposing Academic status for another Party hack, an agricultural propagandist named S. P. Trapeznikov. Khrushchev was incensed at Sakharov's interference in agricultural policy and, according to rumor, told the secret police to "teach Sakharov a lesson." When Khrushchev himself fell from power the move was dropped.

Sakharov knew that others within the scientific and political milieu felt much as he did about the issues with which he was concerned, and he was heartened when the United States and the Soviet Union agreed in 1963 to halt tests in the atmosphere, space, and under water. In fact, he took some credit for this agreement, because he called the attention of Yefim Slavsky, the minister of Medium Machine Building, to the American fall-back position, which President Eisenhower had put forward in 1959 calling for such a ban. The Russian side picked up this idea and the 1963 agreement was achieved.

Sakharov paid a price, however, for his growing political activity. He was dropped a couple of notches in his scientific status and this modified the high-security classification under which he had lived since 1950. But he was able to meet more freely with other Soviet members of the intelligentsia (it was in this period that he first became acquainted with Alexander Solzhenitsyn), and he began to publish once again in scientific journals. Two articles appeared in 1965, two more in 1966, and two in 1967. Moreover, the subjects of his scientific contributions revealed that he was turning from nuclear physics to much broader fields. He was writing about such questions as the quark phenomenon and the ever-expanding universe. From the sub-micro world of the atom he had moved to the macro-world of infinite space.

It is doubtful whether Sakharov envisaged at this point where his broadening exploration of the society in which he lived would lead him. But now, residing in Moscow instead of the cloistered nuclear community in Turkmenia, Sakharov was exchanging ideas with other scientists and a broadening circle of intellectuals, each of whom felt, in one way or another, that basic changes had to be made if the Soviet system was not to sink back into the terror-haunted morass into which Stalin had led it. This conviction found expression in a petition to the Communist Party leadership just before the Twenty-third Party Congress in 1966 in which Sakharov and twenty-four others, including Tamm, Kapitsa, the liberal writers Konstantin G. Paustovsky and Viktor Nekrasov, the ballerina Maya Plisetskaya, the movie director Mikhail I. Romm, and the grand old man of Soviet diplomacy, Ivan M. Maisky, called on the Party not to rehabilitate Stalin. That, they said, "would be a great disaster."

Whether their argument was compelling, whether in fact the Party leadership had planned to put Stalin back on the pedestal, is not known. But he was not rehabilitated and the decisions of the Twenty-second Party Congress condemning him were left on the books unchanged.

By this time certain hypotheses about his own society and about the world had begun to form in Sakharov's mind and, in his careful scientific manner, he started to test out his ideas. He circulated his theses among his friends both in the scientific community and in the new world of dissenting intellectuals. These were the basic ideas that comprised his famous Manifesto—*Progress, Coexistence, and Intellectual Freedom.*

The manifesto bears the date of June 1968. This was to prove a high watermark in the movement for liberalization within the Communist world. Sakharov's views found a ready reception and warm support in many layers of the Soviet intelligentsia and, even, it was whispered, in certain circles high within the government itself. They were widely circulated in *samizdat,* the typewritten self-publication process, which swiftly carried his views to almost every larger community within the Soviet Union. Not that there was unanimity over Sakharov's opinions. The hallmark of the Russian *intelligent* is dispute, challenge, disagreement, and individuality. But the thinking of many was moving in the same direction as that of Sakharov.

What was that direction? His manifesto speaks for itself, but perhaps the tendency may be summed up as calling for genuine coexistence and cooperation on world problems by the United States and the Soviet Union; a belief in the general trend of the two systems to converge; a call for the end of the arms race and a concentration of Soviet-American resources to meet the world's critical problems, which he postulated as hunger and the uneven development of societies, racism, militarism, the wastage of resources.

In order for the Soviet Union to move forward Sakharov believed it had to liberalize internally, opening up conditions for freedom of thought and access to information, ending the censorship, ending all violations of human rights, ending the system of political prisoners, political trials, and political prisons; complete the de-Stalinization process; restrict the influence of neo-Stalinists; and carry out a general reform of the Soviet economic system.

Sakharov emphasized the tentativeness of many of his conclusions and called for frank, open discussion of his ideas with full publicity—not only within the Soviet Union but also throughout the world.

This discussion did not occur. Sakharov's manifesto was published in the United States, western Europe, and ultimately in almost all the world—except the Communist nations. It evoked intense interest in the United States. In many universities small Sakharov groups were formed, often with physicists as their nuclei, hoping to collaborate with Russian colleagues toward Sakharov's goals. But the manifesto was circulated in Russia only by underground means, and it was not discussed publicly except in polemical terms that distorted and concealed the nature of Sakharov's thinking.

The brutal suppression of the Czech government, and the proclamation of the "Brezhnev doctrine," which sought to justify Soviet armed intervention in any Communist country if there was a putative threat to what Moscow defined as the stability of the Communist world, closed off any hope that Sakharov's ideas would be permitted intelligent consideration within the Soviet Union.

The new atmosphere was quickly reflected in Sakharov's own life. He was discharged from the nuclear weapons program in an action taken with typical Soviet brutality. One morning he arrived at the laboratory as usual in his chauffeur-driven car (which he still has, one of the perquisites of being an Academician). But when he approached the working area the guard refused to admit him, saying that his security clearance had been withdrawn. Somewhat later he was told that he no longer had a job. It was nearly a year later that, apparently in embarrassment, Soviet authorities gave him a small position in the Lebedev Institute (where he had started his career) as a senior researcher, the lowest status in which one of his rank as Academician is permitted to be employed.

The new atmosphere found reflection in Sakharov's own conduct. More and more often he signed his name to petitions for intellectuals who had fallen into the hands of the secret police. He began to appear at the trials of writers and poets. When, as often happened, he was not permitted to enter the courtroom, he stood vigil outside in sub-zero temperatures with the handful of other Soviet dissidents who possessed the bravery, the fortitude, and the conviction to stand for hours under the harassment, sometimes physical, of Soviet police and plainclothes thugs.

Sakharov's wife died at this time, and a year later he remarried. He met his second wife on one of the protest vigils. She is Yelena Bonner, half-Armenian, half-Jewish (one of the slanders Soviet propagandists spew against Sakharov is that he is really a Jew named Sugarman), the daughter of a woman who spent sixteen years in Stalinist prison camps and aunt of Eduard Kuznetsov, who received a fifteen-year sentence in the Leningrad hijacking trial.

Exposed to the half-world of Soviet dissidence, Sakharov's views steadily evolved. He directed the force of his analytic powers more and more not at the secrets of atomic nuclei but at the complex and contradictory aspects of Soviet life.

Early in 1970, recognizing that some of the precepts of his manifesto had been overrun by events and also because his own thinking was in a steady process of evolution, Sakharov issued a second programmatic document, this one signed not only by himself but also by the physicist Valentin F. Turchin and the historian Roy A. Medvedev.

The new document, sometimes referred to as Manifesto II, had a different thrust from the first. It was couched in the form of a letter to the Soviet leadership —Leonid I. Brezhnev, Aleksei N. Kosygin, and Nikolai V. Podgorny—and predominantly addressed itself to the major internal problems of the Soviet Union: the slowing down of the economy, Soviet failure to meet the challenge of the computer world, which Sakharov described as "the second industrial revolution," the increasing need for free exchange of information and thought, the stultifying bureaucracy, the adventurous nature of Soviet foreign policy, especially in the Middle East, and the possibility that unless the course was swiftly changed, the Soviet Union would sink rapidly to the status of second-rate power.

"There is no way out of the difficulties facing the

country," Sakharov and his colleagues declared, "except a course toward democratization carried out by the Party in accordance with a carefully worked out program."

This document was forwarded to the Soviet leadership in March 1970 but evoked no response.

Convinced that the core of the problem lay in the consistent, tenacious refusal of the Soviet leadership to grant its people normal freedoms of thought, of speech, of inquiry, of assemblage, of philosophical speculation, of a principled rule of law, Sakharov in 1970 took the remarkable step of forming with two young physicist friends what they called the Committee on Human Rights. The Committee, in its founding declaration signed by Sakharov, A. N. Tverdokhlebov and V. N. Chalidze, November 4, 1970, declared its intent to work within the framework of Soviet law to assist in creating and implementing guarantees of human rights based upon the humanitarian principles of the Universal Declaration of Human Rights adopted by the United Nations in 1948. The Committee proposed to assist persons concerned with the research and study of human rights in a socialist society, to carry on legal education in this field, and to engage in "constructive criticism of the contemporary state of the system of legal guarantees of individual liberty in Soviet law."

Both Tverdokhlebov and Chalidze promptly lost their positions as a result of their membership in the Committee. Chalidze was finally permitted to come to the United States in 1972 with his wife to deliver a series of lectures. Shortly after his arrival two Soviet officials obtained his passport under false pretenses in the lobby of the hotel where he was staying and immediately declared he had been deprived of Soviet citizenship. (A similar trick was played in London on Zhores Medvedev, brother of Roy A. Medvedev, who was associated with Sakharov in signing the 1970 manifesto. Zhores, a biologist, had been briefly confined to a Soviet mental institution as part of the Soviet campaign of repression of intellectuals. He was freed after protests from his brother, Sakharov, Solzhenitsyn, and others. He was then permitted to go to London to engage in scientific work and there, as in the case of Chalidze, a Soviet official persuaded him to hand over his passport and then promptly declared that he had been deprived of citizenship.)

Under the impact of these events Sakharov's scientific career came to a virtual standstill. Through 1973 he continued to go to the Lebedev Institute once a week to participate in a seminar on quantum theory, but he told friends that under the circumstances of his life he was unable to do any really fruitful work. In fact, he expressed concern whether at his age and after such a long interlude he would be able to make any further major contributions to physical theory.

He faced other unpleasantness. The three children of his first marriage, two married daughters and a sixteen-year-old son, began to shun him. The son went to live with his eldest daughter. His stepdaughter, who was studying in Moscow University's journalism school, was dismissed. Her husband, an engineer, lost his job. A sixteen-year-old stepson was barred from Moscow University, his examination papers deliberately tampered with by authorities. Later, the boy was admitted to the Lenin Pedagogical Institute.

None of these discouragements swayed Sakharov from what had become the central purpose of his life—the struggle for the renaissance of Soviet society and the liberation of the system from the repressive framework that he was convinced would produce nothing but disaster.

On March 5, 1971, the eighteenth anniversary of Stalin's death and three years after composing his original manifesto, Sakharov again addressed himself to Party Secretary Brezhnev. Recalling his 1968 Declaration and the letter of 1970 signed by himself, Medvedev, and Turchin, he submitted a new document further refining his views on the critical issues confronting the Soviet Union. He enclosed for Brezhnev's information some basic documentation on the Committee on Human Rights.

Sakharov's goals were unchanged. Once again, he called for a general liberalization, an end to the political prison system, an end to the use of psychiatric institutions to punish sane prisoners, full legal rights for all Soviet citizens, an end to repressions on political, ideological, and religious grounds, freedom of information and press, full restoration of the rights of all nationalities and individuals repressed by Stalin, a rule of law, an end to dogmatism, adventurism, and aggression. He called for basic economic reform, democratic elections, efforts to modernize agriculture, a radical improvement in the educational system, a full-scale anti-pollution and environmental program.

Sakharov had less to say on international relations, but he called for an international conference on the problems of peace, disarmament, economic aid to backward countries, defense of human rights, and protection of the environment. He agreed with the Kremlin that the principal threat to Russia came from China.

Once again, there was no response from Brezhnev.

A year later, in June 1972, he addressed to Brezhnev a fourth memorandum, a postscript to that of March 5, 1971, in which he urged "the democratization of society, the development of openness in public affairs, the rule of law and the safeguarding of basic human rights." These he deemed to be of decisive importance. He sharply criticized Soviet "apathy, hypocrisy, petit bourgeois egoism and hidden cruelty," the secret privileges of the elite, their indifference to human rights, progress, genuine security, and the future of mankind.

"The country's spiritual regeneration," he declared, "demands the elimination of those conditions that drive people into becoming hypocritical and time-serving, and that lead to feelings of impotence, discontent, and disillusionment."

He struck again at the failing Soviet standards of education and public health and expressed alarm at the rising wave of political arrests and repressions.

This time he concentrated almost exclusively on domestic Soviet concerns except for a passing reference to the Soviet industrial-military complex, which, he said, played a role analogous to that of the United States in foreign relations.

By this time the growing police repression against intellectuals had severely reduced Sakharov's circle of friends and associates and had begun to limit his influence within the intelligentsia, and more Soviet citizens began to perceive the potential danger of association with or contact with Sakharov.

The year 1973 was marked by constantly rising struggle. Soviet authorities brought their campaign against Sakharov into the open. Polemic attacks and increased police surveillance became common. Sakharov was called in by Mikhail P. Malyarov, first deputy Prosecutor General, the number two Soviet law enforcement officer, and warned that his conduct was under the strictest government scrutiny. Malyarov hinted that Sakharov might be prosecuted for violation of the Soviet state secrets act.

Simultaneously, a storm was whipped up against Sakharov in the Party press. Party speakers denounced him in their agitational meetings. The stage, it appeared, was being set for the public trial and conviction of Sakharov and his sentencing to the Soviet prison camp system, against which he had so long campaigned.

Then came a sudden turn. Sakharov, mild of manner, shy of appearance, began to fight back. He granted a series of interviews, including a notable discussion over Swedish radio in which he laid his case before world public opinion. He revealed his growing disenchantment with the Soviet system and his increasing doubt that it could, in fact, be regenerated from within. He was, he explained, not a Communist himself. "Philosophically, I am a liberal and a humanist," he said. The Soviet Union, he felt, had drifted away from Marxism and now was marked by intolerance, great-power chauvinism, hypocrisy, brutality, illegality, egoism, and conformism. He saw it as a pragmatic state not a doctrinal one, and he found himself growing more and more skeptical of socialism as a theory. He found less and less in its ability to solve in some special way the great problems of the world. States with socialist systems, he believed, tended to have the same kinds of problems as capitalist states. And the Soviet Union, he believed, was distinguished among all states for the "maximum lack of freedom, maximum ideological rigidity and maximum pretentions about being the best society although it certainly is not that."

Sakharov's thinking in the years of his political awareness has been characterized by deep, continuous development. When he began to move out of the sheltered world of nuclear physics, his first interest lay in the societal problems arising from the development of nuclear weapons. In this his course was clearly comparable to that of Oppenheimer; both felt a rising concern over the implications of a nuclearized world and of the specific consequences of nuclear weapons—fallout, the arms race, the employment of super-weapons for international blackmail. At the same time Sakharov began to turn to other problems of the society in which he lived—problems of education, of scientific development, of professional charlatanism. The deeper he moved into these questions the more his political consciousness expanded. And, much as Oppenheimer had, he began to be concerned with the issues underlying the arms race and the necessity for international collaboration in place of competition and conflict.

The Sakharov manifesto entitled *Progress, Coexistence, and Intellectual Freedom* was permeated with a humanitarian internationalist approach. He believed strongly in the possibility of parallel or converging paths for the Soviet Union and the United States. The heart of his proposal was a joint US–USSR program devised, in essence, to save the world. His domestic program—his concern with civil rights, the liberalization of Soviet society, and the end of repression—was subordinated to internationalist ideals.

With the passage of years Sakharov's emphasis steadily shifted. More and more he became concerned with the essential tyranny and banality of Soviet society and system until in the last of the four programmatic statements he focused almost entirely on Soviet life. He had become convinced that without internal change the great goals of international collaboration could not be achieved and, moreover, that the Soviet Union itself as a world power was headed toward decline and weakness because its technological-scientific intelligentsia was unable to keep the country competitively viable, especially with the United States, so long as it was subjected to the dull and dangerous dregs of the Stalinist terror system.

Throughout this period Sakharov shared Moscow's vision of Peking as the most dangerous enemy and, especially in his early writings, he merely repeated the standardized Soviet view of China as an aberrational power, unpredictable and maniacal. In fact, not until 1973 and rather late in that year did Sakharov frankly retract his early evaluations of China and express the belief that he had wrongly assessed the nature of the Sino-Soviet confrontation.

It is in the light of this evolution that Sakharov's important 1973 declaration on the Soviet-American détente must be understood. From the beginning of his consciousness of world politics he had been an advocate of détente, long before the Soviet government began to take this line and long before the Brezhnev-Nixon conversations brought it toward fulfillment.

Détente and collaboration between the Soviet Union and the United States were perceived by Sakharov as the core of a stable and secure world order. But with the passage of years it became more and more apparent to him that genuine détente could not be achieved when one partner was, in essence, only half free. Only if Russia resolved her internal contradictions, came to grips with the reality of the post-Stalin system of terror, with its police and the prison camps, only if the Soviet moved toward individual freedom, freedom of scientific inquiry, and public debate, and ended the sterility of the single-party system and the authoritarian imposition of the single Party line would the Soviet, in Sakharov's opinion, prove a reliable partner in a genuine détente.

Unless these internal problems were resolved, he was convinced, there was nothing to prevent a Soviet oligarchy from deceptively entering a pseudo-entente with the full intention of overturning it to its own advantage and thus, quite possibly, producing the destruction of the world.

It was this conviction, logically arrived at through the most systematic study, that led Sakharov to his fierce and open battle with the Soviet powers over the issue of liberalization of American trade with the Soviet Union and his opposition to close-knit economic and technological collaboration. He declared that the Soviet should not be given these advantages until or unless there was a reliable guarantee of internal Soviet liberalization.

As his struggle with Soviet authorities grew more intense, Sakharov received an invitation to come to Princeton University with his family for a year's study and lectures. Massachusetts Institute of Technology invited his stepdaughter, her husband, and his stepson to teach and study. Sakharov was reluctant to leave the Soviet Union, even if permission was granted, unless he could be assured of his return. The example of his friends

Chalidze and Medvedev, deprived of their passports and citizenship, was vivid in his mind. There was also the critical question of the Human Rights Movement in the Soviet Union. Through police repression, arrest, intimidation, and enforced deportation, few of the small band remained active in Russia. Would the movement collapse if Sakharov left, possibly never to return? This issue lay at the heart of the dilemma Sakharov faced at New Year's, 1974—a holiday he spent not in traditional celebration, nowhere gayer than in Moscow, but in a hospital with his wife, where both had gone for treatment of serious physical ailments that had begun to sap their strength. They had gone, as well, for a brief respite of calm and comparative serenity in which to review the state of the Soviet Union as it moved into its fifty-seventh year of existence and what they might best do in accordance with the credo of the Russian *intelligent* of self-sacrifice and dedication to the cause of the Russian people.

HARRISON E. SALISBURY

INTRODUCTION

This collection contains the majority of my writings and statements on social, legal, and political subjects for the past several years. Some of them require elucidation, especially for the foreign reader. No doubt the best way to avoid possible misunderstandings would be to give an account, with a maximum of detail and frankness, of the internal and external circumstances that shaped my attitude and position. But at present I do not feel capable of doing this thoroughly, and shall confine myself to the necessary minimum. In giving autobiographical information, I am hoping to put an end to false rumors with respect to facts that have frequently been misrepresented in the press, owing to ignorance or sensationalism.

I was born in 1921 in Moscow, into a cultured and close family. My father was a teacher of physics and the author of several widely known textbooks and popular-science books. From childhood I lived in an atmosphere of decency, mutual help, and tact, a liking for work, and respect for the mastery of one's chosen profession. In 1938 I completed high school and entered Moscow State University, from which I was graduated in 1942. From 1942 to 1945 I worked as an engineer at a war plant, where I developed several inventions having to do with methods of quality control.

From 1945 to 1947 I did graduate work under the guidance of a well-known Soviet scientist, the theoretical physicist Igor Evgenevich Tamm. A few months after defending my dissertation for the degree of Candidate of Doctor of Science, roughly equivalent to an American Ph.D., which occurred in the spring of 1948, I was included in a research group working on the problem of a thermonuclear weapon. I had no doubts as to the vital importance of creating a Soviet super-weapon—for our country and for the balance of power throughout the world. Carried away by the immensity of the task, I worked very strenuously and became the author or co-author of several key ideas. In the Western press I have often been called "the father of the hydrogen bomb." This description reflects very inaccurately the real (and complex) situation of collective invention—something I shall not discuss in detail.

In the summer of 1950, almost simultaneously with the beginning of work on the thermonuclear weapon, I. E. Tamm and I began work on the problem of a controlled thermonuclear reaction; i.e., on the utilization of the nuclear energy of light elements for purposes of industrial power. In 1950 we formulated the idea of the magnetic thermo-isolation of high-temperature plasma,

and completed estimates on the parameters for thermonuclear synthesis installations. This research, which became known abroad through a paper read by I. V. Kurchatov at Harwell in 1956 and through the materials of
the First Geneva Conference on the Peaceful Use of
Atomic Energy, was recognized as pioneering. In 1961 I
proposed, for the same purposes, the heating of deuterium
with a beam from a pulse laser. I mention these things
here by way of explaining that my contributions were not
limited to military problems.

In 1950 our research group became part of a special
institute. For the next eighteen years I found myself
caught up in the routine of a special world of military
designers and inventors, special institutes, committees
and learned councils, pilot plants and proving grounds.
Every day I saw the huge material, intellectual, and nervous resources of thousands of people being poured into
the creation of a means of total destruction, something
potentially capable of annihilating all human civilization.
I noticed that the control levers were in the hands of
people who, though talented in their own way, were cynical. Until the summer of 1953 the chief of the atomic
project was Beria, who ruled over millions of slave-prison-
ers. Almost all the construction was done with their
labor. Beginning in the late fifties, one got an increasingly
clearer picture of the collective might of the military-industrial complex and of its vigorous, unprincipled leaders,
blind to everything except their "job." I was in a rather
special position. As a theoretical scientist and inventor,
relatively young and (moreover) not a Party member,
I was not involved in administrative responsibility and
was exempt from Party ideological discipline. My position

enabled me to know and see a great deal. It compelled me to feel my own responsibility; and at the same time I could look upon this whole perverted system as something of an outsider. All this prompted me—especially in the ideological atmosphere that came into being after the death of Stalin and the Twentieth Congress of the CPSU —to reflect in general terms on the problems of peace and mankind, and in particular on the problems of a thermonuclear war and its aftermath.

Beginning in 1957 (not without the influence of statements on this subject made throughout the world by such people as Albert Schweitzer, Linus Pauling, and others) I felt myself responsible for the problem of radioactive contamination from nuclear explosions. As is known, the absorption of the radioactive products of nuclear explosions by the billions of people inhabiting the earth leads to an increase in the incidence of several diseases and birth defects, of so-called sub-threshold biological effects—for example, because of damage to DNA molecules, the bearers of heredity. When the radioactive products of an explosion get into the atmosphere, each megaton of the nuclear explosion means thousands of unknown victims. And each series of tests of a nuclear weapon (whether they be conducted by the United States, the USSR, Great Britain, China, or France) involves tens of megatons; i.e., tens of thousands of victims.

In my attempts to explain this problem, I encountered great difficulties—and a reluctance to understand. I wrote memorandums (as a result of one of them I. V. Kurchatov made a trip to Yalta to meet with Khrushchev in an unsuccessful attempt to stop the 1958 tests), and I spoke at conferences. I remember that in the summer of

1961 there was a meeting between atomic scientists and the chairman of the Council of Ministers, Khrushchev. It turned out that we were to prepare for a series of tests that would bolster up the new policy of the USSR on the German question (the Berlin Wall). I wrote a note to Khrushchev, saying: "To resume tests after a three-year moratorium would undermine the talks on banning tests and on disarmament, and would lead to a new round in the armaments race—especially in the sphere of intercontinental missiles and anti-missile defense." I passed it up the line. Khrushchev put the note in his breast pocket and invited all present to dine. At the dinner table he made an off-the-cuff speech that I remember for its frankness, and that did not reflect merely his personal position. He said more or less the following: Sakharov is a good scientist. But leave it to us, who are specialists in this tricky business, to make foreign policy. Only force—only the disorientation of the enemy. We can't say aloud that we are carrying out our policy from a position of strength, but that's the way it must be. I would be a slob, and not chairman of the Council of Ministers, if I listened to the likes of Sakharov. In 1960 we helped to elect Kennedy with our policy. But we don't give a damn about Kennedy if he is tied hand and foot—if he can be overthrown at any moment.

Another and no less dramatic episode occurred in 1962. The Ministry, acting basically from bureaucratic interests, issued instructions to proceed with a routine test explosion that was actually useless from the technical point of view. The explosion was to be powerful, so that the number of anticipated victims was colossal. Realizing the unjustifiable, criminal nature of this plan, I made desperate efforts to stop it. This went on for several weeks—

weeks that, for me, were full of tension. On the eve of the test I phoned the minister and threatened to resign. The minister replied: "We're not holding you by the throat." I was able to put a phone call through to Ashkabad, where Khrushchev was stopping on that particular day, and begged him to intervene. The next day I had a talk with one of Khrushchev's close advisers. But by then the time for the test had already been moved up to an earlier hour, and the carrier aircraft had already transported its burden to the designated point for the explosion. The feeling of impotence and fright that seized me on that day has remained in my memory ever since, and it has worked much change in me as I moved toward my present attitude.

In 1962 I visited the minister of the atomic industry, who at that time was in a suburban government sanatorium together with the deputy minister of foreign affairs, and presented an important idea that had been brought to my attention by one of my friends. By then, talks on the banning of nuclear testing had already been going on for several years, the stumbling block being the difficulty of monitoring underground explosions. But radioactive contamination is caused only by explosions in the atmosphere, in space, and in the ocean. Therefore, limiting the agreement to banning tests in these three environments would solve both problems (contamination and monitoring). It should be noted that a similar proposal had previously been made by President Eisenhower, but at the time it had not accorded with the thinking of the Soviet side. In 1963 the so-called Moscow Treaty, in which this idea was realized, was concluded on the initiative of Khrushchev and Kennedy. It is possible that my initiative was of help in this historic act.

In 1964 I spoke at a conference of the Academy of Sciences USSR (in connection with the election of one of Lysenko's companions-in-arms) and publicly touched on the "prohibited" subject of the situation in Soviet biology in which, for decades, modern genetics had been attacked as a "pseudo-science" and scientists working in that field had been subjected to harsh persecution and repression. Subsequently I developed these thoughts in greater detail in a letter to Khrushchev. Both the speech and the letter found a very broad response, and later helped to correct the situation to some extent. It was at this time that my name first appeared in the Soviet press—in an article by the president of the Academy of Agricultural Sciences that contained the most unpardonable attacks on me.

For me, personally, these events had great psychological significance. Furthermore, they expanded the circle of persons with whom I associated. In particular, I became acquainted during the next few years with the Medvedev brothers, Zhores and Roy. A manuscript by the biologist Zhores Medvedev, which was passed from hand to hand, circumventing the censor, was the first *samizdat* work I had read. (*Samizdat* was a word that had come into use a few years before to denote a new social phenomenon.) In 1967 I also read the manuscript of a book by the historian Roy Medvedev on the crimes of Stalin. Both books, and especially the latter, made a very strong impression on me. However our relations may have turned out, and whatever my subsequent disagreements with the Medvedevs on matters of principle, I cannot minimize their role in my own development.

In 1966 I was one of the signers of a collective letter on the "cult" of Stalin sent to the Twenty-third Congress of the CPSU. In that same year I sent a telegram to the Supreme Soviet of the USSR about a new law, then being drafted, which would facilitate large-scale persecutions for one's convictions (Article 190–1 of the RSFSR Criminal Code). Thus, for the first time my own fate became intertwined with the fate of that group of people—a group that was small but very weighty on the moral (and, I dare say, the historical) plane—who subsequently came to be called "dissenters" (*inakomyslyashchie*). (Personally, I am fonder of the old Russian word "freethinkers"— *volnomyslyashchie.*) Very shortly thereafter I had occasion to write a letter to Brezhnev protesting the arrest of four of them: A. Ginzburg, Yu. Galanskov (who perished tragically in a camp in 1972), V. Lashkova, and Dobrovolsky. In connection with this letter and my previous actions, the minister heading up the department for which I worked said of me: Sakharov is an outstanding scientist and we have rewarded him well, but he is "stupid as a politician."

In 1967, for a publication that circulated among my colleagues, I wrote a "futurological" article on the future role of science in the life of society, and on the future of science itself. In that same year, for the *Literaturnaya Gazeta,* the journalist E. Henry (Genri) and I wrote an article on the role of the intelligentsia and the danger of a thermonuclear war. The Central Committee of the CPSU did not authorize publication of the article. But by means unknown to me it got into the *Political Diary*—a supposedly secret publication, something like *samizdat* for higher officials. A year later both of these articles, which remained little known, served as the basis for a work destined to play a central role in my activity for social causes. Early in 1968 I began work on a book I called *Progress, Coexistence, and Intellectual Freedom.* I wanted that book to reflect my thoughts on the most important problems facing mankind: thoughts on war and peace, on dictatorship, on the prohibited subject of Stalinist terror and freedom of thought, on demographic problems and the pollution of the environment, on the role that can be played by science and technological progress. The general tenor of the book was affected by the time of its writing—the height of the "Prague Spring." The basic ideas I tried to develop in the book were neither very new nor original. Essentially it was a compilation of liberal, humanistic, and "scientocratic" ideas based on information available to me and on personal experience. Today I regard this work as eclectic, pretentious in places, and imperfect ("raw") in terms of form. Nonetheless its basic ideas are dear to me. In it I clearly formulated the thesis (which strikes me as very important) that the rapprochement of the socialist and capitalist systems, accompanied by democratization, demilitarization, and social and technological progress, is the only alternative to the ruin of mankind. Beginning in May and June of 1968, *Progress* was widely distributed in the USSR. This was the first work of mine that was taken up by *samizdat.* In July and August came the first foreign reports of my book. Subsequently it was published abroad in large printings and provoked a great flow of responses in the press of many countries. In addition to the content of the work, an important role in all this was undoubtedly played by the fact that it was one of the first sociopolitical works to reach the West and that, moreover, its author was a highly decorated representative of the "secret" and "dread" specialty of nuclear physics. (Unfortunately, this sensationalism still envelops me, especially on the pages of the mass press in the West.)

The publication of this volume abroad immediately resulted in my being taken off secret projects (in August of 1968), and in the restructuring of my entire way of life. It was precisely at that time that I, acting under the influence of impulses I now consider unsound, transferred almost all my savings to a government fund (for the construction of a hospital for cancer patients), and to the Red Cross. At that time I had no personal contacts with people in need of help. Today, constantly seeing around me people who need not only protection but also material help, I often regret my overly hasty gesture.

In 1969 I was sent to work at the Physics Institute of the Academy of Sciences USSR, where I had once done graduate work and then been a collaborator of Igor Evgenevich Tamm. Although this meant a substantial drop in salary and job status, I was still able to continue scientific work in that area of physics most interesting to me: the theory of elementary particles. Unfortunately, however, in recent years I have not been satisfied with my productivity in scientific work. Two things have played a decisive role in this: first, the fact that, as theoretical physicists go, I am well along in years; second, the stressful—and recently very alarming—situation in which people close to me, my family, and I have found ourselves.

Meantime, events in society and an inner need to oppose injustice continued to urge me toward new actions. Early in 1970 another open letter to the leaders of the state was published by Valentin Turchin (the physicist and mathematician), Roy Medvedev, and myself. The subject of the letter was the interdependence of the problems of democratization and techno-economic progress. In June I took an active part in the campaign to free the other Medvedev brother—the biologist Zhores—from illegal confinement in a psychiatric hospital. About that same time I joined in a collective supervisory protest* to the Prosecutor's Office of the USSR on the case of General P. G. Grigorenko, who by decision of a Tashkent court had been sent for compulsory treatment to a special prison-type hospital of the MVD** in the town of Chernyakhovsk. The reason for this was the fact that Grigorenko had repeatedly made public appeals in defense of political prisoners and in defense of the rights of the Crimean Tatars, who in 1944 had been resettled from the Crimea with great cruelties under the Stalinist tyranny, and who today cannot return to their homeland. Our appeal, which pointed out the many patent violations of the law in the Grigorenko case, was never answered (which is also a crude violation of the law). Thus even more closely than in 1968, I was brought into contact with what is perhaps one of the most shameful aspects of present-day Soviet reality: illegality, and the cynical persecution of persons coming out in defense of basic human rights. But at the same time I got to know several of these persons, and subsequently many others. One of those who joined in the collective protest on the Grigorenko case was Valery Chalidze, with whom I became very close.

---

* I.e., a protest demanding that the Prosecutor's office intervene (as it is entitled to do under Soviet law) to order review of a case "by way of supervision." [Translator's note.]
** Ministry of Internal Affairs. [Translator's note.]

I became even more familiar with the problems of defending human rights in October 1970, when I was allowed to attend a political trial. The mathematician Revolt Pimenov and the puppet-show actor Boris Vail had been charged with distributing *samizdat*—giving friends books and manuscripts to read. The items named in their case included an article by Djilas, the Czech manifesto "Two Thousand Words," Pimenov's personal commentaries on Khrushchev's speech at the Twentieth Congress, etc. I sat in a courtroom filled with "probationers" of the KGB, while the friends of the defendants remained in a hallway on the ground floor throughout the trial. This is one more feature of all political trials, without exception. Formally, they are open. But the courtroom is packed in advance with KGB agents specially designated for the purpose, while another group of agents stands around the court on all sides. They are always in civilian clothes, they call themselves *druzhinniki*,* and they are allegedly preserving public order. This is the way it was (with negligible variations) in all cases when I was allowed to enter the courtroom. As for the passes enabling me to attend, they were apparently issued in acknowledgment of my previous services.

Pimenov and Vail were sentenced to five years of exile each, despite the fact that Vail's lawyer, at the appellate hearing, had argued convincingly that he had taken no part at all in the incidents incriminating him. In his concluding remarks Boris Vail said that an unjust sentence has an effect not only on the convicted person but also on the hearts of judges.

* I.e., members of a *druzhina*, or voluntary auxiliary police detachment. [Translator's note.]

From the autumn of 1971 on I was outside the line formed by the *druzhinniki*. But nothing else had changed. At the trial of the well-known astrophysicist Kronid Lyubarsky (who was charged with the same thing—distributing *samizdat*) a very significant and tragic show was put on. We were not allowed in the courtroom. And when the session began, the "unknown persons in civilian clothes" used force to push us out of the vestibule of the court into the street. Then a big padlock was hung on the door leading into the people's court. One has to see all these senseless and cruel dramatics with one's own eyes to feel it to the fullest. But why all this? The only answer I can give is that the farce being performed inside the courthouse is even less intended for public disclosure than the farce outside the courthouse. The bureaucratic logic of legal proceedings looks grotesque in the light of public disclosure, even when there is formal observance of the law—which is by no means always the case.

The sentence received by Pimenov and Vail, so harsh and unjust from the viewpoint of natural human norms, is relatively lenient compared to the decisions of Soviet courts in other cases of a similar nature, especially in recent years. Vladimir Bukovsky, known to the entire world for his protests in defense of people incarcerated in psychiatric hospitals for political reasons, was sentenced to twelve years: two years of prison, five years of camp, and five years of exile. K. Lyubarsky was sentenced to five years of imprisonment. The sentences passed outside of Moscow are even harsher. The young psychiatrist Semyon Gluzman was sentenced to seven years of imprisonment. I once happened to see Semyon for a few minutes at a railroad station, and I was astounded by the purity of his

countenance—by a kind of effective goodness and direct-
ness. At the time I had no way of suspecting that such a
fate was in store for him! It is generally supposed that
the reason for the reprisal against Gluzman was the assumption that he was the author of "Expert Examination
in Absentia in the Grigorenko Case." But at the trial this
charge was not brought. V. Morozov and Yu. Shukhevich,
both authors of memoirs about their terms in camp, were
sentenced by a Ukrainian court to fourteen and fifteen
years, respectively, of imprisonment and exile. And the
number of similar reprisals has grown rapidly.

Before proceeding further, I should like to say a few
words as to why I attach so much importance to the
matter of defending political prisoners—defending the
freedom of one's convictions. In the course of fifty-six
years our country has undergone great shocks, sufferings,
and humiliations, the physical annihilation of millions of
the best people (best both morally and intellectually),
decades of official hypocrisy and demagoguery, of internal
and external time-serving. The era of terror—when tortures and special conferences* threatened everyone, when
they seized the most devoted servants of the regime
simply for the general count and to create an atmosphere
of fright and submission—is now behind us. But we are
still living in the spiritual atmosphere created by that
era. Against those few who do not go along with the
prevalent practices of compromise, the government uses
repression as before. Together with judicial repressions,
the most important and decisive role in maintaining this
atmosphere of internal and external submission is played

* Special conferences (or boards) was the designation given, in the Stalin
era, to secret drumhead courts, or troikas. [Translator's note.]

by the power of the state, which manipulates all economic and social control levers. This, more than anything else, keeps the body and soul of the majority of people in a state of dependence. Another major influence on the psychological situation in the country is the fact that people are weary of endless promises of economic flowering in the very near future, and have ceased altogether to believe in fine words. The standard of living (food, clothing, housing, possibilities for leisure), social conditions (children's facilities, medical and educational institutions, pensions, labor protection, etc.)—all these lag far behind the level in advanced countries. An indifference to social problems—an attitude of consumerism and selfishness—is developing among the broad strata of the population. And among the majority, protest against the deadening official ideology has an unconscious, latent character. The religious and national movements are the broadest and most conscious. Among those who fill the camps or are subjected to other persecutions are many believers and representatives of national minorities. One of the mass forms of protest is the desire to leave the country. Unfortunately, it must be noted that sometimes the striving toward a national revival takes on chauvinistic traits, and borders on the traditional "everyday" hostility toward "aliens." Russian anti-Semitism is an example of this. Thus a part of the Russian opposition intelligentsia is beginning to manifest a paradoxical closeness to the secret Party-state doctrine of nationalism, which in fact is increasingly replacing the anti-national and anti-religious myth of Bolshevism. Among some people the same feeling of dissatisfaction and internal protest takes on other asocial forms (drunkenness, crime).

It is very important that the facade of prosperity and enthusiasm not conceal from the world this real picture of things. Our experience must not come to nothing. And it is equally important that our society gradually emerge from the dead end of unspirituality, which closes off the possibilities not only for the development of spiritual culture but also for progress in the material sphere.

I am convinced that under the conditions obtaining in our country a position based on morality and law is the most correct one, as corresponding to the requirements and possibilities of society. What we need is the systematic defense of human rights and ideals and not a political struggle, which would inevitably incite people to violence, sectarianism, and frenzy. I am convinced that only in this way, provided there is the broadest possible public disclosure, will the West be able to recognize the nature of our society; and that then this struggle will become part of a worldwide movement for the salvation of all mankind. This belief constitutes a partial answer to the question as to why I have (naturally) turned from worldwide problems to the defense of individual people.

The position of those who, beginning with the trials of Sinyavsky and Daniel, Ginzburg and Galanskov, have struggled for justice as they understand it can probably be compared with the position of the world-famous apolitical organization "Amnesty International." In any democratic country the question of the legality of such activity could not even arise. In our country, unfortunately, such is not the case. Dozens of the most famous political trials and dozens of prisoners in psychiatric hospitals of the prison type provide a graphic demonstration of this.

In recent years I have learned a great deal about Soviet juridical practices, through attending trials and receiving information about the course of similar trials in other cities [besides Moscow]. I have also learned a great deal about conditions in places of confinement: about malnutrition, pitiless formalism, and repressions against prisoners. In several statements I called the attention of world public opinion to this problem, which is vitally important for the 1,700,000 Soviet prisoners and indirectly has a deep influence on many important aspects of the moral and social life of the whole country. I have appealed, and I again appeal, to all international organizations concerned with this problem—and especially to the International Red Cross—to abandon their policy of nonintervention in the internal affairs of the socialist countries as regards defending human rights and to manifest the utmost persistence. I have also spoken out on the institution of "conditional release with obligatory assignment to labor," which in a political sense represents a vestige of the Stalinist system of mass forced labor, and which is very frightening in a social sense. It is difficult even to imagine the nightmare of the barracks for the "conditionally released persons," with almost general drunkenness, fistfights, throat-slitting. This system has broken the lives of many people. The preservation of the camp system and forced labor is one of the reasons why extensive regions of the country are off-limits for foreigners. It would appear that the realization of any successful international cooperation in developing our very rich resources is impossible without the abolishment of this system.

Another problem that has claimed my attention in recent years is that of the psychiatric repressions used by organs of the KGB as an important auxiliary means of stifling and frightening dissenters. There is no doubt as to the tremendous social danger of this phenomenon.

The documents brought together in this collection reflect my striving to call attention to this set of problems.

I feel that I owe a debt too great to be repaid to the brave and good people who are incarcerated in prisons, camps, and psychiatric hospitals because they struggled to defend human rights.

□

In the autumn of 1970, V. N. Chalidze, A. N. Tverdokhlebov, and I joined in founding the Human Rights Committee. This act on our part attracted great attention in the USSR and abroad. From the day of the Committee's founding, A. S. Volpin took an active part in its work. This was the first time that such an association had made its appearance in our country; and its members did not have a very precise idea of what they should do and how they should do it. Yet the Committee did a great deal of work on several problems, particularly in studying the question of compulsory confinement in psychiatric hospitals for political reasons. At the present time the work of the Committee is being carried on by I. R. Shafarevich, G. S. Podyapolsky, and myself. As was true of the "Initiative Group" created somewhat earlier, the very existence of the Committee, as a free group of associates independent of the authorities, has a unique and very great moral significance for our country.

□

This collection includes a "Memorandum" written in the first months of 1971 and sent to L. I. Brezhnev in March of that year. In terms of form, the "Memorandum" is a kind of synopsis of an imaginary dialogue with the leadership of the country. I am not convinced that this form is literarily successful, but it is compact. As for the content, I endeavored to set forth my positive demands in the political, social, and economic spheres. Fifteen months later, not having received any reply, I published the "Memorandum," adding a "Postscript," which stands on its own. I call the reader's special attention to it.

In publishing the "Memorandum," I did not make any changes in the text. In particular, I did not change the treatment of the problem of Soviet-Chinese relations—something I now regret. I still do not idealize the Chinese variant of socialism. But I do not regard as correct the evaluation of the danger of Chinese aggression vis-à-vis the USSR that is given in the "Memorandum." In any case, the Chinese threat cannot serve as a justification for the militarization of our country and the absence of democratic reforms in it.

I have already said something about those documents in this collection that are associated with the defense of the rights of individual people. During the past few years I have learned of an increasingly large number of tragic and heroic fates, some of which are reflected in the pages of this collection. For the most part, the documents of this cycle require no commentary.

In April of 1972 I drew up the text of an appeal to the Supreme Soviet of the USSR to grant amnesty to political prisoners and abolish capital punishment. These documents were timed to coincide with the fiftieth anniversary of the USSR. I have already explained why I attribute such prime importance to the first of these questions. As for the latter, the abolishment of capital punishment is an extremely important act, both morally and socially, for any country. And in our country, with its very low level of legal consciousness and widespread animosity, this act would be especially important. I succeeded in gathering about fifty signatures for the appeals. Each of them represented a very ponderable moral and social act on the part of the signer. I felt this with particular force while I was gathering the signatures. Many more people refused than signed, and the explanations offered by some of them clarified for me much regarding the inner reasons for the thoughts and acts of our intelligentsia.

In September 1971 I sent a letter to the members of the Presidium of the Supreme Soviet of the USSR on freedom of emigration and unobstructed return. My letter to the U.S. Congress in September of 1973 was another *démarche* on this same subject. In these documents I call attention to various aspects of this problem, including the important role that its solution would play in the democratization of our country, and in raising its standard of living to the level of the advanced countries. The validity of this idea can be shown by the example of Poland and Hungary, where today freedom to leave the country and return to it is not so heavily encumbered as in our country.

In the summer of 1973 I was interviewed by Olle Stenholm, correspondent for a Swedish radio station, who asked me questions of a general character. This interview had a broad response in the USSR and foreign countries. I received several dozen letters expressing indignation at the "slanderous" line I had taken. (It should be borne in mind that letters of the opposite kind usually do not reach me.) The Soviet *Literaturnaya Gazeta* published an article about me entitled "A Supplier of Slander." The correspondent who had interviewed me and published his text without distortions was recently deprived of his entry visa and the possibility of continuing his work in the USSR. This was an outrageous violation of the rights of an honest and intelligent journalist, who had become a friend of my family. One cannot rule out the possibility that the latter circumstance played its own role in the illegality practiced upon him. The interview was verbal, and neither questions nor answers were discussed in advance. This must be taken into account in evaluating the document, which represents an unconstrained conversation, in a home setting, on very serious, basic problems. In this interview, as in the "Memorandum" and the "Postscript," I went beyond the limits of the subject of the rights of man and democratic freedoms and touched on economic and social problems, which generally speaking require special—and perhaps even professional—training. But these problems are of such vital importance to every person that I am not sorry they came up for discussion. My opponents were especially irritated by my description of our country's system as state capitalism with a Party-state monopoly and the consequences, in all spheres of social life, that flow from such a system.

Important basic problems of the "détente" in international tensions in their connection with a proviso for the democratization and opening up of Soviet society were reflected in the interview of August–September 1973.

In recent years I have carried on my activities under conditions of ever-increasing pressure on me, and especially on my family. In September of 1972 our close friend Yury Shikhanovich was arrested. In October of 1972 Tatyana, my wife's daughter, who was doing very well in her studies, was expelled from the university in her last year under a formal and far-fetched pretext. Throughout the year we were harassed by anonymous telephone calls, with threats and absurd accusations. In February of 1973 the *Literaturnaya Gazeta* published an article by its editor-in-chief, Chakovsky, dealing with a book by Harrison Salisbury. In this article I was characterized as an extremely naïve person who quoted the New Testament, "coquettishly waved an olive branch," "played the holy fool," and "willingly accepted the compliments of the Pentagon." All this was said in connection with my *Progress*, which thus, after five years, was mentioned in the Soviet press for the first time. In March, likewise for the first time, I was summoned to the KGB for a talk on the pretext that my wife and I had jointly offered to go surety for our friend Yury Shikhanovich. In June Tatyana's husband was deprived of work in connection with having made an application to go and study in the United States, pursuant to an invitation. In July the above-mentioned article, "A Supplier of Slander," appeared. Also in July my wife's son Aleksei was refused admission to the university, apparently on special orders from above. In August I was summoned by the deputy prosecutor of the USSR, Malyarov. The basic content of the talk was threats. Then immediately after the interview of August twenty-first on the problems of détente, Soviet newspapers reprinted items from foreign Communist papers and a letter from forty Academicians declaring I was an opponent of relaxation of international tensions. Next came a nationwide newspaper campaign in which I was condemned by representatives of all strata of our society. In late September our apartment, thoroughly observed by the KGB, was visited by persons who called themselves members of the "Black September" organization. They threatened reprisals not only on me but also on the members of my family. In November an investigator who was a colonel in the KGB summoned my wife for repeated interrogations that lasted many hours. My wife refused to participate in the investigation, but this did not immediately put an end to the summonses. Previously she had publicly stated that she had sent to the West the diary of Eduard Kuznetsov, which had come into her hands. But she felt she was entitled not to tell what was done, or how it was done, by way of its distribution. The investigator warned her that her actions made her liable under Article 70 of the RSFSR Criminal Code, with a period of punishment of up to seven years. It seems to me this is quite enough for one family.

Soon after the coup d'état in Chile, the writers A. Galich and V. Maximov joined with me in an appeal to the new government expressing fears for the life of the outstanding Chilean poet Pablo Neruda. Our letter was not political in nature and had no other aims than strictly humane ones. But in the Soviet press and the pro-Soviet foreign press, it provoked an explosion of feigned indignation as allegedly "defending the fascist junta." Moreover, the letter itself was quoted inaccurately, and two of its authors—Galich and Maximov—were in general "forgotten." The aim of the organizers of this campaign—to compromise me at least in this way if it couldn't be done otherwise—was only too obvious.

But to digress from the subject of patently unscrupulous opponents and to turn to opinions that more objectively reflect liberal social opinion in the West, it must be said that this whole story brought to light a typical misunderstanding that merits discussion. As a rule, liberal social opinion in the democratic countries takes an international position, protesting against injustice and violence not only in one's own country but also throughout the world. It was not by accident that I said "as a rule." Unfortunately, it is very frequently the case that the defense of human rights in the socialist countries, by virtue of an opinion as to the special progressiveness of their regimes, falls outside (or almost falls outside) the field of activity of foreign organizations. The greater part of my efforts has been aimed precisely at changing this situation, which has been one of the reasons for our tragedies. However, that is not the point at issue here. Instead I should like to talk about that part of the Western liberal intelligentsia (still a small part) that extends its activities to the socialist countries as well. These people look to the Soviet dissenters for a reciprocal, analogous international position with respect to other countries. But there are several important circumstances they do not take into account: the lack of information; the fact that a Soviet dissenter is not only unable to go to other countries but also is deprived, within his own country, of the majority of sources of information; that the historical experience of our country has weaned us away from excessive "leftism," so that we evaluate many facts differently from the "leftist" intelligentsia of the West; that we must avoid political pronouncements in the international arena, where we are so ignorant (after all, we do not engage in political activity even in our own country); that we must avoid getting into the channel of Soviet propaganda, which so often deceives us. We know that in the Western countries there are vigilant and influential forces that protest (better and more effectively than we do) against injustice and violence there. We do not justify injustice or violence, whereever they appear. We do not feel that there is necessarily more in our country than in other countries. But at the moment our strength cannot suffice for the whole world. We ask that all this be taken into account, and that we be forgiven the errors we sometimes make in the dust kicked up by polemics.

The general position reflected in the materials of this collection is closer to my first book than might appear at first glance. [There are] differences in the treatment of political or politico-economic questions that are of course immediately apparent. But since I lay no claim to the role of discoverer or political adviser, these differences are less essential than the spirit of free debate and the concern for fundamental problems, which, I should like to think, are found both in *Progress* and in the recent writings.

The majority of my writings are either addressed to the leaders of our state or they have a specific foreign addressee. But inwardly I address them to all people on earth, and in particular to the people of my country, because they were dictated by concern and anxiety for my own country and its people.

I am not a purely negative critic of our way of life: I recognize much that is good in our people and in our country, which I ardently love. But I have been compelled to fix attention on negative phenomena, since they are precisely what the official propaganda passes over in silence, and since they represent the greatest damage and danger. I am not an opponent of détente, trade, or disarmament. On the contrary, in several writings I have called for just these things. It is precisely in convergence that I see the only way to the salvation of mankind. But I consider it my duty to point out all the hidden dangers of a false détente, a collusion-détente, or a capitulation-détente, and to call for utilization of the entire arsenal of means, of all efforts, to achieve real convergence, accompanied by democratization, demilitarization, and social progress. I hope that the publication of this collection will be of some use in that cause.

In conclusion, I should like to express my deep gratitude to all those who helped in the preparation and publishing of this collection: to the publisher, Mr. Knopf, to the editors, Messrs. Green and Salisbury, to my wife, and to my many friends in the USSR and other countries.

A. SAKHAROV

December 31, 1973
Moscow

PROGRESS, COEXISTENCE, AND INTELLECTUAL FREEDOM

The views of the author were formed in the milieu of the scientific and scientific-technical intelligentsia, which manifests much anxiety over the principles and specific aspects of foreign and domestic policy and over the future of mankind. This anxiety is nourished, in particular, by a realization that the scientific method of directing policy, the economy, arts, education, and military affairs still has not become a reality.

We regard as "scientific" a method based on deep analysis of facts, theories, and views, presupposing unprejudiced, unfearing open discussion and conclusions. The complexity and diversity of all the phenomena of modern life, the great possibilities and dangers linked with the scientific-technical revolution and with a number of social tendencies demand precisely such an approach, as has been acknowledged in a number of official statements.

In this essay, advanced for discussion, the author has set himself the goal to present, with the greatest conviction and frankness, two theses that are supported by many people in the world. The theses relate to the destruction threatened by the division of mankind and the need for intellectual freedom.

I.

The division of mankind threatens it with destruction. Civilization is imperiled by: a universal thermonuclear war, catastrophic hunger for most of mankind, stupefaction from the narcotic of "mass culture," and bureaucratized dogmatism, a spreading of mass myths that put entire peoples and continents under the power of cruel and treacherous demagogues, and destruction or degeneration from the unforeseeable consequences of swift changes in the conditions of life on our planet.

In the face of these perils, any action increasing the division of mankind, any preaching of the incompatibility of world ideologies and nations is madness and a crime. Only universal cooperation under conditions of intellectual freedom and the lofty moral ideals of socialism and labor, accompanied by the elimination of dogmatism and pressures of the concealed interests of ruling classes, will preserve civilization.

The reader will understand that ideological collaboration cannot apply to those fanatical, sectarian, and extremist ideologies that reject all possibility of rapprochement, discussion, and compromise, for example, the ideologies of fascist, racist, militaristic, and Maoist demagogy.

Millions of people throughout the world are striving to put an end to poverty. They despise oppression, dogmatism, and demagogy (and their more extreme manifestations—racism, fascism, Stalinism, and Maoism). They believe in progress based on the use, under conditions of social justice and intellectual freedom, of all the positive experience accumulated by mankind.

II.

The second basic thesis is that intellectual freedom is essential to human society—freedom to obtain and distribute information, freedom for open-minded and unfearing debate, and freedom from pressure by officialdom and prejudices. Such a trinity of freedom of thought is the only guarantee against an infection of people by mass myths, which, in the hands of treacherous hypocrites and demagogues, can be transformed into bloody dictatorship. Freedom of thought is the only guarantee of the feasibility of a scientific democratic approach to politics, economy, and culture.

But freedom of thought is under a triple threat in modern society—from the deliberate opium of mass culture, from cowardly, egotistic, and philistine ideologies, and from the ossified dogmatism of a bureaucratic oligarchy and its favorite weapon, ideological censorship. Therefore, freedom of thought requires the defense of all thinking and honest people. This is a mission not only for the intelligentsia but for all strata of society, particularly its most active and organized stratum, the working class. The worldwide dangers of war, famine, cults of personality, and bureaucracy—these are perils for all of mankind.

Recognition by the working class and the intelligentsia of their common interests has been a striking phenomenon of the present day. The most progressive, internationalist, and dedicated element of the intelligentsia is, in essence, part of the working class, and the most advanced, educated, internationalist, and broad-minded part of the working class is part of the intelligentsia.

This position of the intelligentsia in society renders senseless any loud demands that the intelligentsia subordinate its strivings to the will and interests of the working class (in the Soviet Union, Poland, and other socialist countries). What these demands really mean is subordination to the will of the Party or, even more specifically, to the Party's central apparatus and its officials. Who will guarantee that these officials always express the genuine interests of the working class as a whole and the genuine interests of progress rather than their own caste interests?

We will divide this essay into two parts. The first we will title "Dangers" and the second "The Basis of Hope." This essay contains much that is controversial and open to question; I invite response and debate.

DANGERS

THE THREAT OF NUCLEAR WAR

Three technical aspects of thermonuclear weapons have made thermonuclear war a peril to the very existence of humanity. These aspects are: the enormous destructive power of a thermonuclear explosion, the relative cheapness of rocket-thermonuclear weapons, and the practical impossibility of an effective defense against a massive rocket-nuclear attack.

□

Today one can consider a three-megaton nuclear warhead as "typical" (this is somewhere between the warhead of a Minuteman and of a Titan II). The area of fires from the explosion of such a warhead is 150 times greater than from the Hiroshima bomb, and the area of destruction is 30 times greater. The detonation of such a warhead over a city would create a 100-square-kilometer [40-square-mile] area of total destruction and fire.

Tens of millions of square meters of living space would be destroyed. No fewer than a million people would perish under the ruins of buildings, from fire and radiation, suffocating in the dust and smoke or dying in shelters buried under debris. In the event of a ground-level explosion, the fallout of radioactive dust would create a danger of fatal exposure in an area of tens of thousands of square kilometers.

□

A few words about the cost and the possible number of explosions.

After the stage of research and development has been passed, mass production of thermonuclear weapons and carrier rockets is no more complex and expensive than, for example, the production of military aircraft, which were produced by the tens of thousands during the war.

The annual production of plutonium in the world now is in the tens of thousands of tons. If one assumes that half this output goes for military purposes and that an average of several kilograms of plutonium goes into one warhead, then enough warheads have already been accumulated to destroy mankind many times over.

□

The third aspect of thermonuclear peril (along with the power and cheapness of warheads) is what we term the practical impossibility of preventing a massive rocket attack. This situation is well known to specialists. In the popular scientific literature, for example, one can read this in an article by Richard L. Garwin and Hans A. Bethe in the *Scientific American* of March 1968.

The technology and tactics of attack have now far surpassed the technology of defense despite the development of highly maneuverable and powerful anti-missiles with nuclear warheads and despite other technical ideas, such as the use of laser beams and so forth.

Improvements in the resistance of warheads to shock waves and to the radiation effects of neutron and X-ray exposure, the possibility of mass use of relatively light and inexpensive decoys that are virtually indistinguishable from warheads and exhaust the capabilities of an anti-missile defense system, a perfection of tactics of massed and concentrated attacks, in time and space, that overstrain the defense detection centers, the use of orbital and fractional-orbital attacks, the use of active and passive jamming, and other methods not disclosed in the press—all this has created technical and economic obstacles to an effective missile defense that, at the present time, are virtually insurmountable.

The experience of past wars shows that the first use of a new technical or tactical method of attack is usually highly effective even if a simple antidote can soon be developed. But in a thermonuclear war the first blow may be the decisive one and render null and void years of work and billions spent on creation of an anti-missile system.

An exception to this would be the case of a great technical and economic difference in the potentials of two enemies. In such a case, the stronger side, creating an anti-missile defense system with a multiple reserve, would face the temptation of ending the dangerous and unstable balance once and for all by embarking on a pre-emptive adventure, expending part of its attack potential on destruction of most of the enemy's launching bases and counting on impunity for the last stage of escalation, i.e., the destruction of the cities and industry of the enemy.

Fortunately for the stability of the world, the difference between the technical-economic potentials of the Soviet Union and the United States is not so great that one of the sides could undertake a "preventive aggression" without an almost inevitable risk of a destructive retaliatory blow. This situation would not be changed by a broadening of the arms race through the development of anti-missile defenses.

In the opinion of many people, an opinion shared by the author, a diplomatic formulation of this mutually comprehended situation, for example, in the form of a moratorium on the construction of anti-missile systems, would be a useful demonstration of a desire of the Soviet Union and the United States to preserve the status quo and not to widen the arms race for senselessly expensive anti-missile systems. It would be a demonstration of a desire to cooperate, not to fight.

A thermonuclear war cannot be considered a continuation of politics by other means (according to the formula of Clausewitz). It would be a means of universal suicide.

Two kinds of attempts are being made to portray thermonuclear war as an "ordinary" political act in the eyes of public opinion. One is the concept of the "paper tiger," the concept of the irresponsible Maoist adventurists. The other is the strategic doctrine of escalation, worked out by scientific and militarist circles in the United States. Without minimizing the seriousness of the challenge inherent in that doctrine, we will just note that the political strategy of peaceful coexistence is an effective counterweight to the doctrine.

A complete destruction of cities, industry, transport, and systems of education, a poisoning of fields, water, and air by radioactivity, a physical destruction of the larger part of mankind, poverty, barbarism, a return to savagery, and a genetic degeneracy of the survivors under the impact of radiation, a destruction of the material and information basis of civilization—this is a measure of the peril that threatens the world as a result of the estrangement of the world's two super-powers.

Every rational creature, finding itself on the brink of a disaster, first tries to get away from the brink and only then does it think about the satisfaction of its other needs. If mankind is to get away from the brink, it must overcome its divisions.

A vital step would be a review of the traditional method of international affairs, which may be termed "empirical-competitive." In the simplest definition, this is a method aiming at maximum improvement of one's position everywhere possible and, simultaneously, a method of causing maximum unpleasantness to opposing forces without consideration of common welfare and common interests.

If politics were a game of two gamblers, then this would be the only possible method. But where does such a method lead in the present unprecedented situation?

VIETNAM AND THE MIDDLE EAST

In Vietnam, the forces of reaction, lacking hope for an expression of national will in their favor, are using the force of military pressure. They are violating all legal and moral norms and are carrying out flagrant crimes against humanity. An entire people is being sacrificed to the proclaimed goal of stopping the "Communist tide."

They strive to conceal from the American people considerations of personal and Party prestige, the cynicism and cruelty, the hopelessness and ineffectiveness of the anti-Communist tasks of American policy in Vietnam, as well as the harm this war is doing to the true goals of the American people, which coincide with the universal tasks of bolstering peaceful coexistence.

To end the war in Vietnam would first of all save the people perishing there. But it also is a matter of saving peace in all the world. Nothing undermines the possibilities of peaceful coexistence more than a continuation of the war in Vietnam.

Another tragic example is the Middle East. If direct responsibility for Vietnam rests with the United States, in the Middle East direct responsibility rests not with the United States but with the Soviet Union (and with Britain in 1948 and 1956).

On the one hand, there was an irresponsible encouragement of so-called Arab unity (which in no way had a socialist character—look at Jordan—but was purely nationalist and anti-Israel). It was said that the struggle of the Arabs had an essentially anti-imperialist character. On the other hand, there was an equally irresponsible encouragement of Israeli extremists.

We cannot here analyze the entire contradictory and tragic history of the events of the last twenty years, in the course of which the Arabs and Israel, along with historically justified actions, carried out reprehensible deeds, often brought about by the actions of external forces.

Thus, in 1948, Israel waged a defensive war. But in 1956, the actions of Israel appeared reprehensible. The preventive six-day war in the face of threats of destruction by merciless, numerically vastly superior forces of the Arab coalition could have been justifiable. But the cruelty to refugees and prisoners of war and the striving to settle territorial questions by military means must be condemned. Despite this condemnation, the breaking of relations with Israel appears a mistake, complicating a peaceful settlement in this region and complicating a necessary diplomatic recognition of Israel by the Arab governments.

In our opinion, certain changes must be made in the

conduct of international affairs, systematically subordinating all concrete aims and local tasks to the basic task of actively preventing an aggravation of the international situation, of actively pursuing and expanding peaceful coexistence to the level of cooperation, of making policy in such a way that its immediate and long-range effects will in no way sharpen international tensions and will not create difficulties for either side that would strengthen the forces of reaction, militarism, nationalism, fascism, and revanchism.

International affairs must be completely permeated with scientific methodology and a democratic spirit, with a fearless weighing of all facts, views, and theories, with maximum publicity of ultimate and intermediate goals, and with a consistency of principles.

INTERNATIONAL TENSIONS
AND NEW PRINCIPLES

The international policies of the world's two leading super-powers (the United States and the Soviet Union) must be based on a universal acceptance of unified and general principles, which we initially would formulate as follows:

All peoples have the right to decide their own fate with a free expression of will. This right is guaranteed by international control over observance by all governments of the "Declaration of the Rights of Man." International control presupposes the use of economic sanctions as well as the use of military forces of the United Nations in defense of "the rights of man."

All military and military-economic forms of export of revolution and counterrevolution are illegal and are tantamount to aggression.

All countries strive toward mutual help in economic,

cultural, and general-organizational problems with the aim of eliminating painlessly all domestic and international difficulties and preventing a sharpening of international tensions and a strengthening of the forces of reaction.

International policy does not aim at exploiting local, specific conditions to widen zones of influence and create difficulties for another country. The goal of international policy is to insure universal fulfillment of the "Declaration of the Rights of Man" and to prevent a sharpening of international tensions and a strengthening of militarist and nationalist tendencies.

□

Such a set of principles would in no way be a betrayal of the revolutionary and national liberation struggle, the struggle against reaction and counterrevolution. On the contrary, with the elimination of all doubtful cases, it would be easier to take decisive action in those extreme cases of reaction, racism, and militarism that allow no course other than armed struggle. A strengthening of peaceful coexistence would create an opportunity to avert such tragic events as those in Greece and Indonesia.

Such a set of principles would present the Soviet armed forces with a precisely defined defensive mission, a mission of defending our country and our allies from aggression. As history has shown, our people and their armed forces are unconquerable when they are defending their homeland and its great social and cultural achievements.

HUNGER AND OVERPOPULATION
(and the Psychology of Racism)

Specialists are paying attention to a growing threat of hunger in the poorer half of the world. Although the 50 percent increase of the world's population in the last thirty years has been accompanied by a 70 percent increase in food production, the balance in the poorer half of the world has been unfavorable. The situation in India, Indonesia, in a number of countries of Latin America, and in a large number of other underdeveloped countries—the absence of technical-economic reserves, competent officials, and cultural skills, social backwardness, a high birth rate—systematically worsens the food balance and without doubt will continue to worsen it in the coming years.

The answer would be a wide application of fertilizers, an improvement of irrigation systems, better farm technology, wider use of the resources of the oceans, and a gradual perfection of the production, already technically feasible, of synthetic foods, primarily amino acids. However, this is all fine for the rich nations. In the more backward countries, it is apparent from an analysis of the situation and existing trends that an improvement cannot be achieved in the near future, before the expected date of tragedy, 1975–80.

What is involved is a prognosticated deterioration of the average food balance in which localized food crises merge into a sea of hunger, intolerable suffering and desperation, the grief and fury of millions of people. This is a tragic threat to all mankind. A catastrophe of such dimension cannot but have profound consequences for the entire world and for every human being. It will provoke a wave of wars and hatred, a decline of standards of living throughout the world, and will leave a tragic, cynical, and anti-Communist mark on the life of future generations.

The first reaction of a philistine in hearing about the problem is that "they" are responsible for their plight because "they" reproduce so rapidly. Unquestionably, control of the birth rate is important and the people, in India for example, are taking steps in this direction. But these steps remain largely ineffective under social and economic backwardness, surviving traditions of large families, an absence of old-age benefits, a high infant mortality rate until quite recently, and a continuing threat of death from starvation.

It is apparently futile only to insist that the more backward countries restrict their birth rates. What is needed most of all is economic and technical assistance to these countries. This assistance must be of such scale and generosity that it is unlikely before the estrangement in the world and the egotistical, narrow-minded approach to relations between nations and races are eliminated. It is impossible as long as the United States and the Soviet Union, the world's two great super-powers, look upon each other as rivals and opponents.

Social factors play an important role in the tragic present situation and the still more tragic future of the impoverished regions. It must be clearly understood that if a threat of hunger is, along with a striving toward national independence, the main cause of "agrarian" revolution, the "agrarian" revolution in itself will not eliminate the threat of hunger, at least not in the immediate future. The threat of hunger cannot be eliminated without the assistance of the developed countries, and this requires significant changes in their foreign and domestic policies.

At this time, the white citizens of the United States are unwilling to accept even minimum sacrifices to eliminate the unequal economic and cultural position of the country's black citizens, who make up 10 percent of the population.

It is necessary to change the psychology of the American citizens so that they will voluntarily and generously support their government and worldwide efforts to change the economy, technology, and level of living of billions of people. This, of course, would entail a serious decline in the United States rate of economic growth. The Americans should be willing to do this solely for the sake of lofty and distant goals, for the sake of preserving civilization and mankind on our planet.

Similar changes in the psychology of people and practical activities of governments must be achieved in the Soviet Union and other developed countries.

In the opinion of the author, a fifteen-year tax equal to 20 percent of national incomes must be imposed on developed nations. The imposition of such a tax would automatically lead to a significant reduction in expenditures for weapons. Such common assistance would have an important effect—that of stabilizing and improving the situation in the most underdeveloped countries, restricting the influence of extremists of all types.

Changes in the economic situation of underdeveloped countries would solve the problem of high birth rates with relative ease, as has been shown by the experience of developed countries, without the barbaric method of sterilization.

Certain changes in the policies, viewpoints, and traditions on this delicate question are inescapable in the advanced countries as well. Mankind can develop smoothly only if it looks upon itself in a demographic sense as a unit, a single family without divisions into nations other than in matters of history and traditions.

Therefore, government policy, legislation on the family and marriage, and propaganda should not encourage an increase in the birth rates of advanced countries while demanding that it be curtailed in underdeveloped countries that are receiving assistance. Such a two-faced game would produce nothing but bitterness and nationalism.

In conclusion on that point, I want to emphasize that the question of regulating birth rates is highly complex and that any standardized, dogmatic solution "for all time and all peoples" would be wrong. All the foregoing, incidentally, should be accepted with the reservation that it is somewhat of a simplification.

POLLUTION
OF ENVIRONMENT

We live in a swiftly changing world. Industrial and water-engineering projects, cutting of forests, plowing up of virgin lands, the use of poisonous chemicals—all such activity is changing the face of the earth, our "habitat."

Scientific study of all the interrelationships in nature and the consequences of our interference clearly lags behind the changes. Large amounts of harmful wastes of industry and transport are being dumped into the air and water, including cancer-inducing substances. Will the safe limit be passed everywhere, as has already happened in a number of places?

Carbon dioxide from the burning of coal is altering the heat-reflecting qualities of the atmosphere. Sooner or later, this will reach a dangerous level. But we do not know when. Poisonous chemicals used in agriculture are penetrating the body of man and animal directly, and in more dangerous modified compounds are causing serious damage to the brain, the nervous system, blood-forming organs, the liver, and other organs. Here, too, the safe limit can be easily crossed, but the question has not been fully studied and it is difficult to control all these processes.

The use of antibiotics in poultry-raising has led to the development of new disease-causing microbes that are resistant to antibiotics.

I could also mention the problems of dumping detergents and radioactive wastes, erosion and salinization of soils, the flooding of meadows, the cutting of forests on mountain slopes and in watersheds, the destruction of birds and other useful wildlife like toads and frogs, and many other examples of senseless despoliation caused by local, temporary, bureaucratic, and egotistical interest and sometimes simply by questions of bureaucratic prestige, as in the sad fate of Lake Baikal.

The problem of geohygiene (earth hygiene) is highly complex and closely tied to economic and social problems. This problem can therefore not be solved on a national and especially not on a local basis. The salvation of our environment requires that we overcome our divisions and the pressure of temporary, local interests. Otherwise, the Soviet Union will poison the United States with its wastes and vice versa. At present, this is a hyperbole. But with a 10 percent annual increase of wastes, the increase over a hundred years will be multiplied twenty thousand times.

POLICE DICTATORSHIPS

An extreme reflection of the dangers confronting modern social development is the growth of racism, nationalism, and militarism and, in particular, the rise of demagogic, hypocritical, and monstrously cruel dictatorial police regimes. Foremost are the regimes of Stalin, Hitler, and Mao Tse-tung, and a number of extremely reactionary regimes in smaller countries, such as Spain, Portugal, South Africa, Greece, Albania, Haiti, and other Latin American countries.

These tragic developments have always derived from the struggle of egotistical and group interests, the struggle for unlimited power, suppression of intellectual freedom, a spread of intellectually simplified, narrow-minded mass myths (the myth of race, of land and blood, the myth about the Jewish danger, anti-intellectualism, the concept of *lebensraum* in Germany, the myth about the sharpening of the class struggle and proletarian infallibility bolstered by the cult of Stalin and by exaggeration of the contradictions with capitalism in the Soviet Union, the myth about Mao Tse-tung, extreme Chinese nationalism and the resurrection of the *lebensraum* concept, of anti-intellectualism, extreme anti-humanism, and certain prejudices of peasant socialism in China).

The usual practice is the use of demagogy, storm troopers, and Red Guards in the first stage and terrorist bureaucracy with reliable cadres of the type of Eichmann, Himmler, Yezhov, and Beria at the summit of deification of unlimited power.

The world will never forget the burning of books in the squares of German cities, the hysterical, cannibalistic speeches of the fascist "führers," and their even more cannibalistic plans for the destruction of entire peoples, including the Russians. Fascism began a partial realization of these plans during the war it unleashed, annihilating prisoners of war and hostages, burning villages, carrying out a criminal policy of genocide (during the war, the main blow of genocide was aimed at the Jews, a policy that apparently was also meant to be provocative, especially in the Ukraine and Poland).

We shall never forget the kilometer-long trenches filled with bodies, the gas chambers, the SS dogs, the fanatical doctors, the piles of women's hair, suitcases with gold teeth, and fertilizer from the factories of death.

Analyzing the causes of Hitler's coming to power, we will never forget the role of German and international monopolist capital. We also will not forget the criminally sectarian and dogmatically narrow policies of Stalin and his associates, setting Socialists and Communists against one another (this has been well related in the famous letter to Ilya Ehrenburg by Ernst Henri).*

Fascism lasted twelve years in Germany. Stalinism lasted twice as long in the Soviet Union. There are many common features but also certain differences. Stalinism exhibited a much more subtle kind of hypocrisy and demagogy, with reliance not on an openly cannibalistic program like Hitler's but on a progressive, scientific, and popular socialist ideology.

This served as a convenient screen for deceiving the working class, for weakening the vigilance of the intellectuals and other rivals in the struggle for power, with the treacherous and sudden use of the machinery of torture, execution, and informants, intimidating and making fools of millions of people, the majority of whom were neither cowards nor fools. As a consequence of this "specific feature" of Stalinism, it was the Soviet people, its most active, talented, and honest representatives, who suffered the most terrible blow.

At least ten to fifteen million people perished in the torture chambers of the NKVD [secret police] from torture and execution, in camps for exiled kulaks [rich peasants] and so-called semi-kulaks and members of their families and in camps "without the right of correspondence" (which were in fact the prototypes of the fascist death camps, where, for example, thousands of prisoners were machine-

---

* Ernst Henri, a German Communist long resident in the Soviet Union, outlined in this letter the role Stalin's policies had played in making possible Hitler's rise—notably his insistence that the German Communist Party view as its chief enemy the German Social Democratic Party rather than Hitler's Nazis. Henri's thesis was that the German Communists and Social Democrats should have formed a united front against Hitler.

gunned because of "overcrowding" or as a result of "special orders").

People perished in the mines of Norilsk and Vorkuta from freezing, starvation, and exhausting labor, at countless construction projects, in timber-cutting, building of canals, or simply during transportation in prison trains, in the overcrowded holds of "death ships" in the Sea of Okhotsk, and during the resettlement of entire peoples, the Crimean Tatars, the Volga Germans, the Kalmyks, and other Caucasus peoples. Readers of the literary journal *Novy Mir* recently could read for themselves a description of the "road of death" between Norilsk and Igarka [in northern Siberia].

Temporary masters were replaced (Yagoda, Molotov, Yezhov, Zhdanov, Malenkov, Beria), but the anti-people's regime of Stalin remained equally cruel and at the same time dogmatically narrow and blind in its cruelty. The killing of military and engineering officials before the war, the blind faith in the "reasonableness" of the colleague in crime, Hitler, and the other reasons for the national tragedy of 1941 have been well described in the book by Nekrich, in the notes of Maj. Gen. Grigorenko, and other publications—these are far from the only examples of the combination of crime, narrow-mindedness, and short-sightedness.*

Stalinist dogmatism and isolation from real life was demonstrated particularly in the countryside, in the policy

---

* A. M. Nekrich, a distinguished Soviet historian, was expelled from the Soviet Communist Party after publishing a study of Stalin's errors and unpreparedness for the Nazi attack of June 1941. Maj. Gen. Pyotr G. Grigorenko, author of a long memorandum supporting Nekrich and a leading Soviet dissident, has been confined as punishment in Soviet mental hospitals.

of unlimited exploitation and the predatory forced deliveries at "symbolic" prices, in almost serflike enslavement of the peasantry, the depriving of peasants of the simplest means of mechanization, and the appointment of collective-farm chairmen on the basis of their cunning and obsequiousness. The results are evident—a profound and hard-to-correct destruction of the economy and way of life in the countryside, which, by the law of interconnected vessels, damaged industry as well.

The inhuman character of Stalinism was demonstrated by the repressions of prisoners of war who survived fascist camps and then were thrown into Stalinist camps, the anti-worker "decrees," the criminal exile of entire peoples condemned to slow death, the unenlightened zoological kind of anti-Semitism that was characteristic of Stalin bureaucracy and the NKVD (and Stalin personally), the Ukrainophobia characteristic of Stalin, and the draconian laws for the protection of socialist property (five years' imprisonment for stealing some grain from the fields and so forth) that served mainly as a means of fulfilling the demands of the "slave market."

A profound analysis of the origin and development of Stalinism is contained in the thousand-page monograph of Roy Medvedev.* This was written from a socialist, Marxist point of view and is a successful work, but unfortunately it has not yet been published. The present author is not likely to receive such a compliment from Comrade Medvedev, who finds elements of "Westernism" in his views. Well, there is nothing like controversy! Actually the views of the

---

* Medvedev's study was published in the United States and Britain in 1972 under the title *Let History Judge*.

present author are profoundly socialist, and he hopes that the attentive reader will understand this.

The author is quite aware of the monstrous relations in human and international affairs brought forth by the egotistical principle of capital when it is not under pressure from socialist and progressive forces. He also thinks, however, that progressives in the West understand this better than he does and are waging a struggle against these manifestations. The author is concentrating his attention on what is before his eyes and on what is obstructing, from his point of view, a worldwide overcoming of estrangement, obstructing the struggle for democracy, social progress, and intellectual freedom.

Our country has started on the path of cleansing away the foulness of Stalinism. "We are squeezing the slave out of ourselves drop by drop" (an expression of Anton Chekhov). We are learning to express our opinions, without taking the lead from the bosses and without fearing for our lives.

The beginning of this arduous and far from straight path evidently dates from the report of Nikita S. Khrushchev to the Twentieth Congress of the Soviet Communist Party. This bold speech, which came as a surprise to Stalin's accomplices in crime, and a number of associated measures —the release of hundreds of thousands of political prisoners and their rehabilitation, steps toward a revival of the principles of peaceful coexistence and toward a revival of democracy—oblige us to value highly the historic role of Khrushchev despite his regrettable mistakes of a voluntarist character in subsequent years and despite the fact that Khrushchev, while Stalin was alive, was one of his collaborators in crime, occupying a number of influential posts.

The exposure of Stalinism in our country still has a long way to go. It is imperative, of course, that we publish all authentic documents, including the archives of the NKVD, and conduct nationwide investigations. It would be highly useful for the international authority of the Soviet Communist Party and the ideals of socialism if, as was planned in 1964 but never carried out, the party were to announce the "symbolic" expulsion of Stalin, murderer of millions of Party members, and at the same time the political rehabilitation of the victims of Stalinism.

From 1936 to 1939 more than 1.2 million Party members, half of the total membership, were arrested. Only fifty thousand regained freedom; the others were tortured during interrogation or were shot (six hundred thousand) or died in camps. Only in isolated cases were the rehabilitated allowed to assume responsible posts; even fewer were permitted to take part in the investigation of crimes of which they had been witnesses or victims.

We are often told lately not to "rub salt into wounds." This is usually being said by people who suffered no wounds. Actually only the most meticulous analysis of the past and of its consequences will now enable us to wash off the blood and dirt that befouled our banner.

It is sometimes suggested in the literature that the political manifestations of Stalinism represented a sort of superstructure over the economic basis of an anti-Leninist pseudosocialism that led to the formation in the Soviet Union of a distinct class—a bureaucratic elite from which all key positions are filled and which is rewarded for its work through open and concealed privileges. I cannot deny that there is some (but not the whole) truth in such an interpretation, which would help explain the vitality of neo-Stalinism, but a full analysis of this issue would go beyond the scope of this essay, which focuses on another aspect of the problem.

It is imperative that we restrict in every possible way the influence of neo-Stalinists in our political life. Here we are compelled to mention a specific person. One of the most influential representatives of neo-Stalinism at the present time is the director of the Science Department of the Communist Party's Central Committee, Sergei P. Trapeznikov. The leadership of our country and our people should know that the views of this unquestionably intelligent, shrewd, and highly consistent man are basically Stalinist (from our point of view, they reflect the interests of the bureaucratic elite).

His views differ fundamentally from the dreams and aspirations of the majority and most active section of the intelligentsia, which, in our opinion, reflect the true interests of all our people and progressive mankind. The leadership of our country should understand that as long as such a man (if I correctly understand the nature of his views) exercises influence, it is impossible to hope for a strengthening of the Party's position among scientific and artistic intellectuals. An indication of this was given at the last elections in the Academy of Sciences when Trapeznikov was rejected by a substantial majority of votes, but this hint was not "understood" by the leadership.

The issue does not involve the professional or personal qualities of Trapeznikov, about which I know little. The issue involves his political views. I have based the foregoing on word-of-mouth evidence. Therefore, I cannot in principle exclude the possibility (although it is unlikely) that in reality everything is quite the opposite. In that pleasant event, I would beg forgiveness and retract what I have written.

In recent years, demagogy, violence, cruelty, and vileness have seized a great country embarked on the path of socialist development. I refer, of course, to China. It is impossible without horror and pain to read about the mass contagion of anti-humanism being spread by "the great helmsman" and his accomplices, about the Red Guards who, according to the Chinese radio, "jumped with joy" during public executions of "ideological enemies" of Chairman Mao.

The idiocy of the cult of personality has assumed in China monstrous, grotesquely tragicomic forms, carrying to the point of absurdity many of the traits of Stalinism and Hitlerism. But this absurdity has proved effective in making fools of tens of millions of people and in destroying and humiliating millions of intelligent citizens.

The full picture of the tragedy in China is unclear. But in any case, it is impossible to look at it in isolation from the internal economic difficulties of China after the collapse of the adventure of "the great leap forward," in isolation from the struggle by various groups for power, or in isolation from the foreign political situation—the war in Vietnam, the estrangement in the world, and the inadequate and lagging struggle against Stalinism in the Soviet Union.

The greatest damage from Maoism is often seen in the split of the world Communist movement. That is, of course, not so. The split is the result of a disease and to some extent represents the way to treat that disease. In the presence of the disease a formal unity would have been a dangerous, unprincipled compromise that would have led the world Communist movement into a blind alley once and for all.

Actually the crimes of the Maoists against human

rights have gone much too far, and the Chinese people are now in much greater need of help from the world's democratic forces to defend their rights than in need of the unity of the world's Communist forces, in the Maoist sense, for the purpose of combating the so-called imperialist peril somewhere in Africa or in Latin America or in the Middle East.

THE THREAT TO
INTELLECTUAL FREEDOM

This is a threat to the independence and worth of the human personality, a threat to the meaning of human life.

Nothing threatens freedom of the personality and the meaning of life like war, poverty, terror. But there are also indirect and only slightly more remote dangers.

One of these is the stupefaction of man (the "gray mass," to use the cynical term of bourgeois prognosticators) by mass culture with its intentional or commercially motivated lowering of intellectual level and content, with its stress on entertainment or utilitarianism, and with its carefully protective censorship.

Another example is related to the question of education. A system of education under government control, separation of school and church, universal free education—all these are great achievements of social progress. But everything has a reverse side. In this case it is excessive standardization, extending to the teaching process itself, to the curriculum, especially in literature, history, civics, geography, and to the system of examinations.

One cannot but see a danger in excessive reference to authority and in the limitation of discussion and intellectual boldness at an age when personal convictions are beginning to be formed. In the old China, the systems of examinations for official positions led to mental stagnation and to the canonizing of the reactionary aspects of Confucianism. It is highly undesirable to have anything like that in a modern society.

Modern technology and mass psychology constantly suggest new possibilities of managing the norms of behavior, the strivings and convictions of masses of people. This involves not only management through information based on the theory of advertising and mass psychology, but also more technical methods that are widely discussed in the press abroad. Examples are biochemical control of the birth rate and biochemical and electronic control of psychic processes.

It seems to me that we cannot completely ignore these new methods or prohibit the progress of science and technology, but we must be clearly aware of the awesome danger to basic human values and to the meaning of life that may be concealed in the misuse of technical and biochemical methods and the methods of mass psychology.

Man must not be turned into a chicken or a rat as in the well-known experiments in which elation is induced electrically through electrodes inserted into the brain. Related to this is the question of the ever-increasing use of tranquilizers and anti-depressants, legal and illegal narcotics, and so forth.

We also must not forget the very real danger mentioned by Norbert Wiener in his book *Cybernetics,* namely the absence in cybernetic machines of stable human norms of behavior. The tempting, unprecedented power that mankind, or, even worse, a particular group in a divided mankind, may derive from the wise counsels of its future intellectual aides, the artificial "thinking" automata, may become, as Wiener warned, a fatal trap; the counsels may turn out to be incredibly insidious and, instead of pursuing human objectives, may pursue completely abstract problems that had been transformed in an unforeseen manner in the artificial brain.

Such a danger will become quite real in a few decades if human values, particularly freedom of thought, are not strengthened, if alienation is not eliminated.

Let us now return for the dangers of today, to the need for intellectual freedom, which will enable the public at large and the intelligentsia to control and assess all acts, designs, and decisions of the ruling group.

Marx once wrote that the illusion that the "bosses know everything best" and "only the higher circles familiar with the official nature of things can pass judgment" was held by officials who equate the public weal with governmental authority.

Both Marx and Lenin always stressed the viciousness of a bureaucratic system as the opposite of a democratic system. Lenin used to say that every cook should learn how to govern. Now the diversity and complexity of social phenomena and the dangers facing mankind have become immeasurably greater; and it is therefore all the more important that mankind be protected against the danger of dogmatic and voluntaristic errors, which are inevitable when decisions are reached in a closed circle of secret advisers or shadow cabinets.

It is no wonder that the problem of censorship (in the broadest sense of the word) has been one of the central issues in the ideological struggle of the last few years. Here is what a progressive American sociologist, Lewis A. Coser, has to say on this point:

"It would be absurd to attribute the alienation of many avant-garde authors solely to the battle with the censors; yet one may well maintain that those battles contributed in no mean measure to such alienation. To these authors, the censor came to be the very symbol of the Philistinism, hypocrisy and meanness of bourgeois society.

"Many an author who was initially apolitical was drawn to the political left in the United States because the left was in the forefront of the battle against censorship. The close alliance of avant-garde art with avant-garde political and social radicalism can be accounted for, at least in part, by the fact that they came to be merged in the mind of many as a single battle for freedom against all repression." (I quote from an article by Igor Kon, published in *Novy Mir* in January 1968.)

We are all familiar with the passionate and closely argued appeal against censorship by the outstanding Soviet writer A. Solzhenitsyn. He as well as G. Vladimov, G. Svirsky, and other writers who have spoken out on the subject has clearly shown how incompetent censorship destroys the living soul of Soviet literature; but the same applies, of course, to all other manifestations of social thought, causing stagnation and dullness and preventing fresh and deep ideas.

Such ideas, after all, can arise only in discussion, in the face of objections, only if there is a potential possibility of expressing not only true but also dubious ideas. This was clear to the philosophers of ancient Greece and hardly anyone nowadays would have any doubts on that score. But after fifty years of complete domination over the minds of an entire nation, our leaders seem to fear even allusions to such a discussion.

At this point we must touch on some disgraceful tendencies that have become evident in the last few years. We will cite only a few isolated examples without trying to create a whole picture. The crippling censorship of Soviet artistic and political literature has again been intensified. Dozens of brilliant writings cannot see the light of day. They include some of the best of Solzhenitsyn's works, executed with great artistic and moral force and containing profound artistic and philosophical generalizations. Is this not a disgrace?

Wide indignation has been aroused by the recent decree adopted by the Supreme Soviet of the Russian Republic amending the Criminal Code in direct contravention of the civil rights proclaimed by our Constitution. [The decree included literary protests among acts punishable under Article 190, which deals with failure to report crimes.]

The Daniel-Sinyavsky trial, which has been condemned by the progressive public in the Soviet Union and abroad (from Louis Aragon to Graham Greene) and has compromised the Communist system, has still not been reviewed. The two writers languish in a camp with a strict regime and are being subjected (especially Daniel) to harsh humiliations and ordeals.*

---

* Yuli M. Daniel and Andrei D. Sinyavsky were convicted in 1966 of smuggling out of the Soviet Union literary works that the authorities contended were slanderous to the Soviet state. The trial aroused widespread concern both within and outside the Soviet Union. After more than five years in Soviet prison camps the men were released. Sinyavsky is now living in France.

Most political prisoners are now kept in a group of camps in the Mordvinian Republic, where the total number of prisoners, including criminals, is about fifty thousand. According to available information, the regime has become increasingly severe in these camps, with personnel left over from Stalinist times playing an increasing role. It should be said, in all fairness, that a certain improvement has been noted very recently; it is to be hoped that this turn of events will continue.

The restoration of Leninist principles of public control over places of imprisonment would undoubtedly be a healthy development. Equally important would be a complete amnesty for political prisoners, and not just the recent limited amnesty, which was proclaimed on the fiftieth anniversary of the October Revolution as a result of a temporary victory of rightist tendencies in our leadership. There should also be a review of all political trials that are still raising doubts among the progressive public.

Was it not disgraceful to allow the arrest, twelve-month detention without trial, and then the conviction and sentencing to terms of five to seven years of Ginzburg, Galanskov, and others for activities that actually amounted to a defense of civil liberties and (partly, as an example) of Daniel and Sinyavsky personally. The author of these lines sent an appeal to the Party's Central Committee on February 11, 1967, asking that the Ginzburg-Galanskov case be closed. He received no reply and no explanations on the substance of the case. It was only later that he heard there had been an attempt (apparently inspired by Semichastny, the former chairman of the KGB) to slander the present writer and several other persons on the basis of inspired false testimony by one of the accused in the Ginzburg-Galanskov case. Subsequently the testimony of that person

—Dobrovolsky—was used at the trial as evidence to show that Ginzburg and Galanskov had ties with a foreign anti-Soviet organization, which one cannot help but doubt.

Was it not disgraceful to permit the conviction and sentencing (to three years in camps) of Khaustov and Bukovsky for participation in a meeting in defense of their comrades? Was it not disgraceful to allow persecution, in the best witch-hunt tradition, of dozens of members of the Soviet intelligentsia who spoke out against the arbitrariness of judicial and psychiatric agencies, to attempt to force honorable people to sign false, hypocritical "retractions," to dismiss and blacklist people, to deprive young writers, editors, and other members of the intelligentsia of all means of existence?*

Here is a typical example of this kind of activity.

Comrade B., a woman editor of books on motion pictures, was summoned to the Party's district committee. The first question was, "Who gave you the letter in defense of Ginzburg to sign?" "Allow me not to reply to that question," she answered.

"All right, you can go, we want to talk this over," she was told.

The decision was to expel the woman from the Party and to recommend that she be dismissed from her job and barred from working anywhere else in the field of culture.

With such methods of persuasion and indoctrination the Party can hardly expect to claim the role of spiritual leader of mankind.

---

* Aleksandr Ginzburg, a young poet, and Yury Galanskov, a poet and editor, were convicted on charges growing out of their protest of the Daniel-Sinyavsky case. Galanskov subsequently died in a prison camp. Vladimir Bukovsky and Yevgeny Kushev were arrested for protesting the Ginzburg-Galanskov case.

Was it not disgraceful to have the speech at the Moscow Party conference by the president of the Academy of Sciences [Mstislav V. Keldysh], who is evidently either too intimidated or too dogmatic in his views? Is it not disgraceful to allow another backsliding into anti-Semitism in our appointments policy (incidentally, in the highest bureaucratic elite of our government, the spirit of anti-Semitism was never fully dispelled after the 1930's).

Was it not disgraceful to continue to restrict the civil rights of the Crimean Tatars, who lost about 46 percent of their numbers (mainly children and old people) in the Stalinist repressions? Nationality problems will continue to be a reason for unrest and dissatisfaction unless all departures from Leninist principles are acknowledged and analyzed and firm steps are taken to correct mistakes.

Is it not highly disgraceful and dangerous to make increasingly frequent attempts, either directly or indirectly (through silence), to publicly rehabilitate Stalin, his associates, and his policy, his pseudosocialism of terroristic bureaucracy, a socialism of hypocrisy and ostentatious growth that was at best a quantitative and one-sided growth involving the loss of many qualitative features? (This is a reference to the basic tendencies and consequences of Stalin's policy, or Stalinism, rather than a comprehensive assessment of the entire diversified situation in a huge country with two hundred million people.)

Although all these disgraceful phenomena are still far from the monstrous scale of the crimes of Stalinism and rather resemble in scope the sadly famous McCarthyism of the cold war era, the Soviet public cannot but be highly disturbed and indignant and display vigilance even in the face of insignificant manifestations of neo-Stalinism in our country.

We are convinced that the world's Communists will also view negatively any attempt to revive Stalinism in our country, which would, after all, be an awful blow to the attractive force of Communist ideas throughout the world.

Today the key to a progressive restructuring of the system of government in the interests of mankind lies in intellectual freedom. This has been understood, in particular, by the Czechoslovaks and there can be no doubt that we should support their bold initiative, which is so valuable for the future of socialism and all mankind. That support should be political and, in the early stages, include increased economic aid.

The situation involving censorship (Glavlit) in our country is such that it can hardly be corrected for any length of time simply by "liberalized" directives. Major organizational and legislative measures are required, for example, adoption of a special law on press and information that would clearly and convincingly define what can and what cannot be printed and would place the responsibility on competent people who would be under public control. It is essential that the exchange of information on an international scale (press, tourism, and so forth) be expanded in every way, that we get to know ourselves better, that we not try to save on sociological, political, and economic research and surveys, that we not restrict our research to that done in a government-controlled program (otherwise we might be tempted to avoid "unpleasant" subjects and questions).

THE BASIS
FOR HOPE

PEACEFUL COMPETITION

The prospects of socialism now depend on whether social-ism can be made attractive, whether the moral attractive-ness of the ideas of socialism and the glorification of labor, compared with the egotistical ideas of private ownership and the glorification of capital, will be the decisive factors that people will bear in mind when comparing socialism and capitalism, or whether people will remember mainly the limitations of intellectual freedom under socialism or, even worse, the fascistic regime of the cult [of personality].

I am placing the accent on the moral aspect because, when it comes to achieving a high productivity of social labor or developing all productive forces or insuring a high standard of living for most of the population, capitalism and socialism seem to have "played to a tie." Let us examine this question in detail.

Imagine two skiers racing through deep snow. At the start of the race, one of them, in a striped jacket, was many kilometers ahead, but now the skier in the red jacket is catching up to the leader. What can we say about their relative strength? Not very much, since each skier is racing under different conditions. The striped one broke the snow, and the red one did not have to. (The reader will understand that this ski race symbolizes the burden of research and development costs that the country leading in technology has to bear.) All one can say about the race is that there is not much difference in strength between the two skiers.

The parable does not, of course, reflect the whole complexity of comparing economic and technological progress in the United States and the Soviet Union, the relative vitality of RRS and AME (Russian Revolutionary Sweep and American Efficiency).

We cannot forget that during much of the period in question the Soviet Union waged a hard war and then healed its wounds; we cannot forget that some absurdities in our development were not an inherent aspect of the socialist course of development but a tragic accident, a serious, though not inevitable, disease.

On the other hand, any comparison must take account of the fact that we are now catching up with the United States only in some of the old, traditional industries, which are no longer as important as they used to be for the United States (for example, coal and steel). In some of the newer fields—for example, automation, computers, petrochemicals, and especially in industrial research and development—we are not only lagging behind but are also growing more slowly, so that a complete victory of our economy in the next few decades is unlikely.

It must also be borne in mind that our nation is endowed with vast natural resources, from fertile black earth to coal and forests, from oil to manganese and diamonds. It must be borne in mind that during the period under review our people worked to the limit of their capacity, which resulted in a certain depletion of resources.

We must also bear in mind the ski-track effect, in which the Soviet Union adopted principles of industrial organization and technology and development previously tested in the United States. Examples are the method of calculating the national fuel budget, assembly-line techniques, antibiotics, nuclear power, oxygen converters in steel-making, hybrid corn, self-propelled harvester combines, strip mining of coal, rotary excavators, semiconductors in electronics, the shift from steam to diesel locomotives, and much more.

There is only one justifiable conclusion and it can be formulated cautiously as follows:

1. We have demonstrated the vitality of the socialist course, which has done a great deal for the people materially, culturally, and socially and, like no other system, has glorified the moral significance of labor.

2. There are no grounds for asserting, as is often done in the dogmatic vein, that the capitalist mode of production leads the economy into a blind alley or that it is obviously inferior to the socialist mode in labor productivity, and there are certainly no grounds for asserting that capitalism always leads to absolute impoverishment of the working class.

The continuing economic progress being achieved under capitalism should be a fact of great theoretical significance for any nondogmatic Marxist. It is precisely this fact that lies at the basis of peaceful coexistence and it suggests, in principle, that if capitalism ever runs into an economic blind alley it will not necessarily have to leap into a desperate military adventure. Both capitalism and socialism are capable of long-term development, borrowing positive elements from each other, and actually coming closer to each other in a number of essential aspects.

I can just hear the outcries about revisionism and blunting of the class approach to this issue; I can just see the smirks about political naïveté and immaturity. But the facts suggest that there is real economic progress in the United States and other capitalist countries, that the capitalists are actually using the social principles of socialism, and that there has been real improvement in the position of the working people. More important, the facts suggest that on any other course except ever-increasing coexistence and collaboration between the two systems and the two superpowers, with a smoothing of contradictions and with mutual assistance, on any other course annihilation awaits mankind. There is no other way out.

We will now compare the distribution of personal income and consumption for various social groups in the United States and the Soviet Union. Our propaganda materials usually assert that there is crying inequality in the United States, while the Soviet Union has something entirely just, entirely in the interests of the working people. Actually both statements contain half truths and a fair amount of hypocritical evasion.

I have no intention of minimizing the tragic aspects of the poverty, lack of rights, and humiliation of the twenty-two million American Negroes. But we must clearly understand that this problem is not primarily a class problem, but a racial problem, involving the racism and egotism of white workers, and that the ruling group in the United States is interested in solving this problem. To be sure, the government has not been as active as it should be; this may be related to fears of an electoral character and to fears of upsetting the unstable equilibrium in the country and thus activating extreme leftist and especially extreme rightist parties. It seems to me that we in the socialist camp should be interested in letting the ruling group in the United States settle the Negro problem without aggravating the situation in the country.

At the other extreme, the presence of millionaires in the United States is not a serious economic burden in view of their small number. The total consumption of the rich is less than 20 percent, that is, less than the total rise of national consumption over a five-year period. From this point of view, a revolution, which would be likely to halt economic progress for more than five years, does not appear to be an economically advantageous move for the working people. And I am not even talking of the bloodletting that is inevitable in a revolution. And I am not talking of the danger of the "irony of history," about which Friedrich Engels wrote so well in his famous letter to V. Zasulich, the "irony" that took the form of Stalinism in our country.

There are, of course, situations where revolution is the only way out. This applies especially to national uprisings. But that is not the case in the United States and other developed capitalist countries, as suggested, incidentally, in the programs of the Communist parties of these countries.

As far as our country is concerned, here, too, we should avoid painting an idyllic picture. There is still great inequality in property between the city and the countryside, especially in rural areas that lack a transport outlet to the private market or do not produce any goods in demand in private trade. There are great differences between cities with some of the new, privileged industries and those with older, antiquated industries. As a result, 40 percent of the Soviet population is in difficult economic circumstances. In the United States about 25 percent of the population is on the verge of poverty. On the other hand, the 5 percent of the Soviet population that belongs to the managerial group is as privileged as its counterpart in the United States.

The development of modern society in both the Soviet Union and the United States is now following the same course of increasing complexity of structure and of industrial management, giving rise in both countries to managerial groups that are similar in social character.

We must therefore acknowledge that there is no qualitative difference in the structure of society of the two countries in terms of distribution of consumption. Unfortunately, the effectiveness of the managerial group in the Soviet Union (and, to a lesser extent, in the United States) is measured not only in purely economic or productive terms. This group also performs a concealed protective function that is rewarded in the sphere of consumption by concealed privileges.

Few people are aware of the practice under Stalin of paying salaries in sealed envelopes, of the constantly recurring concealed distribution of scarce foods and goods for various services, privileges in vacation resorts, and so forth.

I want to emphasize that I am not opposed to the socialist principle of payment based on the amount and quality of labor. Relatively higher wages for better administrators, for highly skilled workers, teachers, and physi-

cians, for workers in dangerous or harmful occupations, for
workers in science, culture, and the arts, all of whom account for a relatively small part of the total wage bill, do not
threaten society if they are not accompanied by concealed
privileges; moreover, higher wages benefit society if they
are deserved.

The point is that every wasted minute of a leading administrator represents a major material loss for the economy, and every wasted minute of a leading figure in the
arts means a loss in the emotional, philosophical, and artistic
wealth of society. But when something is done in secret,
the suspicion inevitably arises that things are not clean, that
loyal servants of the existing system are being bribed.

It seems to me that the rational way of solving this
touchy problem would be not the setting of income ceilings
for Party members or some such measure, but simply the
prohibition of all privileges and the establishment of unified
wage rates based on the social value of labor and an economic market approach to the wage problem.

I consider that further advances in our economic reform and a greater role for economic and market factors
accompanied by increased public control over the managerial group (which, incidentally, is also essential in capitalist countries) will help eliminate all the roughness in our
present distribution pattern.

An even more important aspect of the economic reform for the regulation and stimulation of production is the
establishment of a correct system of market prices, proper
allocation and rapid utilization of investment funds, and
proper use of natural and human resources based on appropriate rents in the interest of our society.

A number of socialist countries, including the Soviet

Union, Yugoslavia, and Czechoslovakia, are now experi-
menting with basic economic problems of the role of planning and of the market, government and cooperative
ownership, and so forth. These experiments are of great
significance.

Summing up, we now come to our basic conclusion
about the moral and ethical character of the advantages of
the socialist course of development of human society. In
our view, this does not in any way minimize the significance
of socialism. Without socialism, bourgeois practices and
the egotistical principle of private ownership gave rise to
the "people of the abyss" described by Jack London and
earlier by Engels.

Only the competition with socialism and the pressure
of the working class made possible the social progress of the
twentieth century and, all the more, will insure the now
inevitable process of rapprochement of the two systems. It
took socialism to raise the meaning of labor to the heights
of a moral feat. Before the advent of socialism, national
egotism gave rise to colonial oppression, nationalism, and
racism. By now it has become clear that victory is on the
side of the humanistic, international approach.

The capitalist world could not help giving birth to the
socialist, but now the socialist world should not seek to
destroy by force the ground from which it grew. Under the
present conditions this would be tantamount to the suicide
of mankind. Socialism should ennoble that ground by its
example and other indirect forms of pressure and then
merge with it.

The rapprochement with the capitalist world should
not be an unprincipled, anti-popular plot between ruling
groups, as happened in the extreme case [of the Soviet-Nazi

rapprochement] of 1939–40. Such a rapprochement must rest not only on a socialist, but also on a popular, democratic foundation, under the control of public opinion, as expressed through publicity, elections, and so forth.

Such a rapprochement implies not only wide social reforms in the capitalist countries, but also substantial changes in the structure of ownership, with a greater role played by government and cooperative ownership, and the preservation of the basic features of ownership of the means of production in the socialist countries.

Our allies along this road are not only the working class and the progressive intelligentsia, which are interested in peaceful coexistence and social progress and in a democratic, peaceful transition to socialism (as reflected in the programs of the Communist parties of the developed countries), but also the reformist part of the bourgeoisie, which supports such a program of "convergence." (Although I am using this term, taken from Western literature, it is clear from the foregoing that I have given it a socialist and democratic meaning.)

Typical representatives of the reformist bourgeoisie are Cyrus Eaton, President Franklin D. Roosevelt and, especially, President John F. Kennedy. Without wishing to cast a stone in the direction of Comrade N. S. Khrushchev (our high esteem of his services was expressed earlier), I cannot help recalling one of his statements, which may have been more typical of his entourage than of him personally.

On July 10, 1961, in speaking at a reception of specialists about his meeting with Kennedy in Vienna, Comrade Khrushchev recalled Kennedy's request that the Soviet Union, in conducting policy and making demands, consider the actual possibilities and the difficulties of the new Kennedy administration and refrain from demanding more than it could grant without courting the danger of being defeated in elections and being replaced by rightist forces. At that time, Khrushchev did not give Kennedy's unprecedented request the proper attention, to put it mildly, and began to rail. And now, after the shots in Dallas, who can say what auspicious opportunities in world history have been, if not destroyed, at any rate set back because of a lack of understanding?

Bertrand Russell once told a peace congress in Moscow that "the world will be saved from thermonuclear annihilation if the leaders of each of the two systems prefer complete victory of the other system to a thermonuclear war." (I am quoting from memory.) It seems to me that such a solution would be acceptable to the majority of people in any country, whether capitalist or socialist. I consider that the leaders of the capitalist and socialist systems by the very nature of things will gradually be forced to adopt the point of view of the majority of mankind.

Intellectual freedom of society will facilitate and smooth the way for this trend toward patience, flexibility, and a security from dogmatism, fear, and adventurism. All mankind, including its best-organized and most active forces, the working class and the intelligentsia, is interested in freedom and security.

A FOUR-STAGE PLAN FOR COOPERATION

Having examined the development of mankind according to the negative alternative, leading to annihilation, we must now attempt, even schematically, to suggest the positive alternative. (The author concedes the primitiveness of his attempts at prognostication, which requires the joint efforts of many specialists and here, even more than elsewhere, invites criticism.)

□

In the first stage, a growing ideological struggle in the socialist countries between Stalinist and Maoist forces, on the one hand, and the realistic forces of leftist Leninist Communists (and leftist Westerners), on the other, will lead to a deep ideological split on an international, national, and intraparty scale.

In the Soviet Union and other socialist countries, this process will lead first to a multiparty system (here and there) and to acute ideological struggle and discussions, and then to the ideological victory of the realists, affirming the policy of increasing peaceful coexistence, strengthening democracy, and expanding economic reforms (1968–80). The dates reflect the most optimistic unrolling of events.

The author, incidentally, is not one of those who consider the multiparty system to be an essential stage in the development of the socialist system, or, even less, a panacea for all ills, but he assumes that in some cases a multiparty system may be an inevitable consequence of the course of events when a ruling Communist Party refuses for one reason or another to rule by the scientific democratic method required by history.

☐

In the second stage, persistent demands for social progress and peaceful coexistence in the United States and other capitalist countries, and pressure exerted by the example of the socialist countries and by internal progressive forces (the working class and the intelligentsia), will lead to the victory of the leftist reformist wing of the bourgeoisie, which will begin to implement a program of rapprochement (convergence) with socialism, i.e., social progress, peaceful coexistence, and collaboration with socialism on a world scale and changes in the structure of ownership. This phase includes an expanded role for the intelligentsia and an attack on the forces of racism and militarism (1972–85). (The various stages overlap.)

□

In the third stage, the Soviet Union and the United States, having overcome their alienation, solve the problem of saving the poorer half of the world. The aforementioned 20 percent tax on the national income of developed countries is applied. Gigantic fertilizer factories and irrigation systems using atomic power will be built [in the developing countries], the resources of the sea will be used to a vastly greater extent, indigenous personnel will be trained, and industrialization will be carried out. Gigantic factories will produce synthetic amino acids and synthesize proteins, fats, and carbohydrates. At the same time disarmament will proceed (1972–90).

□

In the fourth stage, the socialist convergence will reduce differences in social structure, promote intellectual freedom, science, and economic progress, and lead to the creation of a world government and the smoothing of national contradictions (1980–2000). During this period decisive progress can be expected in the field of nuclear power, on the basis of both uranium and thorium and, probably, deuterium and lithium.

Some authors consider it likely that explosive breeding (the reproduction of active materials such as plutonium, uranium 233, and tritium) may be used in subterranean or other enclosed explosions.

During this period the expansion of space exploration will require thousands of people to work and live continuously on other planets and on the moon, on artificial satellites and on asteroids whose orbits will have been changed by nuclear explosions.

The synthesis of materials that are super-conductors at room temperature may completely revolutionize electrical technology, cybernetics, transportation, and communications. Progress in biology (in this and subsequent periods) will make possible effective control and direction of all life processes at the levels of biochemistry and of the cell, organism, ecology, and society, from fertility and aging to psychic processes and heredity.

If such an all-encompassing scientific and technological revolution, promising uncounted benefits for mankind, is to be possible and safe, it will require the greatest possible scientific foresight and care and concern for human values of a moral, ethical, and personal character. (I touched briefly on the danger of a thoughtless bureaucratic use of the scientific and technological revolution in a divided world in the section on "Dangers," but could add a great deal more.) Such a revolution will be possible and safe only under highly intelligent worldwide guidance.

The foregoing program presumes:

1. worldwide interest in overcoming the present divisions;

2. the expectation that modifications in both the socialist and capitalist countries will tend to reduce contradictions and differences;

3. worldwide interest of the intelligentsia, the working class, and other progressive forces in a scientific democratic approach to politics, economics, and culture;

4. the absence of insurmountable obstacles to economic development in both world economic systems that might

otherwise lead inevitably into a blind alley, despair, and adventurism.

Every honorable and thinking person who has not been poisoned by narrow-minded indifference will seek to insure that future development will be along the lines of the better alternative. However only broad, open discussion, without the pressure of fear and prejudice, will help the majority to adopt the correct and best course of action.

A SUMMARY OF PROPOSALS

In conclusion, I will sum up a number of the concrete proposals of varying degrees of importance that have been discussed in the text. These proposals, addressed to the leadership of the country, do not exhaust the content of the article.

□

The strategy of peaceful coexistence and collaboration must be deepened in every way. Scientific methods and principles of international policy will have to be worked out, based on scientific prediction of the immediate and more distant consequences.

The initiative must be seized in working out a broad program of struggle against hunger.

A law on press and information must be drafted, widely

discussed, and adopted, with the aim not only of ending irresponsible and irrational censorship, but also of encouraging self-study in our society, fearless discussion, and the search for truth. The law must provide for the material resources of freedom of thought.

All anti-constitutional laws and decrees violating human rights must be abrogated.

Political prisoners must be amnestied and some of the recent political trials must be reviewed (for example, the Daniel-Sinyavsky and Ginzburg-Galanskov cases). The camp regime of political prisoners must be promptly relaxed.

The exposure of Stalin must be carried through to the end, to the complete truth, and not just to the carefully weighed half truth dictated by caste considerations. The influence of neo-Stalinists in our political life must be restricted in every way (the text mentioned, as an example, the case of S. Trapeznikov, who enjoys too much influence).

The economic reform must be deepened in every way and the area of experimentation expanded, with conclusions based on the results.

A law on geohygiene must be adopted after broad discussion, and ultimately become part of world efforts in this area.

□

With this article the author addresses the leadership of our country and all its citizens as well as all people of goodwill throughout the world. The author is aware of the controversial character of many of his statements. His purpose is open, frank discussion under conditions of publicity.

In conclusion, a textological comment. In the process

of discussion of previous drafts of this article, some incomplete and in some respects one-sided texts have been circulated. Some of them contained certain passages that were inept in form and tact and were included through oversight. The author asks readers to bear this in mind. The author is deeply grateful to readers of preliminary drafts who communicated their friendly comments and thus helped improve the essay and refine a number of basic statements.

June 1968

MANIFESTO II

(AUTHOR'S NOTE: *This was a joint letter and at the present time does not fully express the point of view of at least one of its authors.*)

To the Central Committee of the CPSU, L. I. Brezhnev
To the Council of Ministers of the USSR, A. N. Kosygin
To the Presidium of the Supreme Soviet, N. V. Podgorny

We address ourselves to you on a question having great significance. Our country has achieved a great deal in the development of production, in the fields of education and culture, in the radical improvement of the living conditions of the workers, in the formation of new socialist relations between people. These achievements have worldwide historical importance. They have profoundly influenced events throughout the world and have laid a solid foundation for further successes in the cause of Communism. But we are also faced with serious difficulties and shortcomings.

This letter considers and develops a point of view that briefly can be formulated in the following theses:

□

At the present time it is urgently necessary to carry out a series of measures directed toward the further democratization of public life in the country. This necessity arises from the existence of a close link between the problems of technical-economic progress and scientific methods of management, on the one hand, and questions of information, publicity, and competition on the other. This necessity arises also from other internal and external political problems.

Democratization must facilitate the maintenance and strengthening of the Soviet socialist system, of the socialist economic structure, of our social and cultural achievements and socialist ideology.

Democratization carried out under the direction of the CPSU in cooperation with all levels of society should preserve and strengthen the leading role of the Party in the economic, political, and cultural life of society.

Democratization must be gradual in order to avoid possible complications and disruptions. At the same time, it must be profound and it must be carried out consistently and on the basis of carefully worked-out programs. Without deep-rooted democratization, our society will not be able to solve the problems it faces and will not be able to develop normally.

There is reason to suppose that the point of view expressed in these theses is shared to a greater or lesser extent by a considerable portion of the Soviet intelligentsia and the advanced section of the working class. This point of view finds its reflection in the views of students and working youth and in numerous discussions carried on in private.

However, we consider it appropriate to set forth this point of view in comprehensive written form in order to facilitate, widen, and initiate consideration of important problems. We are seeking to achieve a positive and constructive approach acceptable to the Party-state leadership of the country, and we seek to clarify several misunderstandings and groundless fears.

In the course of the past decade, threatening signs of breakdown and stagnation have been observed in the national economy of our country, although the roots of these difficulties originated in a much earlier period and bear a very profound character. The growth rate of the national income is steadily dropping. There is a widening gap between the requirements for normal development and the real returns from new industrial production. Numerous facts point to errors in determining technical and economic policy in industry and agriculture, as does impermissible red tape in the decision of urgent problems. Defects in the system of planning, accounting, and incentives often lead to a contradiction between local and institutional interests on the one hand and public and state interests on the other. As a result, necessary reserves for the development of production are not available or are not utilized, and technical progress is sharply impeded.

Because of these factors, the natural wealth of the country is frequently destroyed without control and with impunity: forests are cut down; water reservoirs are polluted; valuable agricultural lands are despoiled; soil is eroded and rendered unfit for cultivation; and so forth. It is common knowledge that there is a chronically grave situation in agriculture, especially in livestock. Real income of the population in recent years has hardly risen; nourishment, medical services, and everyday services improve very slowly and unequally between regions. The items of goods in short supply grow. There are obvious signs of inflation. Especially alarming for the future of our country is a slowdown in the development of education. Factually, our general expenditures on education of all types are less than in the United States and are growing more slowly. There is a tragic growth in alcoholism, and narcotics addiction is beginning to make itself felt. In many regions of the country crime is rising systematically, including crime among teenagers and youth. Bureaucracy, compartmentalization, formal attitudes toward jobs, and lack of initiative are growing in the work of scientific and technological organizations.

A decisive factor in the comparison of economic systems is labor productivity. Here the situation is worst of all. Productivity of labor as before remains many times lower than in the developed capitalist countries, and its growth is slowing down. This situation is particularly grave if you compare it with the situation in leading capitalist countries and, in particular, the United States.

By introducing into the economy of the country elements of state regulation and planning these countries have rid themselves of the destructive crises that earlier tore capitalist economies apart. The widespread introduction of automation and computer technology into the economy insures a rapid growth of the productivity of labor, which in turn enables the partial overcoming of severe social difficulties and contradictions (as, for example, ways of establishing unemployment benefits, the shortening of the working day, etc.). Comparing our economy with the economy of the United States, we see that our economy lags not only in quantitative but also—which is saddest of all—in qualitative respects.

The newer and more revolutionary the section of the economy the greater the contrast between the United States and us. We have exceeded America in coal production but lag in extraction of oil, are ten times behind in natural gas and production of electric power, hopelessly behind in the chemical field, and immeasurably behind in computer technology. The last is especially essential, for the introduction of the computer into the economy is a factor of decisive importance, radically changing the character of the system of production and all culture. This phenomenon is justly called the second industrial revolution. Yet the capacity of our computers is hundreds of times less than that of the United States, and as regards utilizing computers in the economy the disparity is so great that it is impossible even to measure it. We simply live in a different epoch.

The situation is no better in the field of scientific and engineering discoveries. Here there is no feeling of a growing vitality in our role. On the contrary, at the end of the 1950's our country was the first in the world to launch Sputniks and send a man into space. At the end of the 1960's we lost our leadership and the first men to land on the moon were American.

This fact is just one of the external evidences of actual and growing disparity, on a wide front, of the scientific and technical level of our country and that of the developed countries of the West. In the 1920's and 1930's the capitalist world suffered a period of crises and depression. At that time we were creating industry at an unbelievable pace, by employing the enthusiasm of the nation that was a result of the revolution. At that time our motto was: Catch up with America and overtake it. And we actually did this for several decades. Then the situation changed. The second industrial revolution began. And now, at the beginning of the 1970's, we can see that we did not catch up with America; we fell behind her more and more.

What is the matter? Why didn't we become the trailblazers of the second industrial revolution? Why couldn't we at least stay even with the most developed capitalist countries? Is it really true that the socialist system provides poorer possibilities than the capitalist for the development of productive force and that in economic competition socialism can't beat capitalism?

Of course not! The source of our difficulties is not in the socialist system. On the contrary, it lies in those qualities and conditions of our life that run counter to socialism and are hostile to it. Their cause—anti-democratic traditions and norms of public life—arose during the Stalin period and has not been completely liquidated to this day. Economic constraints, limitations on the exchange of information, restrictions of intellectual freedom, and other anti-democratic distortions of socialism that took place in Stalin's time are still accepted as a kind of necessary cost of the process of industrialization.

It is supposed that these distortions did not affect seriously the country's economy, although they had extremely serious consequences in the political and military fields, for the fate of wide strata of the population and whole nationalities. We are leaving aside the problem of how far this point of view may have been justified regarding the early stages of development of a socialist economy, but the reduced rate of industrial development in the prewar years testifies to the contrary. There is no doubt that with the beginning of the second industrial revolution these phenomena have become the decisive economic factor and the basic obstacle to the development of the country's productive forces.

Due to the increase in the size and complexity of economic systems, problems of organization and management have taken first place. These problems cannot be solved by one individual or even several individuals who possess power and who "know all." They demand the creative participation of millions of people on all levels of the economic system. They demand a wide exchange of information, and this is what distinguishes contemporary economics from, say, the economics of the countries of the ancient East. But in the process of exchanging information and ideas in our country we face insurmountable difficulties. Negative phenomena and real information about our faults are kept secret because they might be "used for hostile propaganda."

The exchange of information with foreign countries is limited by the fear of "penetration of hostile ideology." Theoretical conceptions and practical proposals that seem somehow too bold are suppressed instantly without discussion, out of fear that they may "destroy the foundations."

One can see clear distrust of creative thinkers, critics, and active personalities. Under these conditions those who advance on the service ladder are not those distinguished by high professional qualities and principles but those who by their words display dedication to the cause of the Party, but who in deeds are distinguished only by dedication to

their own narrow personal interests or by passive performance.

Restrictions on freedom of information not only make
difficult any control over the leadership, not only frustrate
the people's initiative, but also deprive even those heading
middle-level administrations of both rights and information, transforming them into passive bureaucrats. Our
leaders receive incomplete and edited information and are
prevented from using their power effectively. The economic reforms of 1965 were extremely useful and an important beginning, calling for the solution of important
questions in our economic life. But we are convinced that
simple economic measures alone are insufficient for the fulfilling of all these tasks. Moreover, these economic measures
cannot be fully undertaken without reforms in the sphere of
administration, information, and public knowledge. The
same is true of such often-promised initiatives as establishing complex industrial organizations with a high degree of
independence in administrative, fiscal, and personnel questions.

It may be concluded that the solution of all economic
problems requires a scientific answer to such general and
theoretical questions of socialist economics as forms of
management feedback, pricing decisions in the absence of
a free market, general planning principles, etc.

We are talking a lot now about the necessity of the
scientific approach to problems of organization and administration. This, of course, is correct. Only a scientific approach can help overcome difficulties and realize all the
possibilities for the direction of the economy and for the
technological progress which the absence of capitalist ownership ought to make possible. But the scientific approach
requires full information, impartial thinking, and creative

freedom. Until these conditions are met (not just for some individuals, but for the masses) the talk about scientific management will remain empty words.

Our economy can be compared with the movement of traffic through an intersection. When there were few cars, traffic police could handle it quite easily and movement was normal. But the number of cars steadily increased. A traffic jam developed. What can be done? The drivers can be fined or the policemen changed. But this will not save the situation. The only way out is to widen the intersection.

The obstacles that prevent the development of our economy can be found outside it, in the political and public area, and all measures that do not eliminate these obstacles will be ineffective.

The consequences of Stalin's period are still negatively affecting the economy, not only directly because of the impossibility of a scientific approach to the problems of administration and management, but also in no less degree indirectly through the general lowering of the creative potential of representatives of all professions.

But it is creative labor that is becoming more and more important for the economy under the conditions of the second industrial revolution. In this connection it is impossible not to speak of the problem of the relationship between the state and the intelligentsia.

Freedom of information and creativity are essential for the intelligentsia because of the nature of its activities and its social function. The desire of the intelligentsia for greater freedom is legitimate and natural. The state, however, suppresses this desire through all kinds of restrictions —administrative pressure, dismissals from work, and even trials. This brings about mutual distrust and profound mutual misunderstanding, which make most difficult any fruitful cooperation between the Party-state structure and the most active—that is, the most socially valuable—strata of the intelligentsia. In conditions of contemporary industrial society, where the role of the intelligentsia is growing continuously, this gap can only be termed suicidal.

Most of the intelligentsia and youth realize the necessity of democratization, the need for cautious and gradual approaches in this matter, but they cannot understand or justify actions having a clearly anti-democratic character. Actually, how can one justify the imprisonment, the detention in camps and psychiatric clinics, of persons who are oppositionists but whose opposition is still within legal bounds in the area of ideas and convictions? In a series of cases the matter lies not in some kind of opposition, but in a simple desire for information, for frank, impartial discussion of important social questions!

It is impermissible to keep writers in prison because of their work. One cannot understand or justify such stupid, harmful measures as the expulsion from the Writers Union of the greatest and most popular Soviet writer [Alexander Solzhenitsyn], nor the destruction of the editorial board of *Novy Mir,* around which gathered the most progressive forces of Marxist-Leninist socialist direction!

One must speak again of ideological problems.

Democratization with full information and competition must return to our ideological life (social science, art, propaganda) its essential dynamism and creative character, liquidating the bureaucratic, ritualistic, dogmatic, official-hypocritical ungifted style that today occupies so important a place.

A policy of democratization would remove the gap between the Party-state apparatus and the intelligentsia. Mutual lack of understanding would be replaced by close cooperation. A policy of democratization would stimulate enthusiasm comparable to that of the 1920's. The best intellectual forces of the country would be mobilized for the solution of social and economic problems.

To carry out democratization is not easy. Its normal progress will be threatened from one side by individualist, anti-socialist forces and from the other side by those worshipers of "strong power," demagogues of a fascist type who may attempt to utilize the economic difficulties of the country for their own aims, and by mutual misunderstanding and mistrust on the part of the intelligentsia and the Party-state apparatus and the existence in some levels of society of bourgeois and nationalist sentiments.

But we must realize that there is no other way out for our country and that this difficult problem must be solved. Democratization at the initiative of, and under the control of, the highest authorities will allow this process to advance gradually and thus to enable all the links of the Party-state apparatus successfully to change over to the new style of work, which, in contrast with the past, will involve greater public information, openness, and wider discussion of all problems.

There is no doubt that the majority of officials, who are, of course, people educated in a contemporary, highly developed country, are capable of adapting to this style of work and very quickly will feel its advantages. The comparatively small number unable to do so will leave the apparatus—to its advantage. We propose the following tentative measures that could be carried out in the course of four or five years:

□

A statement by the highest party and government organs on the necessity of further democratization, on the tempo and method of achieving it; publication in the press of a number of articles discussing the problems of democratization.

Restricted distribution (through Party and state organs, organizations, and institutions) of information on the state of the country and theoretical work on public problems, which for the time being should not be made a subject of wide discussion. Gradual increase in circulation of such material until it is fully available to everyone.

Widespread organization of industrial establishments with a high degree of independence in questions of industrial planning and production processes, sales and supplies, finances, and personnel, and widening these privileges for smaller units. Scientific determination after careful research of the forms and extent of state regulation.

An end to jamming foreign broadcasts. Free sale of foreign books and periodicals. Accession of our country to the international copyright system. Gradual (over three to four years) expansion and easing of international tourism on both sides. Freer international correspondence and other measures for the expansion of international contacts, particularly in relation to the Comecon countries.

Establishment of an institute for the study of public opinion, restricted at first and then with complete publication of materials, showing the attitude of the population to the most important problems of internal and foreign policy and also other sociological material.

Amnesty for political prisoners. A decree on compulsory publication of full stenographic records of trials of a political nature. Public control over places of imprisonment and over psychiatric institutions.

[The number of political prisoners is not great compared to the Stalin days but totals, by a conservative estimate, several thousand.]

Institution of other measures to improve the work of courts and procurators' offices, and to establish their independence from the executive power, local influence, prejudice, and connections.

Elimination of the nationality designation in passports. A single system of passports for urban and rural areas. Gradual elimination of passport registration, carried out simultaneously with elimination of inequities in regional economic and cultural development.

[Every Soviet citizen must possess an "internal" passport for travel, work, and life within his country. Each passport carries a designation of his "nationality" (Russian, Ukrainian, Uzbek, Jewish, etc.).]

Reforms in the field of education. Greater appropriations for primary and secondary schools, improvement of the material situation of teachers, giving them greater independence and the right to experiment.

Passage of a law on the press and information facilitating the possibility of creating new publishers by public organizations and groups of citizens.

Improvement of the training of leading cadres versed in the art of management. Introduction of practical training for managers. Improvement of the knowledgeability of leadership cadres at all levels, their rights to independence, to experimentation, and to the defense of their opinions and the testing of them in practice.

Gradual introduction into practice of the nomination of several candidates for each office in elections for Party and government organs at all levels, including indirect elections.

Widening the rights of Soviet organs. Widening the rights and responsibilities of the Supreme Soviet of the USSR.

Restoration of the rights of all nations forcibly resettled under Stalin. Restoration of the national autonomy of the resettled peoples. Granting them the possibility of resettling in former homelands (where this has not already been done).

Measures designed to increase public disclosure of the work of the leading organs within limits determined by state interests. Creation of committees composed of highly qualified scientists from different specialties to consult with leading organs at all levels.

□

Of course this plan must be regarded as approximate. It is also clear that it must be supplemented by a plan for economic and social measures worked out by specialists. We emphasize that democratization in itself does not solve economic problems. It only creates preconditions for their solution. But without creation of these preconditions, economic problems cannot be solved. Sometimes we hear our foreign friends comparing the Soviet Union to a powerful truck, whose driver is pressing on the gas with one foot as hard as possible while stepping on the brake at the same time. The time has come to use the brake more sensibly.

The plan we propose shows, in our view, that it is quite possible to outline a program of democratization that is acceptable to the Party and the state and satisfies, as a first approximation, the urgent demands of the nation's development. Naturally, wide discussion, profound scientific, sociological, economic, political, pedagogic, and other research, as well as actual practice, will provide essential corrections and additions. But it is important, as the mathematicians say, to prove "the theorem of the existence of a solution."

We must also consider the international consequences of democratization if it is adopted by our country. Nothing can so well serve our international authority and strengthen progressive Communist forces in the entire world as further democratization, accompanied by an intensification of the technological and economic progress of the world's first socialist country. Doubtless possibilities will increase for peaceful coexistence and international cooperation; the forces of peace and social progress will be strengthened; the attractiveness of Communist ideology will grow; and our international position will become more secure. Particularly vital is the fact that our moral and material position relative to China will be strengthened, making it possible (indirectly, by example of technical aid) to influence the situation in that country in the interests of the peoples of both countries.

A number of correct and necessary foreign policy actions by our government are not properly understood because the information provided to citizens on these matters is incomplete, and in the past there have been cases of plain inaccuracy and tendentious information, which increase the lack of confidence.

One example is the question of economic aid to underdeveloped countries. Fifty years ago the workers of Europe, ravaged by war, helped those dying of hunger in the Volga region. Soviet people today are not callous or egotistical. But they must be sure that our resources are being spent on real aid, on the solution of serious problems, not on the construction of grandiose stadiums and for the purchase of

American cars for local bureaucrats. The situation in the modern world and the opportunities and tasks facing our country demand wide participation in economic aid to the underdeveloped nations in cooperation with other countries. But for a correct understanding of these questions on the part of the public it is not enough to give verbal assurances. Proofs must be given and needs must be shown, and this demands fuller information and democratization.

Soviet foreign policy, in its basic features, is a policy of peace and cooperation.

The public's lack of information causes disquiet. In the past there occurred certain negative phenomena in Soviet foreign policy, which had the character of excessive ambitiousness, messianism, and which force one to the conclusion that it is not only the imperialists who bear the responsibility for international tension. All negative phenomena in our foreign policy are closely connected with the problem of democratization, and this works both ways. Great disquiet is caused by the absence of democratic discussion of such questions as arms aid to a number of countries, including, for instance, Nigeria, where a bloody civil war was in progress whose causes and course were quite unfamiliar to the Soviet public. We are convinced that the resolution of the United Nations Security Council on the problems of the Arab-Israeli conflict is just and reasonable, although it is not definite enough in a number of important points. However, disquiet is caused by the question: Does our position not go substantially further than this document? Is it not too one-sided? Is it always realistic for us to strive to extend our influence in places far from our borders in a time of difficulties in Sino-Soviet relations and in technological and economic development?

Of course in certain cases such a "dynamic policy" is essential, but it must be harmonized not only with general principles but also with the nation's real capabilities. We are convinced that the only realistic policy in an age of thermonuclear weapons is a course aimed at a continued deepening of international cooperation, at determined attempts to find a line of possible convergence in scientific, technological, economic, cultural, and ideological spheres, and the renunciation of weapons of mass destruction as a matter of principle.

We take this opportunity to support unilateral and joint declarations of principle by nuclear powers renouncing the first use of mass-destruction weapons.

Democratization will facilitate a better public understanding of our foreign policy and remove from it all its negative features. This in turn will lead to the disappearance of one of the chief "trumps" held by the opponents of democratization. Another of their "trumps"—the well-known mutual lack of understanding between government-Party circles and the intelligentsia—will disappear at the very first stages of democratization.

□

What awaits our country if a course toward democratization is not taken? We will fall behind the capitalist countries in the course of the second industrial revolution and be gradually transformed into a second-rate provincial power (history has known similar examples); economic difficulties will increase; relations between the Party-state apparatus and the intelligentsia will deteriorate, with dangerous clashes between right and left; and nationality problems will be exacerbated, for in the national republics the movement for democratization, arising from below, inevitably takes on a nationalistic character. The prospect becomes particularly menacing if one takes into consideration the presence of a danger from Chinese totalitarian nationalism (which in a historical context we regard as temporary but very serious in the coming years). We can counter this danger only if we increase or at least maintain the technological and economic gap between our country and China, if we add to the number of our friends in the world at large, and if we offer the Chinese people the alternative of cooperation and aid. This becomes obvious if one takes into consideration the numerical superiority of the potential enemy and his militant nationalism, as well as the great extent of our eastern frontiers and the sparse population of the eastern regions.

Thus, economic stagnation, which slows up the rate of development, in combination with an insufficiently realistic and sometimes too ambitious foreign policy on all continents may lead our country to catastrophic consequences.

□

Respected Comrades:

There is no way out of the difficulties facing the country except a course toward democratization carried out by the Party in accordance with a carefully worked out program. A move to the right, that is, the victory of the tendency toward harsh administrative measures and "tightening the screws," will not solve any problems; on the contrary, it will aggravate those problems to the extreme and lead the country into a tragic blind alley. The tactics of passively waiting to see what happens will lead in the final analysis to the same result. Presently we have a chance to take the right road and carry out the necessary reforms. In a few years, perhaps, it will be too late. This problem must be recognized by the whole country.

It is the duty of everyone who sees the source of the difficulties and the means of overcoming them to point this out to his fellow citizens. Understanding the need and opportunity for a gradual democratization is the first step on the road to its realization.

A. D. SAKHAROV

V. F. TURCHIN

R. A. MEDVEDEV

March 19, 1970

[The following footnote was attached to the letter:]

On January 8, 1970, a "letter to L. I. Brezhnev" was widely distributed in Moscow, signed by the name "Sakarov" or "Academician Sakarov." This "letter" in several variations was published subsequently in the foreign press. In issue No. 1 for 1970 of the anti-Soviet emigré journal Possev was published an article under the pretentious title "The Truth about Contemporary Times" over the signature of "R. Medvedev." This article, a complete fabrication, was broadcast subsequently in the Russian language by Radio Liberty (FRG). We declare we are not the authors of the forementioned letter and article. These documents present us in a completely false light and are evidently distributed with provocational aims. Signed:

R. A. MEDVEDEV

A. D. SAKHAROV

MEMORANDUM

I request a discussion of the general questions partially discussed in a previous letter from R. A. Medvedev, V. F. Turchin, and myself, and in my letter of 1968. I also request the consideration of a number of particular questions of a topical nature that I find extremely disturbing.

I have included below, in two general lists, questions that, although differing in degree of importance and self-evidence, have a definite inner connection. A discussion and partial argumentation of these questions will be found in the above-mentioned letters and in the postscript to this memorandum.

I wish also to inform you that in November 1970, I, together with V. N. Chalidze and A. N. Tverdokhlebov, was involved in the creation of a "Human Rights Committee" for the purpose of studying the problem of safeguarding

human rights and promoting the growth of a legal awareness. I enclose some of the committee's documents. We
hope to be useful to society, and we seek a dialogue with
the country's leadership and a frank and public discussion of problems of human rights.

SOME URGENT PROBLEMS

The problems listed below appear to me to need urgent consideration.

For brevity's sake they have been expressed in the form of proposals. While recognizing that some of these problems require further study, and conscious that the list is of necessity an incomplete and therefore to a certain extent a subjective one (I have tried to set out several equally important questions in the second half of this memorandum, while several could not be included at all), I nevertheless consider that a discussion of the following proposals by the competent authorities is essential.

1. Concerning political persecution. I feel it is high time to consider the pressing problem of implementing a general amnesty for political prisoners, that is, persons convicted under Articles 70, 72, 190–1, –2 and –3 of the RSFSR

Criminal Code and the equivalent articles of the codes of the union republics; persons convicted on religious grounds; persons confined in psychiatric institutions; persons sentenced for attempting to cross the frontier; and political prisoners given an additional sentence for attempting to escape or for disseminating propaganda in their camp.

Measures should be taken to insure real and widespread public access to the hearings of all legal proceedings, especially those of a political character. I consider it important that all judicial verdicts carried in violation of the principle of public access should be reviewed.

I hold inadmissible all psychiatric [methods of] repression on political, ideological, and religious grounds. I am of the opinion that a law must be passed to protect the rights of persons subjected to compulsory psychiatric hospitalization; resolutions must be passed and the necessary legislative measures introduced to protect the rights of persons assumed to be mentally ill in the course of a prosecution on political charges. In particular, private psychiatric investigation by commissions independent of the authorities should be allowed in both cases.

Independently of the general solution of these problems, I request the examination by the competent organs of a number of pressing individual cases, some of which are listed in the attached note.

2. *Concerning publicity, freedom of information exchange, and freedom of beliefs.* A bill concerning the press and the mass media should be submitted for nationwide discussion.

A resolution should be passed calling for greater freedom in the publication of statistical and sociological data.

3. *Concerning nationalities problems and the problem*

of leaving the country. Resolutions and laws should be passed fully restoring the rights of peoples deported under Stalin.

Laws should be passed to insure that citizens may easily and without hindrance exercise their right to leave the country and freely return to it. The directives restricting this right and in contravention of the law should be annulled.

4. Concerning international problems. We should show initiative and announce (or affirm, unilaterally at first) our refusal to be the first to use weapons of mass destruction (nuclear, chemical, bacteriological, and incendiary weapons). We should allow inspection teams to visit our territory for effective arms control (assuming that we conclude an agreement on disarmament or partial limitation of certain types of armaments).

In order to consolidate the results of our changed relations with East Germany we should work out a new, more flexible, and realistic position on the question of West Berlin.

We should alter our political position in the Middle East and in Vietnam, and actively seek, through the United Nations and diplomatic channels, a peaceful settlement in the shortest possible time, on the basis of a compromise, with the renunciation by the United States and the USSR of any intervention, military or political, direct or indirect; the promotion of a program of large-scale economic aid on an apolitical, international basis (through the United Nations?); and the proposal that UN troops be widely used to safeguard political and military stability in these areas.

THESES AND PROPOSALS WITH REGARD TO GENERAL PROBLEMS

By way of preparation for a discussion of the basic problems of the development and foreign policy of our country I have attempted to formulate a number of theses. Some of them are set out in the form of discussion points. I have tried to give the fullest possible exposition of my views, although I realize that some of the theses will seem unacceptable and others uninteresting or insignificant.

1. Since the year 1950 a number of important measures have been taken in our country to eliminate the most dangerous and ugly features of the previous stage of development of Soviet society and state policies. However, at the same time there do occur certain negative phenomena—deviations, inconsistencies, and sluggishness in the implementation of the new line. It is essential to work out a clear-cut and consistent program of further democratization and

liberalization, and to take a number of immediate steps as a matter of urgency. This is required in the interests of technical and economic progress, of gradually overcoming our backwardness and isolation from the advanced capitalist countries, and [in the interests of] the prosperity of large sectors of the population, internal stability, and external security. The development of our country is taking place in the extremely difficult conditions presented by our relations with China. We are faced with serious internal difficulties in the sphere of the economy and the general standard of living, technical and economic progress, culture and ideology.

One must point out the increasingly acute nationalities problem, the complexities of the interrelationship between the Party-state apparatus and the intelligentsia, and of that between the basic mass of the workers, who find themselves relatively worse off with regard to their standard of living and financial status, their prospects for professional promotion and cultural development, and many of whom feel disillusioned with all the "fine words," and the privileged group of "the bosses," whom the more backward sectors of the workers frequently, and chiefly by virtue of traditional prejudices, identify with the intelligentsia. Our country's foreign policy is not always sufficiently realistic. We need basic decisions in order to prevent possible complications.

2. I venture the opinion that it would be correct to characterize as follows the society toward the creation of which urgent state reforms as well as the efforts of citizens to develop a social conscience should be directed:

The basic aim of the state is the protection and safeguarding of the basic rights of its citizens. The defense of human rights is the loftiest of all aims.

State institutions always act in complete accordance with laws (which are stable, and known to all citizens, institutions, and organizations).

The happiness of the people is safeguarded, in particular, by their freedom of work, freedom of consumption, freedom in their private lives, and in their education, their cultural and their social activities, freedom of conviction and of conscience, and freedom of exchange of information, and of movement.

Openness facilitates the social controls safeguarding legality, justice, and the rightness of all decisions taken, contributes to the effectiveness of the entire system, makes for a scientific and democratic system of government, and promotes progress, prosperity, and national security.

Competitiveness, openness, and the absence of privileges insure an equitable distribution of incentives for the labor, personal capabilities, and individual initiative of all citizens.

There is a definite stratification of society based on type of occupation, nature of abilities, and [social] relations.

The basic energies of the country are directed toward harmonious internal development, with the purposeful deployment of labor and natural resources, and this is the basis of its power and prosperity. The country and its people are always ready to enter into friendly international cooperation and aid within the framework of universal brotherhood, but the society is such that it does not need to use foreign policy as a means of internal political stabilization, or to extend its spheres of influence, or to export its ideas. Messianism, delusions as to the uniqueness of a society and the exclusive merits of its own path, as well as the rejection of the paths of other [societies], are alien to [the ideal] society; organically alien to it also are dogmatism, adventurism, and aggression.

In the actual conditions obtaining in our country in particular, we will only overcome our economic difficulties and improve the people's standard of living by a concentration of resources on internal problems, and, given some additional conditions (democratization, the elimination of our people's isolation in terms of access to information from the rest of the world, and economic measures), this alone will give us any hope of gradually narrowing the gap between ourselves and the advanced capitalist countries, safeguard national security in the event of a deterioration in [our relations with] China, and insure that we have ample opportunity to assist countries in need.

3. *Foreign policy.* Our chief foreign policy problem is our relations with China. While offering the Chinese people the alternative of economic, technical, and cultural aid, and fraternal cooperation and progress together along the road of democracy, and always leaving open the possibility of developing relations in this way, we must at the same time display a special concern for the safeguarding of our national security, avoid all other possible complications in our foreign and domestic policies, and implement our plans for the development of Siberia, keeping this element in mind.

We must aim at noninterference in the internal affairs of other socialist countries, and mutual economic aid.

We must take the initiative in calling for the creation (within the framework of the United Nations?) of a new international consultative organ, an "International Council of Experts on the Problems of Peace, Disarmament, Economic Aid to Needy Countries, the Defense of Human

Rights, and the Protection of the Environment," consisting
of authoritative and impartial individuals. The council's
statutes, and the procedure for the election of its members,
must guarantee it maximum independence of the interests
of individual states and groups of states. In deciding the
composition and statutes of the council, it is probably essential to take into account the wishes of the main international organizations. An international pact must be
signed obliging legislative and governmental organs to examine the "council of experts" recommendations, which
must be well founded and open to scrutiny. The decisions of
national organs with regard to these recommendations must
be openly proclaimed, irrespective of whether the recommendations are accepted or rejected.

4. *Economic problems, management, personnel.* Extension of the 1965 economic reform, increase in the economic independence of all units of production, review of a
number of restrictive regulations with regard to the selection of personnel, salaries and incentives, systems of material supply and stocks, planning, cooperation, choice of
output profile, and allocation of funds.

Management and personnel: resolutions should be
passed to make the work of state institutions at all levels
more open to public scrutiny, as far as the interests of the
state will allow. A review of the "behind-closed-doors"
tradition is especially vital. With regard to the problems of
personnel policy, there should be increased open and active
public control over the selection of personnel and there
should be procedures for the election of management personnel at all levels and their replacement if they are found
unsuitable. I also suggest the normal requirement of any
democratic program: the system of holding elections in the

absence of a number of candidates, that is, "election without choice," must be abolished. At the same time the following are essential: increased availability of information; self-sufficiency; the right to experiment; a shift in the center of responsibility toward the subsidiary enterprise and its employees; improved methods of specialist instruction and business training for management personnel at all levels; the abolition of special privileges linked with professional and Party ranking, since these are very harmful in social and working relations; publication of official salaries; reorganization of personnel departments; abolition of the system of *nomenklatura* and other such survivals of the previous epoch; the creation of scientific-consultative councils attached to authorities, to be composed of scholars with various specialist qualifications, and endowed with the necessary independence.

Measures to promote the expansion of agricultural production on private plots belonging to collective farmers, workers on state farms, and individual peasants; changes in fiscal policy; increased land usage in the agricultural sector; changes in the system of supplying this sector with modern, purpose-built agricultural machinery, fertilizers, etc. Measures to improve the supply of building materials and fuel to the village; the expansion of all forms of cooperative farming in the village, with changes in fiscal policy, permission to hire and pay laborers in accordance with the requirements of the job, and changes in the system of supplying materials to the village.

Increased opportunity for and profitability of private initiative in the service industries, health service, small trading, education, and so on.

5. The question of the gradual abolition of the pass-

port regulations should be examined, since these are a serious hindrance to the development of the country's productive resources and a violation of civil rights, particularly those of rural dwellers.

6. *Information exchange, culture, science, and freedom of beliefs.* Freedom of beliefs, the spirit of inquiry, and creative anxiety should be encouraged.

The jamming of foreign radio broadcasts should be stopped, more foreign literature brought in from abroad, the international copyright agreement signed, and foreign travel facilitated, in order to overcome the isolation that is having a pernicious effect on our development.

Resolutions should be passed insuring the real separation of church and state, and real (that is, legally, economically, and administratively guaranteed) freedom of conscience and worship.

A review should be carried out of those aspects of the interrelations between the Party-state apparatus and art, literature, theater, organs of education, and so on that are harmful to the development of culture in our country, reduce the boldness and versatility of the creative endeavor, and lead to conventionality, grayness, and ritual repetition. In the social sciences and the humanities, which play an ever greater role in modern life (philosophy, history, sociology, jurisprudence, etc.), we must insure the elimination of stagnation, a widening of scope in the creative endeavor, an independence of all superimposed opinions, and the use of the entire gamut of foreign experience.

7. *Social policies.* The possibility of abolishing the death penalty should be explored. Special- and strict-regime imprisonment should be abolished, since it conflicts with humaneness. Measures should be taken to perfect the

penitentiary system, utilizing foreign experience and the recommendations of the UN.

A study should be made of the possibility of setting up a public supervisory organ to eliminate the use of physical coercion (assault, starvation, cold, etc.) against detainees, persons under arrest or investigation, and convicted persons.

There must be a radical improvement in the quality of education: increased salaries and independence for schoolteachers and college lecturers should be given; less importance should be attached to the formal role of diplomas and degrees; the educational system should be less monolithic; a wider range of subjects should be studied in schools; there should be increased guarantees of the right of freedom of beliefs.

Intensified measures should be taken in the struggle against alcoholism, including the possibility of public control over all aspects of the problem.

Stronger measures should be implemented in the struggle against noise, air and water pollution, erosion, the salting and chemical pollution of the soil. More should be done to preserve forests and wild and domestic animals, as well as to prevent cruelty to animals.

Reform of the health service, expansion of the network of private polyclinics and hospitals; a more important role for doctors, nurses, and health visitors in private practice; salary increases for health-service employees at all levels; reform of the drug industry; general access to modern medicines and equipment; the introduction of X-ray television equipment.

8. *Legal policies.* All forms of discrimination, overt and concealed, with regard to beliefs, national characteristics, etc., should be abolished.

There should be real openness of legal proceedings, wherever this does not conflict with basic civil rights.

What should be taken up again is the question of the ratification by the USSR Supreme Soviet of the pacts on human rights concluded at the Twenty-first Session of the UN General Assembly, and of [the USSR's] signing the optional protocol to these pacts.

9. *Interrelations with the national republics.* Our country has proclaimed the right of a nation to self-determination, even if this means secession. In the case of Finland, implementation of the right to secede was sanctioned by the Soviet government. The right of union republics to secede is proclaimed by the USSR Constitution. There is, however, some vagueness in the relationship between these guarantees and the procedures regarding preparation for, necessary discussion of, and actual implementation of this right. In fact, the mere discussion of such questions frequently leads to prosecution. In my opinion, a juridical settlement of the problem and the passing of a law guaranteeing the right to secession would be of great internal and international significance as a confirmation of the anti-imperialist and anti-chauvinist nature of our policies. The number of republics tending toward secession is, to all appearances, very small, and these tendencies would doubtless become even weaker with time as a result of the future democratization of the USSR. On the other hand, there can be no doubt that any republic that secedes from the USSR for one reason or another by peaceful, constitutional means would maintain intact its ties with the socialist commonwealth of nations. In this case, the economic interests and defense capabilities of the socialist camp would not suffer, since the cooperation of the socialist countries is by nature complete and all-embracing and will doubtless become

even more extensive in conditions of mutual noninterference in each other's internal affairs. For these reasons, discussion of the question I have raised does not seem to me to be dangerous.

□

If this memorandum appears here and there to be excessively peremptory in tone, that must be put down to its abbreviated form. The problems with which our country is confronted are closely connected with some aspects of the general world crisis of the twentieth century—the crisis of international security, of loss of stability in social development, the ideological impasse and disillusionment with the ideals of the recent past, nationalism, and the threat of dehumanization. The constructive, prudent, flexible, and at the same time decisive solution of our problems will, by virtue of our country's special position in the world, be of tremendous significance for the whole of mankind.

March 5, 1971

POSTSCRIPT
TO
MEMORANDUM

The "Memorandum" was sent to the Secretary General of the CPSU [Mr. Brezhnev] on March 5, 1971. It received no reply. I do not think it would be right for me to delay its publication any longer. The "Postscript" was written in June 1972. It contains some additions to and partly replaces the note "Concerning political persecution" *mentioned in the text.*

I began my activity approximately ten to twelve years ago, when I realized the criminal character of a possible thermonuclear war and of thermonuclear tests in the atmosphere. Since then I have revised my views to a considerable extent, particularly since the year 1968, which began for me with work on *Progress, Coexistence, and Intellectual Freedom,* and ended, as for everybody else, with the rumbling of tanks in the streets of unyielding Prague.

As before, I cannot fail to appreciate the great and

beneficial changes (social, cultural, and economic) that have taken place in our country in the last fifty years, realizing, however, that analogous changes have taken place in many countries and that they are a manifestation of worldwide progress.

As before, I consider that it will be possible to overcome the tragic conflicts and dangers of our time only through the convergence of capitalism and the socialist regime.

In capitalist countries this process must be accompanied by a further improvement in the protection of workers' rights and a reduction in the role of militarism and its influence on political life. In socialist countries it is also essential to reduce the militarization of the economy and the role of a messianic ideology. It is vitally necessary to weaken the extreme forms of centralism and Party-state bureaucratic monopoly, both in the economic sphere of production and consumption, and in the sphere of ideology and culture.

As before, I consider the democratization of society, the development of openness in public affairs, the rule of law, and the safeguarding of basic human rights to be of decisive importance.

As before, I hope that society will evolve along these lines under the influence of technological-economic progress, although my prognoses have now become more cautious.

It seems to me now, more than ever before, that the only true guarantee for the safeguarding of human values in the chaos of uncontrollable changes and tragic upheavals is man's freedom of conscience and his moral yearning for the good.

Our society is infected by apathy, hypocrisy, petit

bourgeois egoism, and hidden cruelty. The majority of representatives of its upper stratum—the Party apparatus of government and the highest, most successful layers of the intelligentsia—cling tenaciously to their open and secret privileges and are profoundly indifferent to the infringement of human rights, the interests of progress, security, and the future of mankind. Others, though deeply concerned in their hearts, cannot allow themselves any freedom of thought and are condemned to the torture of internal conflict. Drunkenness has assumed the dimensions of a national calamity. It is one of the symptoms of the moral degradation of a society that is sinking ever deeper into a state of chronic alcoholic poisoning.

The country's spiritual regeneration demands the elimination of those conditions that drive people into becoming hypocritical and time-serving, and that lead to feelings of impotence, discontent, and disillusionment. Everybody must be assured, in deed and not just in word, of equal opportunities for advancement in his work, in education, and cultural growth; and the system of privileges in all spheres of consumption must be abolished. Full intellectual freedom must be assured and all forms of persecution for beliefs must cease. A radical educational reform is essential. These ideas are the basis of many proposals in the memorandum.

In particular, the memorandum mentions the problem of improvement in the material condition and independence of two of the most numerous and socially significant groups of the intelligentsia, the teachers and medical workers. The sorry state of popular education and of the health service is carefully hidden from the eyes of foreigners, but cannot remain secret from those who wish to see.

A free health service and education are no more than an economic illusion in a society in which all surplus value is expropriated and distributed by the state. The hierarchical class structure of our society, with its system of privileges, is reflected in a particularly pernicious way in the health service and education. The condition of the health service and of popular education is clearly revealed in the rundown state of public hospitals, in the poverty of the village schools, with their overcrowded classes, the poverty and low standing of the teacher, and the official hypocrisy in teaching, which inculcates in the rising generation a spirit of indifference toward moral, artistic, and scientific values.

The most essential condition for the cure of our society is the abandonment of political persecution, in its judicial and psychiatric forms or in any other form of which our bureaucratic and bigoted system, with its totalitarian interference by the state in the lives of the citizens, is capable, such as dismissal from work, expulsion from college, refusal of residence permits, limitation of promotion at work, etc.

The first beginnings of a moral regeneration of the people and the intelligentsia, which resulted from the curbing of the most extreme manifestations of the Stalinist system of blind terror, met with no proper understanding in ruling circles. The basic class, social, and ideological features of the regime did not undergo any essential change. With pain and alarm I have to note that after a period of largely illusory liberalism there is once again an extension of restrictions on ideological freedom, efforts to suppress information not controlled by the state, fresh persecution for political and ideological reasons, and a deliberate aggravation of nationalities problems. The fifteen months since the submission of the memorandum have brought new and disturbing evidence about the development of these tendencies.

The wave of political arrests in the first few months of 1972 is particularly alarming. Numerous arrests took place in the Ukraine. Arrests have also taken place in Moscow, Leningrad, and other regions of the country.

The attention of the public has also been drawn during these months to the trial of Bukovsky in Moscow and of Strokatova in Odessa, and other trials. The use of psychiatry for political purposes is fraught with extremely dangerous consequences for society and constitutes a completely inadmissible interference with basic human rights. There have been numerous protests and pronouncements on this question. At present Grigorenko, Gershuni, and many others are being kept in prison-type psychiatric hospitals, the fate of Fainberg and Borisov is unknown; there are other instances of psychiatric repression (e.g., the case of the poet Lupynis in the Ukraine).

The persecution and destruction of religion, which has been carried on with perseverance and cruelty for decades, has resulted in what is undoubtedly one of the most serious infringements of the rights of man in our country. Freedom of religious belief and activity is an integral part of intellectual freedom as a whole. Unfortunately, the last few months have been marked by fresh instances of religious persecution, in particular in the Baltic states.

In this postscript I am passing over a series of important problems that were dealt with in the memorandum and my other published documents—in the open letter to the members of the Presidium of the Supreme Soviet of the USSR, "On freedom to leave the country," and to the Minister of Internal Affairs, "On discrimination against the Crimean Tatars."

I also pass over the majority of international problems dealt with in the memorandum. I will single out from their number the question of arms race limitations. Militarization of the economy leaves a deep imprint on international and domestic policy; it leads to encroachment on democratic rights, the open conduct of public affairs, and the rule of law; it constitutes a threat to peace. The role of the military-industrial complex in United States policy has been thoroughly studied. The analogous role played by the same factors in the USSR and other socialist countries is less well known. It is, however, necessary to point out that in no country does the share of military expenditure with relation to the national income reach such proportions as in the USSR (over 40 percent). In an atmosphere of mutual suspicion the problem of control mentioned in the memorandum assumes a special role.

I write this postscript a short time after the signing of important agreements on the limitation of ABM and strategic missiles. One would like to believe that political leaders and the people who are active in the military-industrial complexes of the United States and the USSR have a sense of responsibility toward humanity.

One would like to believe that these agreements are not merely of symbolic importance, but will lead to a real curtailment of the arms race and to further steps that would improve the political climate in our long-suffering world.

In conclusion, I consider it necessary to emphasize in particular the importance I attach to the proposal for the setting up of an international consultative committee, "The International Council of Experts," which would have the right to put forward recommendations to national governments that they would be obliged to consider (3. under Theses and Proposals with Regard to General Problems, in the memorandum). I think this proposal is feasible if it receives the wide international support for which I appeal, and I appeal not only to Soviet but also to foreign readers. I hope too that my voice from "inside" the socialist world may contribute in some measure to the understanding of the historical experience of the last decade.

June 1972

LET SOVIET CITIZENS EMIGRATE

The trials of recent months have once again reminded us of the tragic conflicts faced by Soviet citizens who wish to emigrate and resettle in another country as well as the legal, social, psychological, and political aspects of this problem.

Soviet citizens, both Jews and those of other nationalities—Russians, Ukrainians, Germans, Armenians, Lithuanians, Latvians, Estonians, Meskhi Turks, and others—who have sought to leave for personal, ethnic, and other reasons have found their lives transformed into constant torture by years of expectation only to receive unjustified refusals.

There is another side to this problem. Concern can only be caused by the fate of those who, having lost hope of satisfying their aspirations within the framework of the law, decided to break the law in one way or another.

Many of these people have been sentenced to long terms of detention in camps or prisons or have been doomed to the horror of forced psychiatric treatment in such strict-regimen hospitals as the Dnepropetrovsk special psychiatric hospital and others.

The attempts made by these citizens, prompted by extreme necessity, have for the most part been categorized by the courts as betrayal of the Motherland, and have resulted in most severe punishment.

In December 1970, the world was stunned by the sentences in the so-called Leningrad case about an attempted hijacking. Two death sentences were commuted by an appeals court, but the public punishment remained exceptionally strict for the sentenced.

In May 1971, a Lithuanian, Simas Kudirka, whose only guilt was an attempt to remain abroad during a voyage overseas, was sentenced to ten years' detention by a court in Vilna. He was able to jump onto an American warship, but was returned and sentenced for "betrayal of the Motherland."

From a legal viewpoint these trials are similar to one that took place in August 1971 at which the physicist Dmitri Mikheev was sentenced to eight years' detention for attempting to leave the country and exchanging documents with a foreigner, François de Perrego, a Swiss citizen. The latter was sentenced to three years.

Finally, there is yet another side to the problem. Persons attempting to leave, usually without success, find themselves in doing so in the position of second-class citizens with regard to retaining a number of their rights—because of prejudices, traditions, and conformism in our society.

This involves the opportunity of continuing with one's studies or with one's job, and may even result in judicial prosecution. The recent trials of Palatnik in Odessa and Kukui in Sverdlovsk are, in my opinion, examples of such preconceived and obviously unjust approaches.

Commenting on the above aspects of the problem as a whole, I would like to stress that a humane and just solution would be highly important to further democratization of our country, for the final overcoming of our international isolation, for an exchange of people and ideas, and for the defense of the rights of man—that primary and basic value of a socio-political system.

The freedom to emigrate, which only a small number of people would in fact use, is an essential condition of spiritual freedom. A free country cannot resemble a cage, even if it is gilded and supplied with material things.

Respected members of the Supreme Soviet, I appeal to you, I appeal to anyone who wants the citizens of this country to be truly free, to contribute in every way possible to a solution of these problems. In particular, I appeal to you personally to take the initiative in the following:

It is essential to adopt legislation that would resolve the problem of emigration in a democratic spirit so that anyone who desires to leave the country will be given the opportunity to do so and, if he then changes his mind, to return home without hindrance. This would be in keeping with the rights of man that are universally acknowledged.

Further, it is essential that the section of the criminal code on high treason be amended so that it will no longer be interpreted as broadly as has been evident in recent trial practice.

It is essential to grant amnesty to all citizens sentenced

in connection with attempts to leave the country and to release those who, for the same reason, are being subjected to forced treatment in special psychiatric hospitals.

October 7, 1971

INTERVIEW WITH OLLE STENHOLM, SWEDISH RADIO CORRESPONDENT

. . . The most natural thing for anyone in this situation is to regard his system as the best. Thus, any deviation from this view is already some kind of a psychological process. And when in 1968 I wrote my work [*Progress, Coexistence, and Intellectual Freedom*] this process was still in its beginning stages and my own approach was more abstract. My life has been such that I began by confronting global problems and only later on more concrete, personal, and human ones. Thus, in evaluating my essay of 1968 you must understand this and take into account the route I followed from work on thermonuclear weapons to my concern about the results of nuclear tests—the destruction of people, genetic consequences, and all these things.

And I was, as it happened, at that moment very far from the basic problems of all of the people and of the

whole country. I found myself in an extraordinary position
of material privilege and isolated from the people.

But after that?

After that my life began to change in purely personal
terms, psychologically. And the process of development
simply went further . . .

Now, what is socialism? I began by thinking that I
understood it and that it was good. Then gradually I ceased
to understand a great deal—I didn't even understand its
economic [basis]; I couldn't make out whether there was
anything to it but mere words and propaganda for internal
and international consumption. Actually, what hits you in
the eye is the state's extreme concentration—economic,
political, and ideological—that is, its extreme monopoliza-
tion of these fields. One may say, exactly as Lenin did at the
beginning of our revolution, that it is simple state capitalism, that the state has simply assumed a monopoly role
over all the economy. But in that case this socialism contains nothing new. It is only an extreme form of that capitalist path of development found in the United States and
other Western countries but in an extremely monopolized
form. Thus, we should not be surprised that we have the
same kinds of problems—that is, crime and personal alienation—that are to be found in the capitalist world. But our
society represents an extreme case with maximum restraint,
maximum ideological restrictions, and so forth. . . . Moreover, and very characteristically, we are also the most pretentious—that is, although we are not the best society we
pretend that we are much more . . .

*What concrete shortcomings do you see in today's
Soviet society?*

In the lack of freedom, to be certain. In lack of freedom, in the bureaucratization of government, in its extremely irrational and also terribly egoistic—that is, class-egoistic—tendency that actually aims only at preserving the system, maintaining a good appearance to conceal a very unpleasant internal state of affairs. A society on the decline. But I've already written about that. And it must be very widely known to attentive observers that for us all social things are more for show than for reality. This relates to education, to its organization, and to medical services. Very often people from the West say: "Well, you have many faults but at least you have free medical service." But actually it is no more free than in many Western countries and often it is even less free, so to speak, because its general quality is so low.

Do you think that Soviet society today is a class society?
Well, that is again a theoretical question—that is a question requiring a theoretical evaluation. But in any case it is a society of great internal inequality . . . Can we say from this that it has a class structure? It is in a certain sense a distinctive society. It is hard to say whether it should be called a class society. In a sense this is a matter of definition. It's something like our past arguments as to what kind of society could be called fascist. It is also a question of definition, a question of terminology.

But what about the inequality?
Inequality. Inequality arises on a very large number of levels. There is inequality between village people and city people; the collective farmers do not have passports, which means that in practical terms they are bound to their place

of residence on the collective farm. And only if they can get permission (true, it is ordinarily given) may they leave the collective farm. There is inequality among regions: Moscow and the larger cities are favored in the distribution of products, living comforts, cultural services, and so on. And the [internal] passport system strengthens these territorial inequities. Most unfairly treated is . . .

Andrei Dmitrivich, you have yourself said that you are privileged . . .

Yes, I have been privileged, of course, and still am today through inertia. I was privileged in the past, actually hyper-privileged, because I was a worker at the very pinnacle of the arms industry. I had by Soviet standards a colossal salary and bonuses.

And, in your opinion, what privileges do Party figures have in the Soviet Union?

Well, they have great extrafinancial privileges. There are the following: a system of sanitariums, medical services . . . great privileges. Real privileges arise, you might say, from personal connections, personal factors of various kinds. Privileges in work, in one's career. All positions of any importance, like those of factory director, chief engineer, and so on are held only by Party members. Exceptions are very rare. And the shop chief must be a Party member. So everything depends on Party membership, on your situation in the Party structure or your official . . . These things have enormous influence on your career. And, in addition, there is the traditional attitude toward Party cadres that is expressed in what is called *nomenklatura*. This means that even if a person fails in some kind of work, as long as he is a leading Party worker he will be transferred to some other job not very different in material advantages from the one he gives up.

The whole manner of getting a job and advancement is very strongly connected with interrelationships within the system. Each important administrator has attached to him personally certain people who move with him from place to place as he is transferred. There is something irresistible about this and it seems to be a kind of law of our state structure.

But if we talk about material advantages, then the basic advantage consists in the rise of a kind of isolated but more or less well-defined group that has a special relationship to the government. The advantages are determined by Party membership but there are also within the Party very large distinctions. It seems as though something like Orwell's concept of an inner party already exists with us in a certain sense.

And if we talk about people in this inner Party, then they have great material advantages. There exists a system of supplemental pay in [special] envelopes. This system sometimes disappears and then again reappears. I don't know what the situation is at the given moment, but it looks as though the custom has been revived in some places. Then there is the supplemental system of so-called closed shops, where not only is the quality of the products better and the assortment wider but also the price differs from the general price structure so that with the same ruble these people can buy a different product at a different price and that means the arithmetical figure of their wage is not really very significant.*

* After reading the text of the interview Sakharov offered the following clarification: "In that part of the interview devoted to the privileged position of the members of the Party there may be created the false im-

We have talked a lot about shortcomings. Now, of course, we must take up the question of what can be done to correct all this.

What can be done and what should be strived for are different questions. It seems to me that almost nothing can be done . . .

Why not?

Because the system has a very strong internal stability. The less free a system is the greater ordinarily its ability to maintain itself.

And outside forces can do nothing?

We have a very poor understanding of what the foreign world is doing. Possibly the foreign world will soon accept our rules of the game. That would be very bad. But there is, of course, another side to the matter. We are now breaking out of our fifty-year isolation and possibly with time this may even exert a beneficial influence. But how this will all come out—it is very difficult to predict. And if we speak of the West, then it is difficult each time to tell whether they want to help us or whether, on the contrary, there is some kind of capitulation, a game involving the internal interests of the people of the West in which we merely play the role of small change.

Well, those are foreign forces—what about inside the Soviet Union?

Within the Soviet Union certainly some kind of pro-

_____

pression that Party members and non-Party members in the same job receive different salaries. That is not so and I want to correct this inexactitude. However, what is said regarding the influence of Party membership on a career, the Party hierarchy, etc. remains in force."

cess is going on, but so far it is so imperceptible and hidden that it's not possible to forecast anything positive, any general change, and as for positive things . . . well, it's almost impossible. We understand that such a large state as ours can never be homogeneous but in the absence of information and the absence of contacts between separate groups of people it is almost impossible to understand what is going on. But we know that there are very strong nationalistic tendencies on the periphery of our state. Whether they are positive or not is very hard to determine in individual cases. In some cases—for example, in the Ukraine—they have become very strongly interwoven with democratic forces. In the Baltic states it is the same— religious and nationalist forces have become interwoven very naturally and easily with the democratic. But in other places it may not be the same. We don't know in detail.

So you are very skeptical in spite of the fact that you yourself . . .

I am skeptical about socialism in general. I don't see that socialism offers some kind of new theoretical plan, so to speak, for the better organization of society. Therefore it seems to me that while in our diverse system of life we may find some positive variants, on the whole our state has displayed more destructive features than positive ones. The positive features may be said to be the result of more general human factors—and they are not few—but they are human factors, which could have arisen in another environment, while in our society there have arisen such fierce political struggles, such destruction, such bitterness that now we are reaping the sad fruits of all this in a kind of tiredness, apathy, cynicism, a kind of . . . which we find it most difficult to recover, or indeed, to recover in general. What direction of development our society will take is extremely difficult to predict from within. Perhaps it can be done better from the outside, but for this, one requires the maximum in objectivity.

But, Andrei Dmitrivich, you are doubtful that any-thing in general can be done to improve the system of the Soviet Union, yet you yourself go ahead acting, writing declarations, protests—why?

Well, there is a need to create ideals even when you can't see any route by which to achieve them, because if there are no ideals then there can be no hope and then one would be completely in the dark, in a hopeless blind alley.

Moreover, we can't know whether there is some kind of possibility of cooperation between our country and the outside world. If no signals about our unhappy situation are sent out, then there cannot be . . . then even the pos-sibility, which might exist, could not be utilized, because we wouldn't know what it was that needed to be changed or how to change it.

Then there is the other consideration—that the history of our country should be some kind of warning. It should hold back the West and the developing countries from committing mistakes on such a scale as we have done dur-ing our historical development. Therefore, if a man does not keep silent it does not mean that he hopes necessarily to achieve something. These are not the same question. He may hope for nothing but nonetheless speak because he cannot, simply cannot remain silent.

In almost every concrete case of repression we really

have no hope and almost always there is a tragic absence of positive results.

But what is it that you are aiming at?
In what sense? In a social sense?

Yes.
Well, in the sense of an ideal I attempted in my memorandum [to General Secretary Brezhnev] and especially in the postscript to it to express a certain ideal, but in the memorandum there is much I should myself correct, because it was written a long time ago, in 1971, and it was published a year and a half later without changes. For instance, I wrote then about the Chinese problem in a tone I would not use today, because at that time I simply did not understand our relations with China and if you do not understand then it is better not to write. For example, I would not now blame China for aggression. But I didn't say even that very clearly and perhaps there was an element of overemphasis on the Chinese threats. As for China itself, it simply represents a much earlier stage of development in our society and it is directed more toward revolutionary self-assertion both internally and in the outer world than, for example, with achieving prosperity for her people and expanding her territory. Probably they don't see this as a problem. China is very similar to Russia in the 1920's and the beginning of the 1930's.

But if you think that socialism in the Soviet Union has not shown its superiority, does that mean you think that in order to remedy the situation you must therefore reconstruct the whole state or can something be done within the system in order to improve it and eliminate its greatest defects?

That is too difficult a question for me, because to re-organize the state—that is unthinkable; there always must be some kind of continuity and some kind of gradualness, otherwise there would again be the terrible destruction through which we have passed several times and a total collapse. Thus, I, of course, am inclined to gradualness. I am a liberal or a "gradualist," if you please.

Well, what is to be done first?

What must be done? I think that our present system can do nothing or at least very little by its own internal resources. What must be done? We must liquidate the ideological monism of our society.

Excuse me—what?

The ideological structure that is anti-democratic in its very essence—it has been very tragic for the state. Isolation from the outside world. For example, the absence of the right to leave and to return produces a very pernicious effect on the internal life of the country. It is in the first instance a great tragedy for all those who wish to leave for personal or national reasons. But it is also a tragedy for those who remain in the country, because a country from which it is not possible to leave freely, to which it is not possible to return freely is a country that is defective, a closed volume where all processes develop differently from those of an open system.

You know that the right of free exit . . .

. . . is one of the very important conditions for return, for free return.

And what else?

It is one of the conditions the country needs for developing along healthier lines. But there are things of an economic nature that are more important. Our very extreme state socialism has led to the closing down of private initiative in areas in which it would be most effective, just as private initiative has been eliminated in large-scale industry and in transport, in which perhaps the state system of administration is more sensible. Moreover, the simple personal initiative of citizens and their personal freedom have been very restricted. This is reflected negatively in the people's way of living and simply makes life much more boring and dreary than need be. I am talking about personal initiative in the field of consumer goods, education, and medicine. All of this no doubt would have a very positive significance in weakening the extreme monopolistic structure of the state. There are aspects relative to the monopoly of administration—that is, the Party monopoly of administration—which with us have reached unheard-of levels . . . it must even be evident at the leadership level that these aspects are intolerable. It already has begun to influence the effectiveness of administration.

So—what is needed? We need first of all greater openness in the work of the administrative apparatus. Quite possibly the single-party system is excessively and unnecessarily rigid. Even under the conditions of a socialist economic system the one-party system is not necessary. Actually, on some levels of the peoples democracies, the one-party system is not needed. And in some of the peoples democracies some elements, so to speak, of a multiparty system exist although in a semicaricatured style.

We need elections to state organs with a certain

number of candidates. In general, a series of measures that taken individually would have little effect but that in combination might shake that monolith we have created, which is so fossilized and so oppressive on the life of the whole country.

The press must change its character. Now it is so standardized that it has lost any significant informational value. And when it does reflect facts, they are expressed in such a way that they are understandable only to the initiated and reflect a distorted picture of real life in the country. As for intellectual life, it simply does not exist so that there is nothing there that can be distorted since there is no variety in intellectual life.

One thing must be emphasized, and that is the role of the intelligentsia in society. It is quite illegally suppressed. It is materially badly off. It is not distinguished from physical work and is poorly provided for. And in absolute terms its living standard is very low in comparison with Western countries that have reached a comparable stage of development. The oppressed situation of the intelligentsia and its economic oppression as well mean ideological oppression, which is reflected in a certain anti-intellectual atmosphere in the country, in which the intellectual professions, the professions of teachers, of doctors, do not receive the respect they should have. And the anti-intellectualism is reflected in the fact that the intelligentsia itself has begun to retreat into narrow professionalism, into a kind of dual intellectual life at work and at home, into narrow circles of their own friends, where people begin to think in different ways, and this dichotomy leads to hypocrisy and a further fall in the morals and creativity of people. The results are particularly sharp in the humanistic as distinguished from the technical intelligentsia. They feel that they have gotten into a kind of blind alley. As a result, the literature that appears is terribly gray or conventional and generally boring. Literature, art, the cinema begin . . .

Permit me one last question. You personally have never feared for your health and freedom in these years in which you have been so active?

Not very much. I have not feared for myself, but that is, you might say, part of my character and partly because I began from a very high social position, where such fears were perfectly unjustified and irrelevant. But now I have grounds for fearing such forms of pressure, which are not directed against me personally but against members of my family, members of the family of my wife. That is the most painful thing, because it is very real and is coming closer to us. Such things as happened to [Veniamin] Levich [corresponding member of the Academy of Sciences] when his son was picked up; this shows how they go about these things.

July 3, 1973

INTERVIEW WITH MIKHAIL P. MALYAROV, FIRST DEPUTY SOVIET PROSECUTOR

On August 15, I received a telephone call from the Deputy Prosecutor General and was asked to come to see him. He did not say what it was about, asserting simply that it would be a man-to-man talk. I arrived at the Prosecutor's office on August 16 at noon and was met at the gate by an employee who took me into the building; another then accompanied me to an office where I was received by M. P. Malyarov, the Deputy Prosecutor General, and another man who introduced himself only as Malyarov's assistant. He took notes and participated in the conversation.

Below I have reproduced the seventy-minute conversation from memory, and the reconstruction may therefore contain some paraphrases, minor unintentional abridgments, and inversions in sequence.

□

MALYAROV: This conversation is intended to be in the nature of a warning and not all my statements will be supported by detailed proof, but you can believe me that we have such proof. Please listen to me attentively and try not to interrupt.

SAKHAROV: I am listening.

MALYAROV: When you began a few years ago to engage in what you call public activity, we could not possibly ignore it and we paid close attention. We assumed that you would express your opinions as a Soviet citizen about certain shortcomings and errors, as you see them, without attacking the Soviet social and political system as such. To be sure, even then your statements were being published in the anti-Soviet press abroad and they caused noticeable harm to our country. Lately your activity and statements have assumed an even more harmful and openly anti-Soviet character and cannot be overlooked by the Prosecutor's office, which is charged with enforcing the law and protecting the interests of society. You are seeing foreigners and giving them material for anti-Soviet publications. That applies in particular to your interview with the Swedish radio. In that interview you denounced the socialist system in our country, calling it a system of maximum nonfreedom, a system that is undemocratic, closed, deprived of economic initiative, and falling to pieces.

SAKHAROV: I did not say "falling to pieces."

MALYAROV: You keep meeting with reactionary newsmen, like the Swedish radio correspondent Stenholm, and give them interviews that are then used for subversive propaganda and are printed by Possev, the publishing arm of the NTS [a Russian émigré organization with headquarters in Frankfurt, West Germany]. You must be aware that the NTS program calls for the overthrow of the Soviet regime. Possev publishes more of your writings than anyone else, and in your interview you adopted in effect the same anti-Soviet subversive position.

SAKHAROV: I am not familiar with the NTS program. If it does indeed include such a plank, it would be fundamentally opposed to my views, as stated, for example, in the interview with the Swedish Radio. There I spoke about the desirability of gradual change, about democratization within the framework of the present system. Of course, I am also referring to what I consider serious faults in the system and do not conceal my pessimism (with regard to possible changes in the near future). As for those publications, I never handed over any material for the NTS or for Possev, and my writings have appeared in many foreign mass media besides Possev. For example, in *Der Spiegel* [West German news magazine], which the Soviet press has regarded as rather progressive so far.

MALYAROV'S ASSISTANT: But you never protested publication in Possev. We found that most of your writings appeared in Possev, *Grani* [another publication of Possev], and the White Guards newspaper *Russkaya Mysl* [of Paris].

SAKHAROV: I would be very glad to have my writings published in the Soviet press. For example, if, in addition to [Yuri] Kornilov's critical article, *Literaturnaya Gazeta* [Soviet Weekly] had also published my interview [with the Swedish Radio]. In that case Kornilov would not have been able to distort the interview. But that is obviously out of the question. I consider openness of publication of great importance. I consider the content of publications far more important than the place of publication.

MALYAROV'S ASSISTANT: Even if they appear in anti-Soviet publications for anti-Soviet purposes, as in Possev?

SAKHAROV: I consider Possev's publishing activities highly useful. I am grateful to that publisher. I reserve the right not to identify Possev with the NTS and not to approve of the NTS program, with which I am not even familiar, or to condemn those aspects of NTS activities that may be viewed as provocative (like sending Sokolov as a witness to the Galanskov–Ginzburg trial, which did have such consequences). [The reference is to Nicolas Brocks Sokolov, an NTS courier, who was arrested on arriving in the Soviet Union and testified for the prosecution in the 1968 trial of two dissidents.]

MALYAROV'S ASSISTANT: We are not talking about that now, that was a long time ago.

SAKHAROV: To go back, you called Stenholm [of the Swedish Radio] a reactionary journalist. That is unfair. He is a Social Democrat; he is far more of a socialist or Communist than I am, for example.

MALYAROV'S ASSISTANT: The Social Democrats were the ones who murdered Rosa Luxemburg [German Communist, in 1919]. As for that "Communist" of yours, he evidently inserted into your interview that our system was "falling to pieces," if indeed you did not say it.

SAKHAROV: I am convinced that Stenholm quoted me correctly.

MALYAROV: Let me go on. Please listen closely. By nature of your previous work, you had access to state secrets of particular importance. You signed a commitment not to divulge state secrets and not to meet with foreigners. But you do meet with foreigners and you are giving them information that may be of interest to foreign intelligence agencies. I am asking you to consider this a serious warning and to draw your conclusions.

SAKHAROV: I insist that I have never divulged any military or military-technical secrets that I may have known by nature of my work from 1948 to 1968. And I never intend to do so. I also want to call your attention to the fact that I have been out of secret work for the last five years.

MALYAROV: But you still have your head on your shoulders, and your pledge not to meet with foreigners is still in effect. You are beginning to be used not only by anti-Soviet forces hostile to our country, but also by foreign intelligence.

SAKHAROV: As for meetings with foreigners, I know many people who used to be in my position and who now meet freely with foreign scholars and ordinary citizens. I do meet with some foreign journalists, but those meetings have no bearing whatever on any state, military, or military-technical secrets.

MALYAROV'S ASSISTANT: Those meetings are of benefit to our enemies.

MALYAROV: We have now warned you. It is up to you to draw your conclusions.

SAKHAROV: I repeat. I would prefer to be published in the Soviet press and to deal with Soviet institutions. But I see nothing illegal in meeting with foreign journalists.

MALYAROV'S ASSISTANT: But you are still a Soviet citizen. Your qualification shows your real attitude toward our system.

SAKHAROV: Soviet institutions ignore my letters and other forms of communication. If we just take the Prosecutor's office, I remember that in May 1970 (I think it was May 17), several persons, including myself, addressed a complaint to Comrade [Roman A.] Rudenko, the Prosecutor General, in the case of [Maj. Gen. Pyotr G.] Grigorenko [a dissident committed to a psychiatric hospital in 1969]. There were many gross violations of the law in that case. There has been no reply to that complaint to this day. Many times I did not even receive confirmation of the delivery of my letters. The late Academician Petrovsky, who was a member of the Presidium of the Supreme Soviet of the USSR [Ivan G. Petrovsky, rector of Moscow University, died in 1973], promised to look into the case of the psychiatrist Semyon Gluzman, sentenced in Kiev in 1972 in a trial fraught with violations of the law. That was the only time anyone promised to look into a case for me. But Petrovsky is now dead. And how about the Amalrik case? [Andrei A. Amalrik, dissident author.] He was unjustly sentenced to three years, he lost his health, suffered from meningitis, and now he has been sentenced in a labor-camp court to another three years. It is an absolute disgrace. He was in fact sentenced once again for his convictions, which he has refused to recant and does not force on anyone. And a labor-camp court! What kind of public proceeding, what kind of justice is that?

MALYAROV: That Amalrik is a half-educated student. He contributed nothing to the state. He was a parasite. And Böll [Heinrich Böll, West German author] writes about him as if he were an outstanding historian. Is that the kind of information Böll has?

SAKHAROV: Böll and many others demonstrate a great deal of interest in Amalrik's fate. A labor-camp court is in fact a closed court.

MALYAROV: I suppose you would have brought him to Moscow for trial?

SAKHAROV: In view of the wide public interest, that would have made sense. If I had known that I could have attended Amalrik's trial, I would have done so.

MALYAROV: Amalrik caused a great deal of harm to our society. In one of his books he tried to show that Soviet society would not survive until 1984, and in so doing he called for violent action. Any society has the right to defend itself. Amalrik violated the law, and he must take the punishment. In camp he again violated the law. You know the law, I don't have to tell you what it is. Abroad they wrote that Amalrik was deprived of a lawyer. That is a lie. Shveisky [Vladimir Shveisky, Amalrik's lawyer] attended the trial, and you know that.

MALYAROV'S ASSISTANT: In contrast to that dropout, you did make contributions to society.

MALYAROV: Who gave you the right to doubt our system of justice? You did not attend the trial. You base yourself on rumors, and they are often wrong.

SAKHAROV: When proceedings are not public, when political trials are consistently held under conditions allowing for violations, there are grounds for doubting the fairness of the court. I consider it undemocratic to prosecute under Articles 190–1 [on circulating false information defaming the Soviet state] and 70 [on anti-Soviet agitation and propaganda]. All the cases with which I am familiar confirm this. Take the recent case of Leonid Plyushch [a Kiev mathematician]. In that case, the court accepted the most grievous of three contradictory psychiatric findings without checking any of them. Although the court reduced the sentence, it was restored upon protest by the prosecution. Plyushch is being kept in a special [psychiatric] hospital, and his wife has not seen him for more than a year and a half.

MALYAROV: You keep dealing in legal questions, but you don't seem to know them very well. The court has the power to determine the form of compulsory treatment regardless of the findings of an expert commission.

SAKHAROV: I am unfortunately all too familiar with that. And, therefore, even when the expert commission recommends an ordinary hospital, there are grounds for fearing the worst. You say I always rely on rumor. That is not so. I try to get reliable information. But it is becoming increasingly difficult in this country to know what is going on. There is no publication with complete and precise information about violations [of due process].

MALYAROV'S ASSISTANT: You mean the *Chronicle* [the *Chronicle of Current Events,* an underground publication that has not appeared since October 1972]?

SAKHAROV: Of course.

MALYAROV'S ASSISTANT: You will soon be hearing about the *Chronicle*. You know what I mean. But now we are talk-about more important matters.

MALYAROV: You don't seem to like the fact that our [Criminal] Code contains Article 190–1 and 70. But there they are. The state has the right to defend itself. You must know what you are doing. I am not going to try to convince you. I know that would be useless. But you must understand what is involved here. And who is supporting you, anyway, who needs you? Yakir, whom you know well, was written about constantly in the anti-Soviet press abroad as long as he provided it with propaganda. As soon as he changed his views, he was forgotten. [Pyotr Yakir was arrested in June 1972 and is now being tried.]

SAKHAROV: To say that I know him well is not correct. I hardly know him. But I do know that there is great interest in his case. Everyone is wondering when the trial will begin. Do you know?

MALYAROV'S ASSISTANT: No. When the trial starts, you will probably know about it yourself.

MALYAROV: Your friend Chalidze [Valery Chalidze, now living in the United States] was quite famous in the West as long as he came out with anti-Soviet statements, and when he stopped he was also soon forgotten. Anti-Soviet circles need people like [Julius] Telesin, [Vladimir] Telnikov [dissidents living in Great Britain], and Volpin [Alexander Volpin, now living in the United States], who keep slandering their former homeland.

SAKHAROV: I don't think that Chalidze ever engaged in anti-Soviet activity. The same goes for the others. You mentioned Volpin. As far as I know, he is busy with mathematics in Boston.

MALYAROV: That may be, but we also have reliable information about his anti-Soviet activity.

SAKHAROV: You say that no one is supporting me. Last year I took part in two collective appeals, for amnesty and for abolition of the death penalty. Each of these appeals was signed by more than fifty persons.

MALYAROV: Only asking that the matter be considered?

SAKHAROV: Yes. And we were quite distressed when the law on amnesty turned out to be a very limited one, and the death penalty was not abolished.

MALYAROV: You did not seriously expect a change in the law just because you wanted it. This is not the time to abolish the death penalty. Murderers and rapists who commit serious crimes go unpunished. [The death penalty also applies to serious crimes against the state, such as treason and espionage and economic crimes.]

SAKHAROV: I am talking about abolishing the very institution of the death penalty. Many thoughtful people are of the view that this institution has no place in a humane society and that it is immoral. We have serious crime despite the existence of the death penalty. The death penalty does not help make society more humane. I heard that abolition of the death penalty has been under discussion in Soviet legal circles.

MALYAROV: No. One jurist raised the question, but he found no support. The time is not ripe.

SAKHAROV: The issue is now being debated throughout the world. Many countries have abolished the death penalty. Why should we be different?

MALYAROV: They abolished it in the United States, but now they are forced to restore it. You've been reading about the crimes that have occurred there. Nothing like that happens here. You seem to like the American way of life even though they permit the unrestricted sale of guns, they murder their Presidents, and now they've got this demagogic fraud of the Watergate case. Sweden, too, is proud of her freedom, and they have pornographic pictures on every street. I saw them myself. Don't tell me you are for pornography, for that kind of freedom?

SAKHAROV: I am not familiar with either the American or the Swedish way of life. They probably have their own problems and I would not idealize them. But you mentioned the Watergate case. To me, it is a good illustration of American democracy.

MALYAROV: It is calculated to be just a show. All Nixon has to do is show a little firmness, and the whole thing will come to nothing. That's their democracy for you, nothing but a fraud. I think we should end this conversation. There was one more thing. You seem to have a high opinion of Belinkov [Arkady V. Belinkov, a Soviet writer who defected to the West in 1968 and died two years later]. You know that name, don't you?

SAKHAROV: I consider Belinkov an outstanding writer on public affairs. I particularly appreciated his letter to the

Pen Club in 1968 [protesting curbs on intellectual freedom in the Soviet Union].

MALYAROV: Are you aware that Belinkov was once arrested and imprisoned for having distributed leaflets calling for the killing of Communists?

SAKHAROV: I don't know anything about that. That probably happened a long time ago under Stalin. How can you take that seriously? At that time anyone could be arrested as a terrorist.

MALYAROV: No, Belinkov was imprisoned twice, the second time not so long ago. And how about your Daniel [Yuli M. Daniel, dissident writer, who served five years at hard labor, from 1966 to 1970]? Didn't he call openly for the murder of leaders of the Party and government in his story "Day of Open Murders"? And Amalrik, is he any better? You should think about it.

SAKHAROV: "Day of Open Murders" is a work of fiction, an allegory, directed in spirit against the terror of the Stalin years, which was still very fresh at that time, in 1956. Daniel made that quite clear in his trial. As for [Amalrik's] "Will the USSR Survive until 1984?"—that, too, is an allegory. You know that the date stems from Orwell's story.

MALYAROV: We had better stop. I just want you to give serious thought to my warning. Any state has the right to defend itself. There are appropriate articles in the Criminal Code, and no one will be permitted to violate them.

SAKHAROV: I have been listening closely and I will certainly bear in mind every word you said. But I cannot agree that I have been violating the law. In particular, I cannot agree with your statement that my meetings with foreign correspondents are illegal or that they endanger state secrets. Goodbye.

MALYAROV: Goodbye.

August 16, 1973

INTERVIEW WITH FOREIGN CORRESPONDENTS

SAKHAROV: All those present are familiar with the record of my conversation with M. P. Malyarov, the First Deputy Prosecutor General (on August 16). Please consider that record as an introduction to our conversation today.

I would like to make some additional comments:

First, about the practice of issuing "warnings": various forms of "warnings" have been employed recently with dissidents by the State Security Committee (KGB) and associated agencies. In some cases such warnings have preceded arrest, in other cases they have been followed by permission to emigrate. The particular form of warning that I encountered August 16 is undoubtedly more serious than the one given me last March at the KGB, when my wife and I offered to become surety in the case of Yury Shikhanovich [a Moscow University mathematician arrested September

28, 1972, and held incommunicado since then. The Sa-
kharovs' offer of being guarantors was refused].

On the other hand, there are even more serious forms
of warnings. It was learned recently that several persons
had been "warned" that their fates would depend on testimony they gave at forthcoming trials. If their behavior as
witnesses was not satisfactory, it was said, then they would
not "leave the courtroom."

No less ominous, and reviving the institution of hostages, were widely publicized "warnings" that for the appearance of every new issue of the *Chronicle of Current
Events* (the underground news bulletin), appropriate persons would be arrested and those already under arrest
would be sentenced to long terms.

The articles about me that have appeared in the Soviet
press are also likely to be intended as "warnings," from the
standpoint of the KGB. When I discussed the Shikhanovich
case with the KGB, I was told that he had not drawn the
proper conclusions from his "warnings," which in this case
apparently referred to searches of his home.

In general, the system of "warnings" seems designed
to remind people of the existence of a force that will not
tolerate any deviation from a desired line on the presumed
grounds that "a state has the right to self-defense." If this
interpretation of the "warnings" is correct, they are symp-
tomatic of the kind of thinking found in police agencies,
and have nothing in common with democracy or the right
to one's convictions, or the law, or humanity.

Second, regarding the NTS [a Russian émigré organization based in Frankfurt, West Germany] and Possev [its
publishing house]. Accusations that writings or appeals are
being used in anti-Soviet publications of Possev for "anti-

Soviet subversive purposes" have become the principal bogy used by the KGB and its like; they have become the principal accusation and the most important means of intimidation and of exerting pressure on public opinion. Even the most casual possession of a Possev publication is regarded as a crime. It is very important, therefore, that this issue be clarified. As for me, in my conversation in the Prosecutor's office, I welcomed the publishing and enlightenment activities of Possev, without regard to the program of the NTS (which aims at the overthrow of the Soviet regime) or to the actions and statements of particular representatives of that organization, with which I do not necessarily have to sympathize.

Third, as for the Prosecutor's contention that my meetings with foreigners violate previous pledges. In 1950, when I went to work in a classified institution, I did indeed sign an undertaking that made any meetings with foreigners punishable "by administrative procedures." The maximum administrative penalty is dismissal from work. I was dismissed from the job in 1968, after publication of my essay *Progress, Coexistence, and Intellectual Freedom,* long before I ever met any foreigner. I can only repeat here what I told Malyarov, namely that my meetings with foreign journalists have no bearing whatever on any violation of state secrets, which I would never and under no circumstances consider permissible.

Do you regard the talk at the Prosecutor's office and the Tass *attack as a general warning or as directed specifically at your interview with the Swedish radio?*
The interview was evidently the last drop that filled the cup to overflowing. Someone must have authorized the

summons to the Prosecutor's office. It could have been authorized at the highest level. But it could also have been sanctioned at an intermediate level so that no one could be reproached for not having warned me. However, I consider this less likely than the first alternative.

Do you think the authorities distinguish between your work within the Committee for Human Rights and your personal criticism of the Soviet system?
Neither one is evidently acceptable to them, but in different degrees.

Could you develop that thought further?
The Committee, of which I am only a member, is, of course, a totally loyal association. In the interview with the Swedish radio, I expressed my personal opinions. I do not impose these opinions on anyone, but they were evidently found unacceptable in substance.

Do you get the impression that the authorities want you to leave the country? Was it that kind of a warning?
This was never openly suggested to me, nor was it in this latest conversation. In fact, I was told that I am still a Soviet citizen. I interpret this to mean that I should stop doing what I am doing in this country, not that I am invited to leave the country.

Were you threatened in some other way? Directly or indirectly?
No. I tried to write down a full account of the conversation. Nothing else was said. They evidently thought I understood the point well enough.

Have you personally ever considered leaving the Soviet Union?

I have always replied to that question that I am not ripe for such a decision.

What do you think will be the next step?

I have already had the occasion to state that I fear most those forms of pressure that are not directed against me personally but could become indirectly unbearable and intolerable.

Do you mean your family?

I mean my family or other persons dear to me. I can really not predict what may happen. Of course, steps may also be taken against me personally but I like to believe that the loyal character of my activities will ultimately be understood.

Loyal to what?

Loyal in the literal meaning of the word, namely lawful.

I have a more general question. People often wonder what your means of support is and what work you are doing.

First of all, I get a salary from the Lebedev Institute of Physics, where I hold the post of Senior Research Associate, the lowest position that can be given a member of the Academy of Sciences. In addition I receive my honorarium as a member of the Academy.

What amounts are involved?

As a member of the Academy four hundred rubles a

month, and in the Institute job three hundred and fifty rubles. I have already stated that I contributed all my savings in 1969 to a government fund for the building of a new cancer research center.

How much was that?
A very large sum. A hundred and thirty-nine thousand rubles.

What made you contribute such a large sum?
In hindsight, I consider it completely senseless; I do not think I was right to do it so I won't give the reasons.

You say that you are on the staff of the Physics Institute. Does that mean that you are in fact working there?
That is a difficult question for me to answer. In general, productivity in theoretical physics tends to decline at my age. That is the general rule. Furthermore, my work in theoretical physics was interrupted for a long time while I was employed in applied fields. And finally, inner unrest also has not made it any easier. In short, I have not been productive in recent years. I am still hopeful that this is a temporary situation and that I will still accomplish something but I can't pretend to hope too much.

Do you actually go to the Institute?
I do, although a theoretical physicist is actually supposed to work at home, with journals, and with a piece of paper and a pen.

What relations do you have with your former colleagues?

They have become very weak. I see them seldom, and very few of them.

Are your colleagues trying to put pressure on you to induce you to change your position?

No, no one is trying to do that. With only rare exceptions.

Do you interpret their silence as approval of your stand?

Rather as reluctance to get involved in delicate matters. Although both may be true.

How widespread, in your view, is a desire for democratization among the intelligentsia?

It is very difficult for me to speak for the intelligentsia. It would require a major sociological research effort.

How many members of your family have already been under some form of pressure?

Those members of my family on my wife's side. Her daughter [by a previous marriage], Tatyana Ivanovna Semyonova, born in February 1950, has been barred from her last year in the University. Her brother, Aleksei, born in 1956, has been denied admission to the University, which is also a form of pressure. He was told that he was "marked." In a more indirect form, my stepdaughter's husgand, Yefrem V. Yankelevich, twenty-three, was dismissed from his job after he applied to go to the Massachusetts Institute of Technology for study. He graduated from the Institute of Communications and now has a temporary job with a geophysical expedition. All three had been invited by Dr. Jerome B. Wiesner, the president of MIT, with the promise of scholarships. There has been no answer to the applications, which were handed in last April 6. The applications have not even been acknowledged. When I inquired, I was told, "This is not a trip to Penza Province [in central Russia]," and they had to take their time about it.

Is it not unusual for Soviet citizens to apply to go abroad individually for study?
Very unusual. But anywhere else in the world, it is highly usual. Here everything is unusual. Nevertheless, the Soviet Union has an agreement with the United States covering student exchanges, so these applications should not really be considered all that unusual.

Didn't you also have an invitation to go to the United States?
Yes, I did get an invitation from Princeton for one academic year. I was very interested and would be glad to go, but I have not taken any steps so far. The question is a very complicated one.

Do you see any pattern in the tactics now being used toward dissidents? Some are allowed to leave the country. Others are being put on trial. Still others are being committed to mental institutions. How do you explain the various approaches being used?
I believe many considerations enter into each particular case. The combination of all three techniques seems to offer the greatest flexibility.

Even among those who are allowed to leave the country and whose Soviet citizenship is then canceled, the approach also seems to differ. Valery Chalidze was deprived of his citizenship promptly upon his arrival in the United States. Zhores Medvedev had to wait much longer.

Yes, evidently here, too, no standard method is being followed.

What is your general evaluation of the present state of the democratic movement in the Soviet Union?

I have always found it difficult to consider it a movement as such. I have viewed it essentially as an expression of concern for the fate of particular persons who have become the victims of injustice. I have considered it mainly as an effort to protest against unfair trials, unjustified commitments to mental institutions, to help the families of the persons concerned. It is certainly not a movement of any kind. It is normal human activity that cannot be regarded as political. There is, of course, also another aspect. There are people who want to assert the right to freedom of conviction for themselves and for others. These convictions may also vary widely, so that here again it would be difficult to speak of a movement as such. So that if you view the situation from the bottom up, there is no movement that may be regarded as pursuing a particular political goal, such as a struggle for power. Even if you were to view the situation from the top, it seems to me that it would be difficult to discern a movement. So that the authorities really have no grounds for concern, especially not for any repressions. If there are any grounds for concern, these must be within their minds.

But if you compare the present situation to the past, say, two years ago, there was more of the type of activity you have described.

If we take those about whose fate we have been concerned I must admit that their ranks have been thinned simply as a result of intensified repression. It represents an injustice, a great personal tragedy for a large number of people. It has had a negative impact on the psychological climate within the country. It has also had a negative impact on the international situation. On the whole, I do not consider the intensification of repressions to have been a sensible decision by the authorities. Just as I did not see any sense in the events whose fifth anniversary we are marking today. I am referring to the news learned on August 21, 1968, by Soviet citizens that a group of political figures had appealed for help to protect the gains of socialism in Czechoslovakia. Exactly five years ago Czechoslovakia was invaded. Now we've all forgotten about it.

If you do not consider the present policy [toward dissidents] to be sensible, why do you think it is being pursued?

I believe that the people at the top of our society have developed a particular way of thinking. They probably see no other way of reacting to the present situation.

May I ask you about your essay Progress, Coexistence, and Intellectual Freedom, *which was published five years ago? If you think back to the analysis of world prospects you then presented, how has the situation in fact evolved, in your view?*

I discussed the possible evolution of events in terms of certain time spans, and these should be viewed as allegorical. But my basic premise still holds true, namely that the world faces two alternatives—either gradual convergence with democratization within the Soviet Union, or increasing confrontation with a growing danger of thermonuclear war. But reality has turned out to be trickier, in the sense that we now face a very specific issue: Will rapprochement be associated with democratization of Soviet society or not? This new alternative, which at first sight may seem a halfway measure, better than nothing, in fact conceals within itself a great internal danger.

What alternative are you now referring to?

I mean rapprochement without democratization, rapprochement in which the West in effect accepts the Soviet Union rules of the game. Such a rapprochement would be dangerous in the sense that it would not really solve any of the world's problems and would mean simply capitulating in the face of real or exaggerated Soviet power. It would mean an attempt to trade with the Soviet Union, buying its gas and oil, while ignoring all other aspects. I think such a development would be dangerous because it would have serious repercussions in the Soviet Union. It would contaminate the whole world with the anti-democratic peculiarities of Soviet society. It would enable the Soviet Union to bypass problems it cannot resolve on its own and to concentrate on accumulating further strength. As a result, the world would become disarmed and helpless while facing our uncontrollable bureaucratic apparatus. I think that if rapprochement were to proceed totally without qualifications, on Soviet terms, it would pose a serious threat to the world as a whole.

In what way?

It would mean cultivation and encouragement of a closed country, where everything that happens may be shielded from outside eyes, a country wearing a mask that hides its true face. I would not wish it on anyone to live next to such a neighbor, especially if he is at the same time armed to the teeth. I think that most of the political leaders in the West understand the situation, at least the Helsinki Conference seemed to suggest an awareness that rapprochement must be associated with simultaneous liquidation of [Soviet] isolation. Adoption of the Jackson Amendment [by the United States Senate, linking easier trade to unrestricted emigration from the Soviet Union] strikes me as a minimal step that would be significant not only by itself, but also as a symbolic expression of the view that rapprochement must involve some sort of control to insure that this country will not become a threat to its neighbors. As for the emigration of Jews . . .

Excuse me, the Jackson Amendment does not refer specifically to Jews. It deals with freedom of emigration as such.

I know, but the Jackson Amendment is often cited in the context of Jewish emigration. Such a narrowing of the issue is very useful to Soviet propaganda, although it is, of course, quite misleading. I do not mean to belittle the Jewish emigration problem in any way. It has been an important, and totally justified, phenomenon in Soviet life, which derives from many factors in the history of the Jewish people and from conditions in the Soviet Union. But the emigration problem is, of course, much broader than that.

But what would happen if, say, 10 to 20 percent of Soviet scientists decided they wanted to emigrate?

In the first place, I don't think that the idea would ever occur to even ten percent. The premise is not realistic. But, in general, it is quite natural for scientists to want to move from country to country. A lot is being written about the brain drain, but in fact it does not lead to any catastrophic consequences. Science is international. Technology, too, is becoming international, and the place of residence of any particular scientist should become a matter of personal choice.

With regard to forthcoming trials, do you know when they might begin and why such trials would be staged in the first place?

Apparently some trials are scheduled for the near future, maybe in September, judging from indirect indications.

What trials are you referring to?

Yakir and Krasin. The trials have apparently been postponed a number of times. We do not know what preparation may have been necessary. It is hard for me to predict how they will finally turn out; probably plans have been changed several times. The point that will evidently be made is that the activities of Yakir, Krasin, and their associates were used for anti-Soviet purposes by anti-Soviet organizations. What I said in the introductory statement today reflects my own point of view on that issue.

Have you had any news about Grigorenko [retired Maj. Gen. Pyotr G. Grigorenko, committed to a mental institution in 1969]?

The news is that there has been no news. He is still in Chernyakhovsk [Kaliningrad Province, the former East Prussia] under horrible conditions, and although he was to have been transferred to a normal hospital by decision of an appeals court, the transfer is being postponed. When his wife inquired about the reasons for the delay, she was told that the director of the present hospital, Bochkov, was away and would be back on September 1. We still hope that Grigorenko will be transferred. That would make it a bit easier for him. He has been undergoing horrible sufferings for the last four years.

One final question. What specific reasons led you to call this news conference?

I felt that my summons to the Prosecutor's office contained a certain threat both for me and for members of my family. And then I felt that my conversation there had raised several important issues that required further clarification.

August 21, 1973

A CLARIFICATION

The newspaper campaign [in the Soviet Union] with respect to my recent interviews employs as its fundamental argument the accusation that I am supposedly speaking against the relaxation of international tension, almost in favor of war. This is an unscrupulous play on the anti-war feelings of the nation that suffered the most from the Second World War, that lost millions of its sons and daughters. This is a deliberate distortion of my position.

Beginning in 1958 I have spoken out both in print and in private for ending nuclear tests in the atmosphere. I believe these efforts made their contribution to the conclusion in 1963 of the historic Moscow Treaty banning tests in three environments.

In my fundamental public statements—my *Progress, Coexistence, and Intellectual Freedom* "Memorandum" and

"Postscript"—I have written about elimination of the mortal danger of thermonuclear war as the main problem facing mankind. Therefore I have always welcomed and welcome now the relaxation of international tension and the efforts of governments toward rapprochement of states, toward limitation of the arms race, toward elimination of mutual mistrust. I have believed and believe now that the only real way to solve world problems is the movement of each side toward the other, the convergence of the capitalist and socialist systems accompanied by demilitarization, reinforcement of the social protection for workers' rights, and creation of a mixed type of economy.

This has been my consistent position and it was restated again in my recent interviews with foreign correspondents in Moscow. In these interviews I also emphasized the importance of mutual trust, which requires extensive public disclosure and an open society, democratization, free dissemination of information, the exchange of ideas, and respect for all the fundamental rights of the individual—in particular, respect for everyone's right to choose the country in which he wishes to live.

I call attention to the danger of a supposed détente not accompanied by increased trust and democratization. I consider this warning my right and my duty. Is this warning really a statement against détente?

I am speaking up for the trampled rights of my friends in camps and psychiatric hospitals, for Shikhanovich, Bukovsky, Grigorenko, Plyushch, Amalrik, Borisov, Fainberg, Strkata, and many others. I cannot consider these statements slanders of our system as the newspapers describe them. I deem it important that human rights in our country should be afforded no worse protection than in the countries entering into new, more friendly relations with us, that our towns, our countryside, and our internal life be open, as in those countries, to foreigners and our own citizens as well, including such institutions as places of confinement, psychiatric hospitals, and places of residence and work of those freed on probation. Let the presence of the Red Cross lead to the removal of iron shutters from the windows of Soviet prisons and stay the hand of the criminals who gave haloperidol to Leonid Plyushch in the hell of Dnepropetrovsk prison psychiatric hospital.

The newspaper campaign involving hundreds of persons, among them many honest and intelligent individuals, has deeply grieved me as still another manifestation of brutal coercion of conscience in our nation, coercion based on the unrestricted material and ideological power of the state.

I believe not my statement, but just this newspaper campaign, so foolish and so savage with respect to its participants, can harm international détente.

September 12, 1973

A LETTER
TO THE
CONGRESS
OF THE
UNITED STATES

At a time when the Congress is debating fundamental issues of foreign policy, I consider it my duty to express my view on one such issue—the protection of the right to freedom of residence within the country of one's choice. That right was proclaimed by the United Nations in 1948 in the Universal Declaration of Human Rights.

If every nation is entitled to choose the political system under which it wishes to live, this is true all the more of every individual person. A country whose citizens are deprived of this minimal right is not free even if there were not a single citizen who would want to exercise that right.

But, as you know, there are tens of thousands of citizens in the Soviet Union—Jews, Germans, Russians, Ukrainians, Lithuanians, Armenians, Estonians, Latvians, Turks, and members of other ethnic groups—who want to leave the country and who have been seeking to exercise that right for years and for decades at the cost of endless difficulty and humiliation.

You know that prisons, labor camps, and mental hospitals are full of people who have sought to exercise this legitimate right.

You surely know the name of the Lithuanian Simas A. Kudirka, who was handed over to the Soviet authorities by an American vessel, as well as the names of the defendants in the tragic 1970 hijacking trial in Leningrad. You know about the victims of the Berlin wall.

There are many more lesser-known victims. Remember them, too.

For decades the Soviet Union has been developing under conditions of intolerable isolation, bringing with it the ugliest consequences. Even a partial preservation of those conditions would be highly perilous for all mankind, for international confidence and détente.

In view of the foregoing, I am appealing to the Congress of the United States to give its support to the Jackson Amendment, which represents in my view and in the view of its sponsors an attempt to protect the right of emigration of citizens in countries that are entering into new and friendlier relations with the United States.

The Jackson Amendment is made even more significant by the fact that the world is just entering on a new course of détente and it is therefore essential that the proper direction be followed from the outset. This is a fundamental issue, extending far beyond the question of emigration.

Those who believe that the Jackson Amendment is likely to undermine anyone's personal or governmental prestige are wrong. Its provisions are minimal and not demeaning.

It should be no surprise that the democratic process

can add its corrective to the actions of public figures who negotiate without admitting the possibility of such an amendment. The amendment does not represent interference in the internal affairs of socialist countries, but simply a defense of international law, without which there can be no mutual trust.

Adoption of the amendment therefore cannot be a threat to Soviet-American relations. All the more, it would not imperil international détente.

There is a particular silliness in objections to the amendment that are founded on the alleged fear that its adoption would lead to outbursts of anti-Semitism in the USSR and hinder the emigration of Jews.

Here you have total confusion, either deliberate or based on ignorance, about the USSR. It is as if the emigration issue affected only Jews. As if the situation of those Jews who have vainly sought to emigrate to Israel were not already tragic enough and would become even more hopeless if it were to depend on the democratic attitudes and on the humanity of OVIR [the Soviet visa agency]. As if the techniques of "quiet diplomacy" could help anyone, beyond a few individuals in Moscow and some other cities.

The abandonment of a policy of principle would be a betrayal of the thousands of Jews and non-Jews who want to emigrate, of the hundreds in camps and mental hospitals, of the victims of the Berlin wall.

Such a denial would lead to stronger repressions on ideological grounds. It would be tantamount to total capitulation of democratic principles in the face of blackmail, deceit, and violence. The consequences of such a capitulation for international confidence, détente, and the entire future of mankind are difficult to predict.

I express the hope that the Congress of the United States, reflecting the will and the traditional love of freedom of the American people, will realize its historical responsibility before mankind and will find the strength to rise above temporary partisan considerations of commercialism and prestige.

I hope that the Congress will support the Jackson Amendment.

September 14, 1973

STATEMENT OF THE HUMAN RIGHTS COMMITTEE

The Committee once again draws the attention of public opinion to the continuing use of psychiatric institutions for political ends in our country. The Committee notes that persons prosecuted in connection with their convictions are, as frequently as before or indeed more frequently, being ruled mentally ill and sent for compulsory treatment, mainly to special prison hospitals. We are firmly convinced that in the overwhelming majority of cases there are no medical grounds for such measures.

Our conviction is based on a great deal of direct and indirect evidence. The very fact of the exceptionally wide-spread occurrence of this form of repression is highly indicative. In a number of cases we have documentary evidence, and in other cases reliable oral testimony, that it is precisely the person's opinions and nothing else that are viewed by experts as evidence of illness. In numerous cases copies of the official psychiatric reports are available, and these can themselves be regarded as proof of such a biased and unscrupulous approach.

A collection of such reports was sent to the West earlier by Bukovsky, who quickly became a victim of judicial revenge for this revelation. We should also mention here that the psychiatrist Gluzman has become another victim of judicial revenge. Reports indicate that the reason was his authorship of an anonymous *in absentia* report on the Grigorenko case. Such acts of revenge for public disclosure are also indicative.

We think it very important that we ourselves personally know many of those who have been declared ill, and in these cases, on the basis of our personal observation as corroborated by their wholly normal life and work, we are convinced of their mental health.

The Committee recalls the names of some of the individuals who have been declared mentally ill for political motives: Grigorenko, Fainberg, Borisov, Gershuni, Ubozhke, Shikhanovich, Plyushch, Starchik, Lupynis, Belov, Kukobaka, Lysak, Mukhamedyarov, Zheleznov, Montlevich, Butkus, and Lavrev.

The Committee notes that persons sent for compulsory treatment have no protection in practice against nonobjective psychiatric examinations, against unfounded, unlimited extension of their hospitalization, against arbitrariness, against harsh and humiliating treatment. Their right to defend their beliefs, and the lawfulness of their actions founded on those beliefs, turn out to be violated, as the court, acting moreover in their absence, regards these beliefs as both evidence of and a consequence of their mental illness.

The Committee urges the following:

1. Demand that relatives of persons undergoing psychiatric examination have the right to select psychiatric experts of their choice, including the right to request foreign psychiatric experts, especially in cases attracting public attention and in cases where a basis exists to doubt the objectivity of the examination; and demand, in particular, examination by a commission of experts, including foreign psychiatrists for the persons named above.

2. Demand—when the public becomes concerned about the use of psychiatry for repressive purposes in any country or about harsh treatment insulting to the dignity of mentally ill persons—the formation of an international commission organized by WHO [the World Health Organization], the Red Cross, and other international organizations and including psychiatrists. In particular, regard as essential the international investigation of the special psychiatric hospitals of the USSR Ministry of Internal Affairs in Dnepropetrovsk, Sychevka, Orel, Kazan, Leningrad, and Chernyakhovsk.

3. Recommend to foreign psychiatric agencies and organizations that they insistently request the transfer of some patients from Soviet psychiatric hospitals, including special hospitals, for observation in foreign hospitals and, if necessary, for treatment there; in particular, insist on the transfer of the individuals named above.

4. Organize in international and national psychiatric organizations discussion of the state of Soviet psychiatry, and, in particular, discussion of the personal role of the psychiatrists who serve on commissions in political cases.

The Committee appeals to international and national psychiatric organizations and asks for discussion and support of the proposals listed above, and also for constructive counterproposals. The Committee calls on psychiatrists throughout the world to speak out in defense of their colleague Semyon Gluzman and of Vladimir Bukovsky.

ANDREI SAKHAROV

GRIGORY PODYAPOLSKY

IGOR SHAFAREVICH

October 1, 1973

INTERVIEW
WITH A
LEBANESE
CORRESPONDENT

The events in the Near East alarm me greatly. I do not know if words can be important at such a moment but I am ready to answer your questions.

How do you appraise the events in the Near East?
This war, which began with simultaneous large-scale Egyptian and Syrian military operations, is a great tragedy both for Arabs and for Jews. But for Israel in this war, just as in the wars of 1949, 1956, and 1967, what is at stake is the very existence of the state, the right to life. I believe that for the Arabs this war is basically a result of the play of internal and external political forces, of considerations of prestige, of nationalistic prejudices. I believe that this difference exists and must be taken into account when appraising these events.

What can the Arabs and Israelis do to end this conflict?

Immediately agree to a cease-fire and sit down to negotiations. The Arabs should clearly and unequivocally declare that they recognize Israel's right to existence within borders insuring its military security, fundamental economic interests, and prospective immigration. Israel should give guarantees in return. With these conditions the honorable peace long wished for by both parties is possible.

What steps can the United States and Western nations take to terminate the war?

Call upon the USSR and socialist countries to abandon the policy of one-sided interference in the Arab-Israeli conflict, and take retaliatory measures if this policy of interference continues. Use all means, including diplomatic, for an immediate cease-fire and for the initiation of direct peace negotiations between the Arabs and Israel. Make effective use of the United Nations Charter to safeguard peace and security.

Which is better for socialist countries and countries of the third world—an Israeli victory or an Arab victory?

The people of all countries are interested not in military victories but in peace and security, in respect for the rights and hopes of all nationalities, in tolerance and in freedom.

How can you, as a defender of human rights, help the Arab countries?

I speak out for the democratization of life in our country, and this is closely related to our foreign policy and the relaxation of international tensions. The Arab countries, as countries throughout the world, have an interest in this as one of the conditions for development free from external forces.

At the present time do you intend to criticize the policy of Israel's leaders?

No. That country, which is the realization of the Jewish people's right to a state, is today fighting for its existence surrounded by enemies who exceed it in population and material resources many times over. This hostility was stirred up to a considerable extent by the imprudent policies of other states. All mankind has on its conscience the Jewish victims of Nazi genocide during the Second World War. We cannot permit a repetition of that tragedy today.

October 11, 1973

STATEMENT ON RECEIVING THE AWARD OF THE INTERNATIONAL LEAGUE FOR THE RIGHTS OF MAN

I accept this prize with deep gratitude and emotion.

I am thinking at this moment of hundreds of my friends and people of like persuasion who are in camps, prisons, and psychiatric hospitals and who, through their courage and suffering, are affirming the defense of human rights as a supreme goal of society.

In 1948 the United Nations adopted a great humanistic document of the era—the Universal Declaration of Human Rights. The UN thereby took upon itself the defense of human rights in every country. In those years the Stalinist dictatorship was committing unprecedented crimes in our country, trampling human rights underfoot at every step. Now times have changed in many respects. But as before, the international defense of human rights is very important to the citizens of our country. Still unsolved are problems

of great importance to the spiritual, political, and economic
health of society, such as assuring freedom of one's convictions and conscience, assuring public disclosure, freedom of
the press and information. Still unsolved are many problems
of national equality. The Crimean Tatars, the Volga Germans, and the Meskhi Turks, resettled under the Stalinist
tyranny, cannot return to their homelands. Such a key problem for our country as that of assuring freedom of emigration is still unsolved.

I would like to believe that the awarding to a Soviet
citizen of the International Human Rights Prize demonstrates that international attention to assuring human rights
in our country will increase and have a deep influence.

A. SAKHAROV

December 5, 1973

[*Read on behalf of Andrei Sakharov by his representative,
Dr. Herman Feschbach, at a session of the International
League for the Rights of Man.*]

DECLARATION ON SOLZHENITSYN

We are deeply perturbed and exasperated by the new threats to Alexander Solzhenitsyn contained in a recent Tass statement. Tass declares that Solzhenitsyn is a "traitor to the Motherland" who libels its past. But how is it possible to affirm that the "mistakes made" have been condemned and corrected and, at the same time, to characterize as libel an honest attempt to gather and publish historical and folkloric information on a part of those crimes that burden our collective conscience? After all, it cannot be denied that there actually were mass arrests, tortures, executions, forced labor, inhuman conditions, and the deliberate annihilation of millions of people in camps. There was the dispossession of the kulaks, the persecution and annihilation of hundreds of thousands of believers, forcible resettling of peoples, anti-worker and anti-peasant laws, and the persecution of those who had returned from prisoner-of-war camps. And there were other crimes whose harshness, perfidy, and cynicism were astounding.

The right of an author to write and publish that which is dictated by his conscience and duty as an artist is one of the most basic in civilized society. This right cannot be limited by national boundaries. A *fortiori*, the opportunity to set such limits cannot be given to the All-Union Agency for the Protection of Copyright, that allegedly social organization which in fact performs the functions of political censorship and currency speculation on an author's work.

We are convinced there are no legal grounds for prosecuting* Solzhenitsyn for his having published his new book, *The Gulag Archipelago*, abroad, just as there are no grounds for prosecuting anyone for similar acts. We know, however, that in our state prosecutions are possible even without such grounds. We call upon honest people throughout the world to resist this danger—to protect the pride of Russian and world culture, Alexander Solzhenitsyn.

ANDREI SAKHAROV

ALEXANDER GALICH

VLADIMIR MAXIMOV

VLADIMIR VOINOVICH

IGOR SHAFAREVICH

January 5, 1974

* Also translatable as "persecuting." [Translator's note.]

APPENDIX

I ask you to use your influence and authority to have
the sentence passed on Vladimir Bukovsky set aside and
Bukovsky himself released. . . . It is in the interests of the
healthy elements of the leadership of the country and
among our people that this unjust sentence should be set
aside, and in a broader context that this country, which has
endured so much suffering and degradation, should undergo a moral regeneration. For only the moral health of the
people is a true guarantee of the viability of the country in
creative labor and in the face of coming trials.

Restore legality and justice!

January 18, 1972

TO: THE HUMAN RIGHTS COMMITTEE

FROM: COMMITTEE MEMBER A. D. SAKHAROV

ON THE PROBLEM OF RESTORING THE RIGHTS OF PERSONS AND PEOPLES VIOLATED IN THE COURSE OF FORCIBLE RESETTLEMENT.

The Committee has received documents from representatives of the Crimean Tatar people and the Meskhi-Turkic people in which the Committee's attention is drawn to the important problem of restoring the rights of persons and peoples violated in the course of resettlement. The Committee is aware that a situation requiring the restoration of rights also exists with respect to the Volga German people.

I propose that the Committee consider the following problems:

1. The circumstances of the forcible resettlement of peoples—Volga Germans, Kalmyks, Circassians, Karachai, Balkars, Crimean Tatars, Meskhi, Greeks, and also the Koreans resettled before the war.

2. An analysis of the violations of legality and humanity committed in the course of forcible resettlement.

3. The circumstances of the forcible detention of resettled persons in their places of residence, the presence of special commandant's offices and other extralegal restrictions on rights, aggravating the already frightful situation of the resettled persons and leading to mass mortality.

4. An analysis of the situation existing at the present moment; in particular, discriminatory restrictions as regards residence permits, employment, education, the right to acquire property, etc., vis-à-vis the Crimean Tatars, the Volga Germans, and the Meskhi.

5. a) An analysis of the causes which led the Stalinist administration to commit the crimes of genocide named in paragraphs 1, 2, and 3.

b) An analysis of the causes conducive to delays in the restoration of the rights of resettled persons at the present time.

I propose that we discuss the role of the following factors: the role of the general–ideological course of great-power chauvinism; visible violence as a means of the political manipulation of prejudices and low instincts; the role of economic and social factors; the role of the general political and psychological situation in a time of war.

6. The persecution of persons who have supported the restoration of the rights of resettled peoples.

7. What *démarches* and documents of the Committee might help in the resolution of the problem.

March 16, 1972

TO THE PRESIDIUM OF THE SUPREME SOVIET USSR

At the request of interested parties, the Human Rights Committee has familiarized itself with the problem of restoring the rights of forcibly resettled peoples and ethnic groups. While expressing satisfaction at the restoration of the rights of several such peoples, we call upon the Presidium of the Supreme Soviet to help restore the rights of the Crimean Tatars and the Meskhi (and other peoples and groups) to live on the territory from which they were forcibly and illegally resettled.

We call upon the Presidium of the Supreme Soviet to

take steps to see that all citizens of our country can fully exercise their right freely to choose a place of residence; that in particular this right can be exercised by citizens of these nationalities pending general settlement of the question of the return of their territory to them: to settle on that territory, to acquire housing, and to work.

A. D. SAKHAROV

A. N. TVERDOKHLEBOV

V. N. CHALIDZE

I. R. SHAFAREVICH

April 21, 1972

These two petitions, drafted and circulated by Andrei Sakharov and signed by more than fifty Soviet intellectuals, were sent to the USSR Supreme Soviet in autumn, 1972.

TO THE USSR SUPREME SOVIET: AN APPEAL FOR AMNESTY

In the anniversary year of the formation of the Union of the Soviet Socialist Republics, we call on you to adopt decisions that correspond in their humanity and democratic thrust to the fundamental interests of our society.

We call on you to adopt, among such decisions, a law on amnesty.

We believe that this law should provide particularly for the release of those convicted for reasons directly or indirectly connected with their beliefs and specifically: those convicted under Articles 190-3 and Articles 70 and 72 of the RSFSR Criminal Code, and under the corresponding articles of the Codes of other Union Republics; all those convicted in connection with their religious beliefs; and all those convicted in connection with an attempt to leave the country. We call on you also to review the decisions made on similar grounds to confine people in special "prison" or ordinary psychiatric hospitals.

Freedom of conscience and freedom to express and defend one's opinions are each man's inalienable rights. These freedoms are, moreover, a guarantee of a society's vitality.

We also consider that a law on amnesty, in conformity with juridical norms and humanity, should provide for the release of all individuals who have served a term of imprisonment in excess of the present maximum of fifteen years on the basis of sentences pronounced before the adoption of the Fundamental Principles of Legislation now in force.

TO THE USSR SUPREME SOVIET: ON ABOLITION OF THE DEATH PENALTY

Many people have long sought the abolition of the death penalty, believing that it contradicts moral sensibility and cannot be justified by any general social considerations. The death penalty has now been abolished in many countries.

On the anniversary of the formation of the Union of Soviet Socialist Republics, we call on the USSR Supreme Soviet to adopt a law abolishing the death penalty in our country.

Such a decision would promote the extension of this humane act throughout the world.

[Telegram]

TO L. I. BREZHNEV, GENERAL SECRETARY OF THE CC CPSU

TWO YEARS AGO I ADDRESSED MYSELF TO YOU IN CONNECTION
WITH THE CASE OF FRIEDRICH RUPPEL, WHO WANTED TO BE
REPATRIATED WITH HIS FAMILY TO THE FEDERAL GERMAN
REPUBLIC. IN 1941 HIS MOTHER WAS SHOT ON THE BASIS OF
A FALSE CHARGE. HE HIMSELF, AS A BOY, SPENT TEN YEARS IN
A CAMP AS THE RESULT OF A SENTENCE BY AN OSO.* TODAY,
THE DAY OF YOUR ARRIVAL IN BONN, AFTER FOUR YEARS OF
EFFORTS, RUPPEL'S REQUEST WAS REFUSED. I ASK YOU TO IN-
TERVENE AND PUT AN END TO VIOLATIONS OF HUMAN RIGHTS
WHICH DO DAMAGE TO THE PRESTIGE OF OUR NATION.

RESPECTFULLY,

SAKHAROV, ACADEMICIAN

May 18, 1973

TO THE SECRETARY-GENERAL OF THE UN, MR. KURT WALD-
HEIM

In 1968–9 several Soviet citizens who were endeavoring,
from a position loyal to the state, to defend victims of un-
lawful repressions, submitted detailed protests to your
predecessor in the post of Secretary-General of the UN. In
subsequent years the majority of these people, who call
themselves the Initiative Group for the Defense of Human
Rights, have themselves become the victims of equally un-

* A "special conference [board]," or "troika," of the secret police.
[Translator's note.]

lawful repressions. We consider the defense of these people a duty of the organization that proclaimed the Universal Declaration of Human Rights, and a matter involving its prestige.

In this appeal we ask you to come forward in defense of two members of the Initiative Group who have been sentenced to an especially terrible fate—indefinite incarceration in a psychiatric prison. We refer to Vladimir Borisov, arrested in 1969, who has already languished for more than three years in a Leningrad special [i.e., administered by the MVD] prison-type hospital; and Leonid Plyushch, arrested in January of 1972. The investigation and trial of their cases abounded with impermissible violations of legal norms—in particular, of the right to public disclosure and the right to a defense—and in violation of medical ethics. The public is aware of Borisov's heroic struggle and his prolonged political hunger strikes, together with Victor Fainberg, for the right to a hearing in court. This struggle has provoked unconcealed hatred toward Borisov on the part of those in whose hands he finds himself.

At the present time we are especially alarmed about the fate of the Kiev mathematician Leonid Plyushch. His case has been characterized by determined efforts at concealment that are unusual even under our conditions, and that compel one to surmise a desire to conceal even more serious violations of the law. Plyushch's trial took place in an empty hall in the absence of the accused and his representative. Defense counsel had only one brief meeting with his client. The court, basing its decision on an experts' report that was not read out during the hearing, and that, moreover, was drawn up without any personal examination of Plyushch, sent him to a special psychiatric hospital. The appeals court mitigated this decision, changing the type of hospital. However, even though this decision has now entered into legal force, Plyushch is still in an investigation prison of the KGB; and his wife is not allowed to visit her husband, whom she has not seen for a year and a half. Recently, in accordance with a protest lodged by the prosecutor's office, a new appellate review was ordered, so that Plyushch is again threatened with a special hospital. No results have been forthcoming from the numerous appeals made to individual authorities and Soviet agencies in connection with the Borisov and Plyushch cases.

We ask you to come forward in defense of Vladimir Borisov and Leonid Plyushch. This is important in order to not only save these individuals and lessen the tragedy of those close to them but also prevent similar violations of human rights in our country.

We attach a letter from T. Khodorovich, a member of the Initiative Group, which contains important details on the case of L. I. Plyushch.

> Respectfully,
>
> ANDREI SAKHAROV
> GRIGORY PODYAPOLSKY

Moscow
June 25, 1973

APPEAL TO THE CHILEAN GOVERNMENT ABOUT PABLO NERUDA

Worried about the fate of the outstanding contemporary poet and winner of the Nobel Prize for Literature, Pablo Neruda, we appeal to you to fulfill the duties of the position you have occupied and to safeguard the freedom and security of your remarkable citizen. One may agree or not agree with his world view and political position, but by his whole life and creative work he has proved to mankind the sincerity and purity of the beliefs he has propounded.

Pablo Neruda is not only a great Chilean poet but also the pride of all Latin-American literature. His glorious name is indissolubly bound up with the struggle of the peoples of Latin America for their spiritual and national liberation. The violent death of this great man would darken for a long time what your Government has proclaimed as the rebirth and consolidation of Chile.

Humanity and magnanimity on your part to one of your best fellow countrymen would undoubtedly promote normalization and relaxation of tensions both in your own country and in the whole world.

ANDREI SAKHAROV

ALEXANDER GALICH

VLADIMIR MAXIMOV

September 18, 1973

IN SUPPORT OF THE APPEAL OF THE INTERNATIONAL COMMITTEE FOR THE DEFENSE OF HUMAN RIGHTS

The proposals of the International Committee aimed at creating conditions for the free exchange of people and ideas between the countries of the West and the socialist countries, free tourism, free choice of country of residence, free exchange of books, manuscripts, films, and other things

of cultural value are extremely important. The implementation of these proposals would create a new situation
in the world—one in which mutual understanding and trust
would rule out the possibility of military conflicts. The
implementation of these proposals is impossible without
strong pressure by the peoples on their own governments
and those of all European countries, including the governments of the countries of eastern Europe. I call upon all
honest people throughout the world to support the proposals of the International Committee for the Defense of
Human Rights, and to help with their efforts to realize
them.

ANDREI SAKHAROV, ACADEMICIAN

Moscow
December 29, 1973

After the Death of God

After the Death of God

John D. CAPUTO and Gianni VATTIMO

Edited by Jeffrey W. ROBBINS

With an Afterword by Gabriel VAIIANIAN

Columbia University Press   New York

Columbia University Press
Publishers Since 1893
New York   Chichester, West Sussex

Copyright © 2007 Columbia University Press

Library of Congress Cataloging-in-Publication Data

Caputo, John D.
After the death of God / John D. Caputo and Gianni Vattimo /
edited by Jeffrey W. Robbins.
p. cm.
Includes bibliographical references and index.
ISBN-13: 978-0-231-14124-6 (cloth : alk. paper)
1. Philosophy and religion. 2. Death of God. 3. God (Christianity)
4. Christianity—Philosophy. 5. Deconstruction.
6. Postmodernism—Religious aspects. 7. Postmodern theology.
8. Belief and doubt. I. Vattimo, Gianni, 1936—
II. Robbbins, Jeffrey W., 1972– III. Title.
B56.C27   2007
211—dc22   2006036009

Casebound editions of Columbia University Press books are printed on
permanent and durable acid-free paper.

Printed in the United States of America

c 10 9 8 7 6 5 4 3 2 1

For Jacques Derrida

Contents

Acknowledgments

First and foremost, the editor would like to express his deepest gratitude to Gianni Vattimo and John D. Caputo, who generously gave of their time and energy to make this book possible. Their collegiality is a model for the intellectual life, their commitment is a model for responsible political and ethical engagement, and this book is both a testament to my appreciation to them and as a faithful record of the dialogical spirit that animates their thought and work. A special thanks as well to Gabriel Vahanian for lending his theological perspective with a postscript that helps make the connection between the original vitality and excitement that characterized the death of God movement in its earliest days to the present.

I must kindly thank others as well who were integral to this project: Gary Grieve-Carlson, who provided invaluable assistance in the original conception of the project and contributed his insight for the respective interviews; Jordan Miller for his assistance with the transcriptions; Carissa Devine for her work on the index; and Wendy Lochner for her encouragement, enthusiasm, and professionalism throughout the process of seeing this project to completion.

The dialogue with Gianni Vattimo took place in Rome, May 21, 2005, and the dialogue with John D. Caputo took place at Villanova University on August 19, 2004.

Finally, credit must be given to Lebanon Valley College for its 2004–2005 colloquium on "God in the Twenty-first Century." This project grew out of the conversation sparked by this year-long colloquium, which hosted a number of key figures who are exploring the changing nature of contemporary religious thought and practice. I would like to thank the college, most especially President Stephen MacDonald, for this valued institutional support apart from which this book would not have been possible.

After the Death of God

Introduction

After the Death of God

> In religion's perpetual agony lies its philosophical and theoretical relevance. As it dies an ever more secure and serial death, it is increasingly certain to come back to life, in its present guise or in another.
>
> —HENT DE VRIES, *Philosophy and the Turn to Religion*

I

Is God Dead?

> So that, in truth, Thou didst Thyself lay the foundation for the destruction of Thy kingdom, and no one is more to blame for it. Yet what was offered Thee? There are three powers, three powers alone, able to conquer and to hold captive for ever the conscience of these impotent rebels for their happiness—those forces are miracle, mystery, and authority. Thou has rejected all three and hast set the example for doing so.
>
> —DOSTOYEVSKY, "The Grand Inquisitor"

On April 8, 1966, the cover of *Time* asked, "Is God Dead?" When published, it was the best-selling issue in the magazine's history. It announced to the public a theological movement that was making its way into the mainstream—namely, radical death of God theology. This theological movement was in fact a collection of various disparate voices and perspectives. It ranged from the cultural theologians' grappling with what they termed

the "post-Christian era,"[1] to the largely Jewish effort at developing a "post-Holocaust theology,"[2] to the popular reformational
efforts of the Anglican bishop John Robinson's book *Honest to
God* and Harvey Cox's *Secular City*,[3] and, finally, to the metaphysical death of God theology of Thomas J. J. Altizer.[4]

What they all shared in common was a collective sense that
Western culture in general, and the Judeo-Christian tradition in
particular, had entered a profound "ideological crisis."[5] Either
religious language had lost its meaning or, even worse, the inherited meanings had grown perverse in the wake of a long list
of modern atrocities. World wars, genocides, nuclear armament,
and the cold war standoff between the East and the West—together these twentieth-century realities turned the optimism associated with the modern period to a deep and lasting pessimism.
As the contemporary political philosophers Antonio Negri and
Michael Hardt have written:

> Modern negativity is located not in any transcendent realm
> but in the hard reality before us: the fields of patriotic bat-
> tles in the First and Second World Wars, from the killing
> fields at Verdun to the Nazi furnaces and the swift annihi-
> lation of thousands in Hiroshima and Nagasaki, the carpet
> bombing of Vietnam and Cambodia, the massacres from
> Setif and Soweto to Sabra and Shatila, and the list goes on
> and on. There is no Job who can sustain such suffering![6]

Those who spoke of the death of God, therefore, were attempting to locate themselves within this "hard reality before us," and,
like the ancient book of Job from the Hebrew Scriptures, they
were asking the age-old question of theodicy about the meaning
of suffering and the reasons for God's apparent silence in the
midst of it all. They were acknowledging that the old moral and
theological platitudes had somehow fallen short and admitting

that the Bible's answer of vicarious suffering is perhaps inadequate in the face of the twentieth century's experience of genocide and potential for nuclear annihilation. To borrow a phrase from the German theologian Dietrich Bonhoeffer, we can consider the death of God movement as a "coming-of-age," an effort at honoring our history by following a certain cultural and theological rite of passage.

In this sense, even though the preoccupation of contemporary theology no longer centers around the death of God, this radical theological movement still speaks to us today as it testifies to a moment of transition and crisis within Western religious consciousness and thereby helps to establish the genealogy that would develop into what we now know as postmodern theology. Indeed, two of the main theorists of postmodern theology, Carl Raschke and Mark C. Taylor, both suggested a direct link between the death of God and postmodern deconstructive philosophies. As Taylor wrote in his landmark work, *Erring*, from 1984, "Deconstruction is the 'hermeneutic' of the death of God."[7] In addition, the death of God theologies came to be associated with a certain spirit of secularism that permeates almost all facets of contemporary Western society.

Of course, long before theologians explicitly took up this thematic of the death of God in the 1960s, philosophers, historians, novelists, and cultural observers had already made this connection between the collapse of Christendom and the birth of a new, more secular culture. Indeed, the distinction between Christendom and Christianity can be seen as one of the defining features of the Christian faith in the late modern and postmodern world and is certainly integral for establishing the cultural conditions for radical theology.[8] This distinction between Christendom and Christianity spawns from a well-known historical narrative that refers to the imperial religion of Christianity that began in the fourth century CE when the Emperor Constantine effectively established Christianity as the religion of the Roman Empire. Constantine's edict of toleration in 312 CE ended nearly three centuries of sporadic, though at times quite severe, state-sanctioned Christian persecution. By the end of the fourth century, however, Christianity had become both the dominant and official religion of the Roman Empire and, with the possible exception of the few hangers-on such as the desert monks and a select group of monastics, the Christian church had fully embraced its newfound alliance with the powers that be. As the church historian Hugh McLeod explains, this alliance established a "pattern of relations between church and state and between church and society" that would prevail for at least the next fifteen hundred years as "most Christians learnt and practiced their faith in the context of 'Christendom.'" McLeod continues: "That is, they lived in a society where there were close ties between the leaders of the church and those in positions of secular power, where the laws purported to be based on Christian principles, and where, apart from certain clearly defined outsider communities, every member of society was assumed to be a Christian."[9]

By wedding the church with the Roman Empire or, more broadly, with Western culture, the Constantinian revolution successfully harnessed the three powers identified by Dostoyevsky by adding the authority of the state to that of the church's already firm grasp on miracle and mystery. In so doing, the power of the church was consolidated in the creation and spread of a distinctively Christian culture. Along the way, however, the witness of Christ—especially his suffering and death—was lost in his exaltation by the now triumphant church. It would seem, therefore, and this is something that Dostoyevsky's Grand Inquisitor knew well: that the glory of the church was built on its rejection of Christ as the persecuted became the persecutors, and the servant the new Lord and master. From death, to resurrection, to exaltation—here we have the death of God in Christ twice over.

(Religion) In the Shadow of Christendom

> We are not working with Thee, but with him—that is our mystery.
> It's long—eight centuries—since we have been on his side and not
> on Thine. Just eight centuries ago, we took from him what Thou
> didst reject with scorn, that last gift he offered Thee, showing
> Thee all the kingdoms of the earth. We took from him Rome and
> the sword of Caesar, and proclaimed ourselves sole rulers of the
> earth, though hitherto we have not been able to complete our
> work. But whose fault is that? Oh, the work is only beginning, but
> it has begun. It has long to await completion and the earth has yet
> much to suffer, but we shall triumph and shall be Caesars, and then
> we shall plan the universal happiness of man.
>
> —DOSTOYEVSKY, "The Grand Inquisitor"

It is a fine line between the servant becoming the master and the
exchange of one master for another. Perhaps, as Dostoyevsky
suggests, the Christianization of culture was a devil's bargain
from the start. Such is the argument of those like Elaine Pagels
whose appreciation of the early Gnostic literature points to a
time *before* the Christian community came to be defined by a
specific set of authorized beliefs. As Pagels tells it and as our increasing knowledge of the Gnostic literature confirms, the first
centuries of the church was a time of great diversity in terms of
beliefs and practices. It was also a time during which many different Christian communities seemed to flourish, even in the face
of official state persecution. But eventually this diversity came
to be seen more as a threat than as a sign of the vitality of the
church. In order to prevent what was called the "wild readings"
of the gospel and "evil exegesis" of the scriptural tradition, a line
was drawn identifying what was formerly thought of as hetero-
doxy now as heresy. "But," as Pagels writes, "it would take more
than theological argument for [this] viewpoint to prevail. . . . It

would take, in fact, the revolution initiated by the Roman emperor Constantine."[10] A devil's bargain that gave the leaders of the church the needed authority not only to define orthodoxy but also to enforce their vision of the church's proper uniformity and homogeneity. Through this newly established framework of canon, creed, and ecclesiastical authority, the world could now be made in the image of the church, the kingdom of God would now (finally) come.

Or if not a devil's bargain then perhaps a fool's dream. To be fair, this dream or ideal of Christendom—namely, that society would be made in the image of the church and that the Christian faith would permeate all aspects of social, cultural, religious, and even political life—was never fully realized. This is the case not simply because of the external challenge that was posed by non-Christians (whether they were in the image of pagans, Jews, Muslims, or primitives) but also because of the internal debate that existed amongst Christians themselves about the proper relation between church and society and the proper understanding of the Christian identity. As McLeod writes:

> At most points of Christian history there have been those who have opposed the identity between church and society or over-close links between church and state, or between the church and social elites. From the fourth century onwards there have been Christians who saw these associations as damaging to the church: "Christendom" meant that the church was subject to state interference, that it was forced to admit into membership those who were not true Christians, and that it was under pressure to condone contemporary customs and values that were unchristian.[11]

While this characteristic tension between the faith of Christianity and the culture of Christendom has been central to the history of Christianity in the West, ever since the Protestant Reformation of the sixteenth century there has been a steady dismantling of the old Constantinian alliance, leading to the eventual collapse of Christendom in the modern era. This collapse of Christendom (which is credited for a whole spectrum of aspects from our contemporary culture ranging from the principle of religious liberty and toleration to the extreme religious skepticism, cynicism, or even nihilism of the modern mind) becomes final or absolute in the first half of the twentieth century as supposedly civilized, and nominally Christian, nations turn against one another in total warfare. In other words, the ideal of Western civilization held together by a common Christian heritage and identity gets turned against itself in its full destructive potential. In the process, Christendom is revealed as "no more than a phase in the history of Christianity, and it represents only one out of many possible relationships between church and society. Yet in Western Europe this phase lasted for more than a thousand years, and we are still living in its shadow."[12]

Not only Christian theology, but the very practice and piety of contemporary religiosity have been greatly determined by the shadow cast by this collapse of Christendom. It is why twentieth-century Christian observers such as Dietrich Bonhoeffer, in his *Letters and Papers from Prison*, began speaking of a "religionless Christianity."[13] Bonhoeffer posed this possibility of a religionless Christianity while living out the final days of his life in a prison cell, before his martyrdom for his involvement in an assassination plot against Hitler. As such, his words had an added moral credibility, especially by those like the death of God theologians who were troubled by the moral ineptitude, if not outright complicity, of the church. For Bonhoeffer, this effort at purging Christianity of the comforts of religion would be a risky faith without assurances, one that severs the ties between Christ's call to discipleship and Christianity's association with the offices of power and the religious identification with the cultural trappings of civilization. Bonhoeffer's words and observations came to the world as a prophetic voice from the grave and became the link between, on the one hand, a world-weary faith in shock and horror at its own moral failure and impotence and, on the other, an emergent religious and cultural sensibility that was now forced to pick up the broken pieces and to imagine, if not craft, an alternative future—a future in the wake of the death of God and after the collapse of Christendom. For many, therefore, Bonhoeffer was seen as a precursor to the death of God theologians.[14]

Another important precursor was the nineteenth-century existentialist Christian philosopher Søren Kierkegaard. Kierkegaard has always been known as a great literary stylist. His use of pseudonyms, irony, and satire had long since been a source of confusion and frustration for modern rationalists. His religious writings, on the other hand, were another matter. Unlike many Enlightenment and post-Enlightenment thinkers, Kierkegaard seemed to be genuinely appreciative of the religious sentiment. At the same time, few have written such a scathing critique of Christendom and the modern-day church as Kierkegaard accomplished in his *Attack Upon Christendom*.[15] Kierkegaard, like Bonhoeffer and the death of God theologians who followed, gave voice to the new anti-institutional, individualized Christian faith that stood in opposition to the easy alliance between religion and society. It was a radical faith purged of any vestige of authoritarianism and triumphalism that was unafraid to call into question the very meaning and purpose of the church both by being willing to admit the failures of its own tradition and by seeing the great success of the state churches as their great failure. In other words, for Kierkegaard, the apparent Christianization of culture and politics made it virtually impossible to live up to the radical existential demands of a truly biblical faith.

While Bonhoeffer and Kierkegaard were both religious thinkers who each in his own way tried to restore the integrity of the Christian faith, there were other nonreligious, or perhaps even antireligious, thinkers who also informed the eventual shape of the radical death of God movement. It is no surprise, after all, that the death of God movement is celebrated as the embrace and culmination of the modern trend toward a fully secularized culture—or if not fully secularized, at least a culture that had become increasingly suspicious of the institution of religion. That is because, in addition to the theological critiques of Bonhoeffer and Kierkegaard, there were also those such as Marx, Nietzsche, and Freud who were known generally for their "hermeneutics of suspicion" and more specifically for their critique, if not hostility to, religion. In the midst of this cultural milieu the death of God movement lends a sympathetic voice. It speaks of a world in which God, through the act of kenosis, has fully emptied Godself. It admits that the idea of God is often no more than a human projection. It calls for human responsibility and accountability. It points to the fact that religion has just as often been the problem as it has been the solution to human conflict throughout the ages. This radical death of God theology, therefore, represents a critical and prophetic voice in the midst of a culture and faith in crisis, one that was moving away from the old religious certainties and assurances and toward a transformed religious sensibility. Further still, it is perhaps the quintessential representative theology for a Christian faith waking up to its new cultural reality in the shadow of Christendom. The irony is that by embracing a culture that was increasingly hostile toward religion, the death of God theology not only helps to lay the groundwork for postmodernism by its early critique of the moral-metaphysical God of ontotheology but also sets the conditions for a recovery of a distinctly biblical faith that gives emphasis not to the power and glory of God but to God's suffering and love—from the being of God to the story of God's being with the poor, the hungry, and the outcast.

The Postmodern Return of Religion

> When the Inquisitor ceased speaking he waited some time for his Prisoner to answer him. His silence weighted down upon him. He saw the Prisoner had listened intently all the time, looking gently in his face and evidently not wishing to reply. The old man longed for Him to say something, however bitter and terrible. But He suddenly approached the old man in silence and softly kissed him on his bloodless ageless lips. That was all His answer. The old man shuddered. His lips moved. He went to the door, opened it, and said to Him: 'Go, and come no more. . . . Come not at all, never, never!' And he let Him out in to the dark alleys of the town. The Prisoner went away.
>
> —DOSTOYEVSKY, "The Grand Inquisitor"

On the one hand, there is the almost two millennia of the power, authority, and triumph of the church. On the other, there is the almost silent witness of Christ. The former bears the heavy weight of history; the latter, the weight of the cross. The genius of Dostoyevsky's Grand Inquisitor is that we can sympathize with his plight and the plight of his church. It is true, as the Grand Inquisitor so mournfully describes, that we human beings are weak and needy. We long for a God who will deliver us to the promised land, not a God who dies and thereby unveils the structure of violence and injustice that reins supreme in this fallen world. We want someone who will save us from ourselves because, try as we might, we continue to botch our freedom. We continue to fight, kill, and hate—sometimes even in the name of God. Perhaps the Grand Inquisitor was right—we human beings cannot be trusted. We must be directed and ruled. We must be fed and clothed. And if not by the church, then by whom? And even if the church has lost its way, who among us is really willing to follow the way of the cross? Therefore, when the Grand Inquisitor speaks, we hear his sadness, pathos, and even resignation. *Ecce homo*—"behold the man"—the one who betrays his true love, the one who suffers for our sakes so that in our weakness we might be saved, the one who knows the truth while the rest of us live by our illusions. Behold the man—the one who suffers the kiss of Christ and who must send Christ on his way and banish him from ever returning again. This is the sad truth and tragedy of religion as revealed by him.

Of course, the prisoner has heard these charges before. He mounts no defense. His only response is that of a kiss and thereby he embodies the essence of his teaching—to love, even one's enemies, even those who condemn him to death. This is a story beyond belief. Who could dare fathom, let alone follow? The strange and unexpected thing is how that kiss, illustrative of the love of Christ, lives on even after the death of the moral-meta-physical God. The irony of Dostoyevsky's story is that though the Grand Inquisitor intends it as an indictment against Christ, it lays bare his desperate desire for him all the same. A similar ironic reversal can be seen in our own modern history. For when examining the current state of theology, philosophy of religion, and contemporary religious thought and practice, the future as charted by the champions of secularism, death of God theologians, and deconstructive philosophers has given way to a new "postsecular" understanding of the postmodern condition in which the return of religion is more determinative than the collapse of Christendom. Indeed, in both philosophical and popular cultural circles, God now seems alive and well, and as the *New York Times* proclaimed in a feature Sunday magazine article from 1998, "religion is making a comeback."[16] In the process, perhaps the most fundamental assumption of the modern mind has been brought into critical relief—namely, the identification of modernization with secularism.

It had long been assumed by sociologists, philosophers, and theologians alike that the more modern we became, the less religious we would become. Our increased technological proficiency and scientific knowledge were thought to translate into a decreased dependency on outdated religious beliefs in God and supernaturalism. Indeed, the most prominent Enlightenment philosopher of them all, Immanual Kant, defined the very project of Enlightenment by this most fundamental of all modern assumptions when he wrote that Enlightenment is the release from all forms self-incurred tutelege. What he had in mind, in addition to various forms of political authoritarianism, was the religious authoritarianism and dogmatism that for centuries had discouraged critical scientific inquiry. According to Kant, the enlightened subject would be one who could think for himself, and one in whom religion might still play a part, but only in the private sphere of personal morality.[17] This modern philosophical anticipation of an autonomous subject not constrained by determinative religious beliefs has come under increased scrutiny as contemporary theorists from various disciplines have seemingly reversed the course of modern subjectivity by demonstrating how personal and social identity is a product of social construction, how knowledge is intertwined with power, and how the presumably private and interior life of religion is always already public and political.

What we see, therefore, is a strangely disjointed history. These modern, secularist assumptions, which are now being questioned and brought into doubt more and more, certainly pervade much if not all the radical death of God theologies of the 1960s. The question, which will become the central question that this volume seeks to address, is the following: *How do we get from the post-Christian, post-Holocaust, and largely secular death of God theologies of the 1960s to the postmodern return of religion?* Put otherwise, what happens when we move from the early claim that deconstruction is the hermeneutic of the death of God to the subsequent effort at deconstructing the death of God? What happens when the critical linking of the death of God with deconstruction comes full circle? And finally, how is it that this question of the return of religion is transmitted not by theologians and/or religious leaders but by and through philosophers and cultural theorists who heretofore had little or no expressed interest in religious or theological questions?

II

This transition from the death of God to postmodern faith (or, if you will, from secularism to postsecularism) is one of the defining chapters in contemporary religious thought. John Caputo and Gianni Vattimo, each in their turn, stand as representative voices of these distinct, though profoundly interrelated, modes of thinking through, and thinking about, the relation of religion to society and the continued viability of theological thinking. The dialogue between them should tell us a great deal not simply about the similarities and differences between two thinkers, the one from the United States and the other from Italy, and two religious perspectives, but even more about the broader currents of our contemporary culture, about how we have moved from religious skepticism (if not outright antagonism toward religion), which is reflective of modernity, to an apparent re-embrace of religion in the postmodern world. Also, what sort of changes, alterations, distortions, or reforms were introduced into this postmodern faith as a result of its passing through the crucible of the death of God critiques? To Vattimo, Caputo will submit his death of God philosophy to a deconstructive critique. To Caputo, Vattimo will offer his interpretation of the death of God and the modern processes of secularization as a faithful recovery of kenotic Christianity and a reorientation toward the very essence of the Christian faith—namely, that of *agape*.

While each may speak of the philosophical and theological significance of the death of God differently, there are at least three major overlapping areas of interest between Caputo and Vattimo. First and foremost, both Caputo and Vattimo have long been engaged in the effort to radicalize hermeneutic philosophy. For Caputo, this has meant forging a closer collaboration between hermeneutics and deconstruction as both signal a departure from, and work to overcome, the metaphysics of presence.[18] While this linking of hermeneutics with Derridean deconstruction might lead to a certain unknowing, or an epistemological undecidability, for Caputo this should not be understood as an exercise in nihilism.

It is this latter point where Vattimo parts company with Caputo. Like Caputo, he has expressed great appreciation and admiration for Derrida and deconstruction, but, unlike Caputo, Vattimo has argued for the positive contribution that nihilism plays both for an understanding of contemporary hermeneutic philosophy and in the process of emancipation. The contribution nihilism makes is not in the sense that it functions as a new philosophical doctrine or a new truth as it were. On the contrary, nihilism is the name for the series of negations that contemporary thought has undergone from the strong metaphysical assumptions associated with ancient philosophy and carried forward through the Enlightenment rationalistic period to the weak, anti-authoritarian strand of the interpretative philosophy of hermeneutics. As written by his friend and frequent collaborator Richard Rorty, and as demonstrated by his recent book of essays in political philosophy, Vattimo has shown that "nihil-

ism and emancipation do, in fact, go hand in hand."[19] In Vattimo's own words, "Nihilism acquires the sense of emancipation"
when we realize that "it is the dissolution of foundations . . . that
brings freedom."[20] That is because, as Vattimo writes, "a weak
ontology, or better an ontology of the weakening of Being, supplies philosophical reasons for preferring a liberal, tolerant, and
democratic society rather than an authoritarian and totalitarian
one."[21] In addition, Vattimo also sees nihilism as synonymous
with hermeneutics as both acknowledge that any argument is
always historically and culturally situated and as both recognize
the necessity for dialogue. In this way Vattimo identifies hermeneutics as "the thought of accomplished nihilism, thought that
aims to reconstruct rationality in the wake of the death of God
and opposes any current of negative nihilism, in other words the
desperation of those who continue to cultivate a sense of mourn-
ing because 'religion is no more.'"[22]

This leads to the second overlapping area of interest between
Caputo and Vattimo—namely, that of weak thought.[23] Both Caputo and Vattimo have spoken about, and examined the consequences of, the weakening of thought. For Caputo, this interest
in weak thought has accompanied his increased attention to the
religious question in recent years, which was first signaled by
his enormously successful and influential study of the religious
dimension to the deconstructive philosophy of Derrida.[24] Since
that first sustained philosophical turn to religion, Caputo has
published a great deal about religion and postmodernism, and,
largely due to the great success he has had in organizing the biannual conferences on this subject, first at Villanova and now at
Syracuse University, he has helped to spearhead and define the
burgeoning field of continental philosophy of religion. But when
Caputo speaks about the postmodern return of religion, he almost invariably invokes the qualifier he learned from Derrida—
namely, "religion without religion." In contrast to the variant of

contemporary religiosity that asserts itself strongly and triumphantly, Caputo offers a postcritical religion in the sense that he wants to affirm faith, though without absolute or certain knowledge, and he seeks to value religious tradition, while keeping his distance from the actual historic faith communities. In short, his is not a theology of power but a theology of weakness that connects the weakness of God with the ethical imperative to serve the poor and needy. In contrast to the historical determinacy and specificity of the strong Christian, Jewish, or Islamic theologies, Caputo offers a more open-ended theology "weakened by the flux of undecidability and translatability." According to Caputo's description, it as a "theology of the event," which we can think of ironically as a "theology without theology."[25]

The origin of Vattimo's interest in weak thought precedes his own philosophical turn to religion. Indeed, the very phrase *weak thought* is perhaps Vattimo's primary contribution to contemporary philosophy and the means by which he has informed and shaped the contemporary reading of the legacy of Nietzsche, Heidegger, and postmodernism. The phrase *weak thought* refers to the gradual weakening of being that has transformed contemporary philosophy from its former obsession with the metaphysics of truth to its current and more limited understanding of itself strictly as an interpretative exercise. The irony is that this weak ontology also weakens the strong metaphysical reasons for atheism and the rationalist repudiation of religion. So not only does weak thought precede the philosophical turn to religion but, according to the narrative offered by Vattimo, it actually establishes the philosophical precondition for the postmodern return of the religious. Vattimo argues that in the postmetaphysical age not only is the world desacralized, and not only does faith lose its assurances, but along with this secularization of religion—which he sees as the truth of the gospel and the destiny of the West—there also occurs the breakdown or dissolution of

the tyranny of reason from which the modern critique, dismissal, or reduction of religion derived. In other words, as Vattimo
puts it, "The end of metaphysics and the death of the moral
God have liquidated the philosophical basis of atheism."[26] In this
sense atheism is nothing but the flip side of theism, with neither
understanding the true nature of belief, because both according
to Vattimo's analysis still rely on absolutist claims characteristic
of scientific positivism or transcendent authority.[27] Now that we
live in the postmetaphysical age in which there are no absolute
truths, only interpretations, the category of belief can again be
taken seriously as constitutive of our lived traditions.

Third, Caputo and Vattimo are two of the world's chief theorists of postmodernism in general—and the possibility of postmodern religion more specifically. Regarding a general theory or
praxis of postmodernism, Caputo's radical hermeneutics can be
seen as an effort to update hermeneutic philosophy for what has
become a vastly different cultural milieu from its origins with its
altered modes of intelligibility associated with the postmodern
condition. In this sense to radicalize hermeneutics is to show its
continued relevancy in the postmodern world. Similarly, with
his effort at "demythologizing Heidegger," Caputo shows the
same knack for rejuvenation by acknowledging the greatness of
Heidegger and at the same time critically examining the source
for his personal flaws and political blindness. In doing so, Caputo demonstrates how postmodern deconstruction is not strictly
a negative philosophy but instead an attempt to read the tradition against itself—indeed, even to read a single thinker against
himself. In this way postmodern deconstruction is necessarily
a twofold operation. As Caputo describes it with respect to his
deconstructive reading of Heidegger:

It is not only a negative work of exposing the insinuations of
the myth of Being into the question of Being, of mercilessly

suspecting everything, even what appears to be innocent. It is also at the same time the positive production of another Heidegger, another reading of Heidegger, of a Heidegger *demythologized*, of a Heidegger read against Heidegger. In this way, demythologizing and deconstructing, reading carefully and re-reading, are positive and even remythologizing operations.[28]

Likewise with his major contribution to the field of postmodern ethics, by his attack "against ethics" (at least as it was rather being simplistically understood and employed by those well-meaning scholars seeking to fix responsibility and establish a moral guidebook for a life without blame), Caputo took a stand for the prior commitment of postmodern deconstruction—namely, that of justice.[29] Finally, with regard to postmodernism and religion, how is it possible that a figure such as Derrida who says of himself that he rightly passes for an atheist should be read as a *religious* thinker? For Caputo, at least, therein lies the great paradox and value of postmodern philosophy. Not that Derrida himself would claim to be either a postmodern or a religious thinker, but by reading Derrida through the lens of postmodernism it is shown how even (or perhaps especially) someone like him can help to create the open space by which a tradition can live up to its promise.

As Caputo tells us, at its most basic, religion is about the love of God, a love that is beyond human measure and that breaks free from all human constraints. The love of God is a love without category or, better, a love that exceeds all categorization—whether religious or secular, whether theist or atheist, and whether Christian, Muslim, Buddhist, Jewish, etc. As such, postmodern deconstruction is not the world-denying, radically skeptic, and antireligious movement that its detractors made it out to be. On the contrary, it can only be understood by recognizing its animating and fundamentally affirmative passion, its radical and unconditional Yes to the promise of life. This Yes holds the promise of distinctively postmodern faith and, even more, helps us to better understand the paradox of how the postmodern—by extending and radicalizing the modern critique of religion—has actually set the cultural conditions the contemporary resurgence of religion.

In this way Caputo identifies the postmodern with the post-secular wherein the death of God ironically realizes its full iconoclastic potential by actualizing what Caputo calls the "death of the death of God." His book, *On Religion*, describes this process playfully when he writes about "How the secular world became post-secular."[30] Here Caputo equates modernity with secularization and postmodernity with desecularization. The transitional figures in this historical transformation, the ones about whom Caputo refers as "our prophets," are Kierkegaard and Nietzsche. As Caputo writes:

> In Kierkegaard and Nietzsche, the world of Enlightenment Reason and Hegelian Absolute Knowledge is left far behind. They each foresee in his own way the madness of the twentieth century whose genocidal violence made a mockery of Hegel's sanguine view of history as the autobiography of the Spirit of time. This is why the twentieth century took them as its prophets. Kierkegaard and Nietzsche sketch the lines of a world after the Enlightenment, after Hegel, after Philosophy, writ large. (55)

In this post-Enlightenment world after Kierkegaard and Nietzsche, the Enlightenment critique of religion boomerangs back against itself. Whether talking about Nietzsche, Marx, or Freud, the postmodern world becomes suspicious of their hermeneutics of suspicion with the realization that their critiques were "*also* perspectives, *also* constructions, or fictions of grammar." In Caputo's words:

> Marx and Freud, along with Nietzsche himself, find themselves hoisted with Nietzsche's petard, their critiques of religion having come undone under the gun of Nietzsche's critique of the possibility of making a critique that would cut to the quick—of God, nature, or history. Enlightenment secularism, the objectivist reduction of religion to something other than itself—say, to a distorted desire for one's mommy, or to a way to keep the ruling authorities in power—is one more story told by people with historically limited imaginations, with contingent conceptions of reason and history, of economics and labor, of nature and human nature, of desire, sexuality, and women, and of God, religion, and faith. (59–60)

In short, Caputo sees postmodernity as "a more enlightened Enlightenment [that] is no longer taken in by the dream of Pure Objectivity. . . . It has a post-critical sense of critique that is critical of the idea that we can establish air-tight borders around neatly discriminated spheres or regions like knowledge, ethics, art, and religion" (61). And, finally, this "opens the doors to another way of thinking about faith and reason," which for Caputo translates not into relativism, irrationalism, or nihilism "but [into] a heightened sense of the contingency and revisability of our constructions, not the jettisoning of reason but a rediscription of reason, one that is a lot more reasonable than the bill of goods about an overarching, transhistorical Rationality that the Enlightenment tried to sell us" (63).

Thus from modernity to postmodernity, from secularization to a process of desecularization through which religion has moved from being on the defensive for having to answer to reason to its contemporary rebound where it has recovered its proper sense as a faith rather than some lesser form of knowledge. As Caputo writes in his conclusion to *On Religion*, "Religious truth is a truth without Knowledge" (115). And further, "Undecidability is the place in which faith takes place, the night in which faith is conceived, for night is its element. Undecidability is the reason that faith is faith and not Knowledge, and the way that faith can be true without Knowledge" (128).

Vattimo, on the other hand, has an alternative reading of postmodernism that rests on a very different, more positive, understanding of the modern processes of secularization. As he states in the interview that follows, "Real religiosity relies on secularization." By this he is referring to the modern fragmentation of religious authority that has both positive and negative consequences. Positively, it safeguards religious belief from coercion and at least provides the possibility that believers might recognize the contingency and historicity of their own beliefs. But, on the flip side, a religion severed from institutional control means that like most everything else in contemporary society it becomes just another commodity in the world of mass communication. For Vattimo, this is at least part of the explanation for the wild popularity of Pope John Paul II. As he says, "People are more interested in the religious show than they are in religious engagement." And later in the conversation, as if to underscore the point of the pope's status as a media star, "Many people watch TV, but not so many attend church."

With this in mind, to what extent does he share Caputo's linking of the postmodern with the postsecular? And if we are living in a postsecular world, does this mean that the postmodern has inaugurated a process of desecularization? With regard to the first question, Vattimo answers in the affirmative in the sense that in the contemporary postmodern society, we are witness to a certain rebirth of religiosity. The postmodern is postsecular in the sense that secularization establishes the conditions of possibility for the religious, and, more strongly, as he argues elsewhere, secularization is the destiny of the Christian West.[31] But Vattimo does not accept the linking of the postsecular with a process of desecularization, for this would imply a reversal that belies the actual historical tradition and a denial of how the West has rediscovered its own Christian origins. Because secularization is the destiny of the Christian West, we remain bound within that tradition, and the postmodern return of religion lives as its response.

If not desecularization, then what is the postmodern? Vattimo provides his most direct answer to this question in the opening chapter of *The Transparent Society*. In this early engagement with the meaning of the postmodern condition, Vattimo writes that if the term *postmodern* is to have any meaning at all, it must be "linked to the fact that the society in which we live is a society of generalized communication. It is the society of the mass media."[32] In addition, whatever else is meant by the term *postmodern*, it at least implies, "in some essential way, that modernity is over" (1). By modernity, Vattimo is referring to the spirit of the Enlightenment, which made a "cult of the new," and most important, viewed history as a unilinear process of emancipation. "Modernity ends," Vattimo writes, "when—for a number of reasons—it no longer seems possible to regard history as unilinear" (2). Among the number of reasons why this is no longer possible is that the ideological character of this reading of history has been exposed, whether in the positing of Jesus' birth as the zero point of history or the depiction of the West as the center of civilization. In contrast to this ideological image of history that valorizes the Christian West, Vattimo writes, "There is no single history, only images of the past projected from different points of view. It is illusory to think that there exists a supreme or comprehensive viewpoint capable of unifying all others" (2). Along with this crisis in the notion of a unilinear and unifying history comes the related crisis in the notion of progress. For Vattimo, this postmodern realization becomes important as a critique of the Eurocentrism that fueled the colonialism and imperialism associated with the modern period.

To return to the earlier point, though the ending of this modern sensibility with regard to history is important, the meaning of the term *postmodern* is not complete for Vattimo without an appreciation of the advent of the society of mass communication:

> What I am proposing is: (a) that the mass media plays a decisive role in the birth of a postmodern society; (b) that they do not make this postmodern society more transparent, but more complex, even chaotic; and finally (c) that it is in precisely this relative "chaos" that our hopes for emancipation lie. (4)

Thus, in contrast to Theodor Adorno and Max Horkheimer, who predicted that modern communication would "produce a general homogenization of society," Vattimo sees a "general explosion and proliferation of *Weltanschauungen*, of world views" (5). In later works he frequently refers to this proliferation of worldviews as the "Babel-like pluralism" of postmodernity. The point is that, with today's mass communication, its "myriad forms of reality" render any single worldview or any unilinear history impossible. In this way the postmodern produces an alternative model of emancipation. In contrast to the model of lucid consciousness as reflected in Hegel's Absolute Spirit or Marx's conception of humanity liberated from false consciousness, Vattimo's model of postmodern emancipation is "based on oscillation, plurality and, ultimately, on the erosion of the very 'principle of reality'" (7). In other words, the postmodern is postmetaphysical, wherein freedom "does not lie in having a

perfect knowledge of the necessary structure of reality and con-
forming to it," but instead is conceived as disorientation by virtue of the dissolution of reality. As Vattimo writes, "If, in the
multicultural world, I set out my system of religious, aesthetic,
political and ethnic values, I shall be acutely conscious of the
historicity, contingency and finiteness of these systems, starting
with my own" (9).

This more positive reading of the history of secularization and
more hopeful, if not optimistic, reading of the postmodern as
the postmetaphysical leads to Vattimo taking distance from what
he calls the "tragic and apocalyptic Christianity of Dostoevsky[33]
with whom we began and about whom Caputo will conclude
our dialogue. Although Dostoevsky's tale of the Grand Inquisitor certainly employs the tragic in this most existential spiritual
crisis, it also anticipates a history—namely, our history of the
postmodern return of a religion based in the love of Christ. On
that, both Caputo and Vattimo can agree.

In the pages of this book that follow, our quest for a new philosophy of religion will pass through the radical hermeneutics
of John Caputo and Gianni Vattimo, through the movement of
the death of God to the postmodern realization of the death of
the death of God, from secularism to the return of religion, and
beyond. In the process, and by virtue of the open form of the
dialogues that follow, both Caputo and Vattimo will be given the
chance to think "otherwise" by thinking in conversation with
one another. To return to the epigraph from Hent de Vries: what
follows represents the perpetual agony of a conversation without
end as we explore the contours of the seeming impossible—a
theology after the death of God and a philosophy of religion
without religion.

I

Toward a Nonreligious Christianity

GIANNI VATTIMO

Knowledge and Interpretation

Let us start from an observation that may help us to understand what the meaning of interpretation is and the role it has to play in what we call knowledge. From a hermeneutical perspective, we must say that knowledge requires a perspective, that in knowing anything I must choose a perspective. But some may object, what about the case of scientific knowledge? Is scientific knowledge also perspectival? My answer is that because scientists have chosen not to have anything to do with their own private interest, and describe only what concerns their science, their knowledge as such is deliberately limited. They never know everything.

Those familiar with the hermeneutical tradition know that this is the point where Heidegger's objection to metaphysics begins—namely, in the decision to be objective, we cannot help but assume a definite position, de-fined, in other words, a point of view that limits, but also helps in a decisive way, our encounter with the world. While Heidegger's critique of metaphysics begins here in the critique of the metaphysical definition of truth as an objective datum, his critique also moves beyond this point in its eventual focus on the ethical-political nature of metaphysics, the "rationalization" of modern society against which the vanguards during the first part of the twentieth century were fighting. Heidegger also realized that the scientific claim of objectivity (which is also what Lukacs says under a Marxist's profile) is inspired from a determined interest: for example, to describe a natural phenomenon in a way that others could also speak of it in the same way and develop this self-same knowledge. In other words, scientists are not moved by the impulse of truth. The relation between the world and the knowledge of the world does not function as a mirror. Instead, there is the world and someone who is "in the world," which means someone who orients himself in and to the world, someone who uses his own capacities of knowledge, hence someone who chooses, reorganizes, replaces, represents, etc.

The concept of interpretation is all here: there is no experience of truth that is not interpretative. I do not know anything that does not interest me. If it does interest me, it is evident that I do not look at it in a noninterested way.

For Heidegger, this concept of interpretation also makes its way into his reflection on the historical sciences, as one can see reading not only the first parts of *Being and Time* but also so many other essays of that period. For Heidegger, then, it comes down to the following: I am an interpreter as long as I am not someone who looks at the world from the outside. I see the external world because I am inside it. As a being-in-the-world, my interests are very complicated. I cannot say precisely how things are, but only how they are from this point of view, how they seem to me and how I think they are. If an experiment moved by one of my ideas works, it does not mean that I have exhausted the objective knowledge on that aspect of reality. Rather, as even the philosophy of science has later realized, I have made the experiment function under certain expectations and premises. When

I conduct an experiment, after all, I already have a whole set of criteria and instruments thanks to which I may determine—always with another someone who comes to the experiment with other interests and thus, by definition, does not think exactly as I do—whether my experiment works or not. From the beginning, the criteria and the instruments are left out of the discussion. No scientist studies all physics from scratch. Nearly all of them trust handbooks, and, with the help of the inherited knowledge contained therein, they develop still others.

This point made by Heidegger almost a century ago is an accepted fact by now—scientists do not objectively describe the world. On the contrary, their description of the world depends on their specific usage of precise instruments and a rigorous methodology, all of which is culturally determined and historically qualified. Of course, I realize that not all scientists would accept these words. But even the very conditions of possibility for verifying a scientific proposition (or falsifying, as Popper would have it) depend on the fact that we speak the same language, we use the same instruments, we take the same measures, etc. If any of this were different, not only would we not understand each other, but we would not even have the possibility of understanding each other. And, further, these criteria and this paradigm have not been invented from scratch. On the contrary, we have inherited them.

Again, this is interpretation: being inside a situation, facing it not as someone who comes from Mars but as someone who has a history, as someone who belongs to a community.

There are some people who believe that to study physics is not to study the truth of physics, but to learn the secret skills and practices and to endure the various rites of initiation, like an athlete getting in shape or an initiate becoming a member of a secret society. It makes sense when one considers the difficulty in getting someone to understand a scientific demonstration. In order to understand the truth of the theory, one must first teach the rudiments of the discipline. These rudiments are presumed to be "natural." But, when we take a closer look, isn't it the case that the knowledge belonging to a particular science could also be different? In all this we must consider something further—namely, the emergence of structuralism as a movement within anthropological study of culture. Heidegger was not yet acquainted with the structuralism of Levi-Strauss, but what is the difference between Kant and Heidegger? Put simply, there is the nineteenth century wherein we have the scientific and/or anthropological "discovery" of other cultures.

This nineteenth-century discovery dramatically alters our understanding of how knowledge is constructed. According to Kant, in order to know the world, one needs some a priori structures that cannot be recuperated from experience and through which experience itself is organized. But what does this mean? Space, time, and the categories of understanding, these are things that constitute myself as the universal structures of reason. In other words, for Kant and many neo-Kantian philosophers, reason was thought to be always the same. Cultural anthropology, on the other hand, reveals differences by showing the various ways that societies, cultures, and diverse individuals face the world. We could say, then, that the philosophy of the twentieth century, as reflected in Heidegger's existentialism, is the result of a Kantian philosophical sensibility passing through the crucible of anthropological culture. If I am a finite human being, I will be born and die at a certain point in history. Is it possible then that I am the carrier of this absolute that I may unconditionally affirm without any doubts? Are these categories and is this structure of the mind no different than the truth that two plus two equals four? After all, there are cultures that eat their own, not to mention the many differences that exist even within European culture and thought.

The first wave of cultural anthropology acknowledged the existence of other cultures but, at the same time, emphasized their "primitive" status—that is, they were examples of an earlier or previous form of human relations. Basically, it was thought that the "primitives" did not know about mathematics; once we get there we teach them sciences and install our governments. But, today, where are these "primitives"? To whom can we teach all these things?

The matter of interpretation is now configured in this way: interpretation is the idea that knowledge is not the pure, uninterested reflection of the real, but the interested approach to the world, which is itself historically mutable and culturally conditioned.

The Advent of Christianity and the Birth of the Subject

But what does any of this have to do with Christianity, let alone the nonreligious interpretation of Christianity I am proposing here? And what right do I as a philosopher have to declare such things?

According to other philosophers with whom Heidegger was quite similar—most notably, Wilhelm Dilthey—Christianity accomplished the first attack against metaphysics construed exclusively as objectivity. Accordingly, Kant only taught us centuries later what Christianity had already affirmed, hence the idea of Saint Augustine that *in interiore homine habitat veritas* ("truth lives in the inner human"). Christianity announces the end to the Platonic ideal of objectivity. It cannot be the eternal word of forms outside ourselves that saves us, but only the eye directed toward the interior and the searching of the deep truth inside us all. According to Dilthey's schema of history (which, even though Heidegger never said this explicitly, is the schema of history that Heidegger follows), the thing that is most decisive in the event of

Christianity is precisely this attention toward subjectivity, which, incidentally, also brings with it the concern for the poor, weak, and outcasts.

In other words, as Erich Auerbach demonstrates in a beautiful book, each of us is just like the other.[1] To be fair, the philosophies of the late antiquity are also like this: Epicureanism and stoicism are both philosophies much more oriented toward the subject. But none more so than Christianity, which consistently questions the fixation on the object in favor of its own attention on the subject. And in this way, at least according to Dilthey's schema, we arrive at Kant and at the truth, which is not in things, not outside ourselves, and which, therefore, comes forward always in an accidental way. Instead, truth is found in the reason of man, which, once it turns back on itself, once it becomes truly reflexive, shows how the mind itself actually contributes to the knowledge of truth.

The philosophers of science of today also talk about the fact that single phenomena (a kettle of water that boils at 100 degrees) are not somehow *better* known whenever science is able to generalize them in formulas. By generating formulas, science in some way transcends the single phenomenon and places it inside a complete artificial system. The thermometer is not useful because it allows me to better know the boiling of the water; it serves me only to generalize this discourse in a wider sphere. In other words, abstraction is not intended to penetrate into the phenomenon and find its true essence. The essence we reach is only the general structure of a certain world of phenomena that become truth in some way having nothing to do with individuality.[2] We are not always looking at the kettle, but we measure it, we link it to some system. In a certain way this is again a Kantian way of thinking. Regarding the immediacy of what I see, I construct a system made of connections, a calculus, through which knowledge is mediated. This is Kant in a nutshell.

Returning to the crucible of cultural anthropology, and with the increased appreciation for the finitude of existence, perhaps now even mathematics is revealed as only *a* mathematics. This is seen in the beginning of the twentieth century with the development of alternative mathematics, non-Euclidean geometries. I must confess that I do not know why people invent these things, but it is always about systems, about logical mathematical connections that really do work and through which it is possible to demonstrate certain truths. When it is discovered that perhaps they can be applied more adequately to some natural phenomenon than others—for instance, some suggest that certain non-Euclidean geometries apply better to cosmic space—one begins to understand that there might be different languages that deal with phenomena in different ways.

Wittgenstein, who was not a great friend of Heidegger (in fact, I do not think that Heidegger ever read him), says, for example, that if someone puts forward a mathematical formula that gives different results from mine, I may always ask myself if he is getting the calculus wrong or if he is applying a different mathematical language. This is already a way to understand the idea of interpretation. That does not imply that if we accept the idea of interpretation, then "everything goes" and anyone can say whatever he wants. Regardless, there are rules, but the rules themselves are relative to language. This is the importance of the later Wittgenstein's insight into language games, wherein every language functions like a game with its own rules. Obviously, you cannot apply to a game of basketball the rules of baseball. Otherwise, the norms of basketball would be violated. This does not mean the baseball rules are wrong, but it means that each language has its own norms.

So Christianity contributes to a philosophy of interpretation for many reasons.[3] One of these is that Christianity turns the mind inward and thus, say the historians of thought, makes possible the

Kantian subject and anticipates modern philosophies of subjectivity. Indeed, even the very possibility of theorizing this is due to the fact that we live in a Christian civilization (even if we do no longer live in the era of Christendom in the global sense). All the discourse concerning the biblical view of creation, which is put forward in mythological form, stands at odds with the compact metaphysics of Plato, Aristotle, etc. Not to mention the more extravagant, or mind-bending, episodes from the New Testament, such as the story of the virgin birth or the Holy Spirit descending onto the apostles at Pentecost. What does all this mean? How are we to understand it? Jesus gives us some clue when he foretells the day of Pentecost when the apostles would be baptized by the Holy Spirit. Here Jesus sends to the apostles what his father had promised so that they might finally understand all that he had taught them. As Jesus anticipated the age of the spirit, he recognized and justified the later transformation of the Christian truths. The message of Christ is true even as he introduced himself as someone with the authority to interpret the inherited tradition and the sacred writings of the past (which Christians now refer to as the Old Testament). In this way Christ is seen as the agent of interpretation. As such, he is not unlike Moses, who, to be realistic, did not simply transcribe the literal words of God. Rather, the commandments brought down by Moses were also the product of interpretation.

My Jewish colleagues remind me that hermeneutics does not, and did not, begin with the New Testament. For the writings contained within the Hebrew Scriptures are nothing if they are not an example of this continual act of interpretation and reinterpretation. They are correct, of course. For example, we see in Water Benjamin, who was a great intellectual of the philosophy of the twentieth century, that he thought about everything in Talmudic terms. That is to say, his thinking was a form of commentary reflecting on that which has been already handed down.

The history of the origin of the idea of interpretation is inescapable.[4] Consider the New Testament gospels, none of which
were written before 60 ce. In other words, as is well chronicled,
the stories of Jesus as the Christ were written sufficiently *after* the time of Jesus such that it is reasonable to conclude that
none are eyewitness accounts and that none preserve for us a
journalistic record of the actual happenings. One of the reasons
why Heidegger chose to comment on Saint Paul's Letters to the
Thessalonians, in his "The Phenomenology of Religious Life"
course of 1919–1920,[5] is because they are the oldest writings
from the New Testament and thus represent the earliest layer
of Christian history we can now access. All of which is to say
that even when we are referring to the canonical gospels—those
texts that the church has long since established as authoritative
and trustworthy—they are at best written reports based on an
oral tradition.

I recognize that these are all scattered observations and premises drawn from the history of interpretation and its battle against
objectivity. But what is its significance? The answer is that Christianity is a stimulus, a message that sets in motion a tradition of
thought that will eventually realize its freedom from metaphysics. Does this mean that metaphysics should have never existed,
that Aristotle was somehow wrong or misguided? No, because
to say that would be to fall into the trap of metaphysics. It would
be an example of typical metaphysical reasoning—namely, affirming that it is an eternal truth that metaphysics is a mistake.
I cannot and would not say this, but, in order to say something,
or anything, I must draw on particular words, and, in order for
those words to make sense, they must be drawn from some particular tradition. If you were to ask me why I feel so confident
as to preach this message of freedom from metaphysics without
falling into the trap of metaphysics, I would offer you a litany:
"Did you read this or that?" In other words, the only arguments

I can offer are not those that are traditionally recognized as such by those who police the rules of logic. My argument is not traditional, but one of transmission, of language, and of the culture in which we live together.

For instance, when I say that I am certain that God created me, I recognize that if I were to strip myself of the biblical world of meaning and reference, I would strip myself of meaning altogether. So to take away the Bible is to take away meaning. It would be like taking Dante away from the history of Italian literature. Dante, like Shakespeare, is written in such a way that, if you did not read the Bible, you would not understand anything. But you can read the Bible without reading Dante or Shakespeare. This means that to profess faith in Christianity is first of all to profess faith in the inevitability of a certain textual tradition that has been passed down to me. Take away the Bible and I would not be what I am. Perhaps I would be something or someone else, but it would be useless for me to think that I could just as easily be a native of the Amazon. It is true that I could be, but how does that help me to understand who I *actually* am? If I reflect on my existence, I must realize that without the text of the Bible I would be bereft of the very instruments I have in order to think and to talk.

The twentieth-century Italian philosopher and political figure Benedetto Croce once said, "We cannot but call ourselves Christians."[6] I have referred to this statement many times, pulling it in different directions, even taking it to an extreme position that Croce probably would not share. For instance, when he says that "we cannot but call ourselves Christians," I say more extremely that we cannot even speak but from a Christian point of view. That is because we are fundamentally incapable of formulating ourselves, fundamentally incapable of articulating a discourse, except by accepting certain culturally conditioned premises.

Think here of Voltaire: For many, Voltaire is considered an enemy of religion. But I say that Voltaire was a good Christian

precisely because he demanded freedom against authoritarianism, even if it just so happened that it was the Jesuits who were in
authority at that particular time and place. By standing unconditionally for freedom and against authoritarianism, he stood for
Christianity. In this way perhaps true Christianity must be nonreligious. In Christianity there is a fundamental commitment to
freedom. And, to add a bit of scandal, by standing for freedom,
this includes freedom from (the idea of) truth. After all, if there
really is an objective truth, there will always be someone who is
more in possession of it than I and thereby authorized to impose
its law obligation on me.

Look around, all forms of authoritarianism are founded on
some premises of a metaphysical nature, if for no other reason
but the fact that authority is easier to explain and apparently
more binding if it is construed metaphysically rather than a government or philosophical official trying to persuade you that a
certain action, policy, or belief is in your own best interest. If
you were to go and explain to President Bush, for instance, that
the risks of the war in Iraq are too monumental, he will respond:
"But they are terrorists." I can try to understand the sentiment
that they might be terrorists, but only within a logic that Bush
himself established. Even the document 1441 of the United Nations, which authorized military action in Iraq, is of the United
Nations as determined by the Security Council. In other words,
it reflects the will of the winners of the World War II. It is not
the voice of God! So even though it is the only form of global le-
gitimacy that we have in place, its importance must not be exaggerated to the point of being sacralized. Recognizing this helps
us to recognize the illegitimacy of a preemptive war.

To offer a different example: If Christianity did not liberate
us from objective truth, how could we even maintain our belief in Scripture, or how could we prevent Scripture from being logically inconsistent, if not utterly absurd? For instance, I

have a colleague in Turin who has written a book in which he actually calculated the height Mary would have reached when she was taken to heaven with her body. The problem, of course, with such calculations is that they generate more questions than they answer. For instance, where is Mary's body now? How do we know that she didn't just disappear? She was taken with the body, but where did she end up? Why are such calculations and questions even necessary in the first place? How can Scripture be saved from such absurdities? In short, to believe in the gospel in today's day and age, one must first understand that language does not only denote objective realities. There is also another language that says other things. Just as it is when I affirm a scientific proposition: I accept the fact that its truth rests on a certain conception of knowledge, a certain accepted code of experimentation, and the use of certain instruments. In this way, I may accept the truth of science without being a scientist myself—that is, I do not have to personally recreate the conditions of an experiment to accept its findings. If not, I would be caught in an infinite regress. It is no different when we come to the discourse of values. I cannot speak outside a certain linguistic tradition without drawing on a certain encyclopedia of knowledge and a dictionary of terms. These are all the basis of my existence.

Likewise, with the language of the gospel, I can only understand it as that which is not ontic, not given in the external world, nor is it meant to be interpreted realistically. Instead, it talks of my destiny. When you say "I love you" on Valentine's Day, this "I love you" does not describe any objective phenomenon. Perhaps you might point to the rapid beating of your pulse as objective evidence of your feeling of love, but so too might it be evidence of something else. Once again we find ourselves in this discourse of interpretation. Until Galileo it was not so easy to be Kantian in science. Only with modern science, with Bacon, but most of all from Galileo onward, has this world been seen and understood from a scientific perspective in such a way that it seems perfectly suited for the philosophy of Kant. Also this seems to be confirmation of what Dilthey said of Christianity, as the Christian message eventually realizes its destiny when we become aware of our action in the world.

Charity and the Future of Christianity

Where will it all end? And where are we going to end up? We are moving toward secularization, which may also be called nihilism. Hence, the idea is that objective being has gradually, little by little, consumed itself.

In a beautiful passage from *The Twilight of the Idols*, Nietzsche tells us how the real world has become a dream. It was the Platonic world of ideas that gave us the idea of the real world in the first place. Later, the real world was construed as the promised world after death (at least for the righteous). Still later, in the mind of Descartes, the thought of the real world was evidence of clear and distinct ideas (but only in my mind). With positivism the real world became the world of experimental verified truths and then a product of the experimental scientist (after all, the modern scientist is not someone so much who looks at nature as someone who stimulates it, teases it, pulls it, and wants some specific thing to come from it). At this point, the so-called real world has become a story that we tell each other. It is difficult to accept all this, but we live today in a story-world of this kind.

Living in this story-world of our creation, we do not see nature anymore. Instead, we mostly see our world, a world that has been increasingly organized through a whole series of technological entities. When we talk about our natural needs, we list such things as the elevator or the cinema—things that are in no real sense natural but have become perfectly natural and apparently indispensable for us. What would become of us if we had to survive in a world in which we were left entirely alone? Our natural needs are defined by whatever it is in which we are immersed. But they are not natural at all. They are, instead, stimulated by advertising, conditioned by technology, etc. Our world has become a dream in so many ways. You see a car accident and you run home to see it on television. What is seen on television is then thought to have some heightened sense of reality. It is through television that you are able to see the accident in its full reality instead of the limited vantage point by which you saw it from the road. We live this televised reality locally and globally day after day.

That the real world becomes a dream can also be expressed in terms of Nietzsche's nihilism. As the objective world consumes itself, it gives way to a growing subjective transformation not of individuals but of communities, cultures, sciences, and languages. This is what I theorized with the notion of weak thought. If there is a possible line of emancipation in our human history, emancipation comes not through the final realization of an essence that was given at the beginning once and for all (which therefore would mean that we must somehow return to our state of original innocence before original sin). We must realize a bigger transformation as the natural gives way to the cultural or the material to the spiritual. This is what Hegel meant when he spoke about making the world into the house of man. It is not unlike the effort of making one's house into a home. When decorating a house, it is not just a matter of providing comfortable furniture or a welcoming environment. Once everything is arranged, if something is then missing or out of place you cannot help but notice its absence immediately. What makes your house a home is the artificial order you establish.

Baudelaire wrote a wonderful thing: "Where I have encountered virtue, I have always encountered against-nature."[7] It is exactly like this: nature is the world in which the big fish eats the small one. It is not at all a place of laws. Virtue is different as it is determined not by nature but by culture. It is also something that transcends. In this sense, emancipation actually consists in pursuing secularization, which is to say, emancipation relies on the process of desacralization, in having a better understanding of the spiritual sense of Scriptures by reading them *spiritually*. Max Weber explained that the capitalist world founded itself on the basis of a certain interpretation of Protestant ethics. Thrift, self-discipline, saving, repressing one's immediate impulses are all fundamental to the constitution of the order of capital. As such, the modern world has been formed by applying, transforming, and sometimes even mistaking the content of its tradition, which is primarily that of its own biblical heritage.

At what point does this continual process of transformation end? What are its limits? Or have we now reached a point where there are no more limits, where we may simply do whatever it is we like? No, because though the event of Christianity sets in motion the processes of secularization, we may also find in Scripture a limit to secularization, hence a guide to desacralization—namely, that of charity.[8] If you read the gospels or the fathers of the church carefully, at the end, the only virtue left is always that of charity. From Saint Paul we learn that the three greatest virtues are faith, hope, and love, "but the greatest of these is love." Even faith and hope will end at one point or another. As Saint Augustine instructs, "Love and do what you want."

While this is a liberating message, it is also a discomforting one, in the sense that it suggests, in relation to love, that everything else associated with the tradition and truth of Christianity is dispensable and may rightfully be called mythology. For instance, I do not know if God is really three persons in one, as defined by classical trinitarian theology. It might seem indispensable to think this way, but surely today we would no longer burn as a heretic someone who does not believe in the trinity.

Instead of applying the heavy hand of church authority to enforce doctrinal conformity, today we would invite the dissenters to think about the matter a bit more. But that being said, when one does think about these matters, instead of settling the debate, it oftentimes raises further difficulties. For example, when I think about the masculine language of God as father, I cannot help but wonder why God must be father and not mother or some other form of parenthood. The language of God as father is so obviously an allegoric language. Once you begin down this road, you do not know where you are going to end up.

The question, then, is whether one can still pray the Lord's Prayer after recognizing that even it too is culturally conditioned. My answer is Yes, because, when I pray, I know precisely that the words I am using are not intended to convey some literal truth. I pray these words more for the love of a tradition than I do for the love of some mythic reality. It is like the relationship you have with an aged relative. It is senseless to demand that your grandparents share your political ideas. Certain matters are best when left unsaid. You may have a special respect for their experience and the language they have inherited. In this sense, interpersonal relationships are much more about charity than truth.

Are scientists scientists out of their love for truth or because they love to be inside a scientific community, which allows them to develop certain discourses and in which they find certain interlocutors? Even when a philosopher such as Jürgen Habermas affirms rationality, he admits that rationality consists in introducing arguments that may be reasonably supported in dialogue with others. He does not say that rationality or truth is that which corresponds to the "thing itself."

The notion of truth has changed from Saint Augustine's understanding. But Augustine's turn inward is already a step forward with respect to the notion of objective truth, because once you turn inward you must also try to listen to others like you.

Today, truth is increasingly determined by agreement with others. We have said, "We do not, and perhaps cannot, agree when we have found the truth, but we may say that at least we have found some truth when we have agreed upon something." This also means that in the place of truth we have put charity. It is like what Dostoevsky wrote a century ago, that, if forced to choose between Christ and the truth, he would choose Christ. Contrast this sentiment with what Aristotle had to say about his teacher Plato: "Amicus Plato sed magis amica veritas" (Plato is a friend, but truth is a greater friend).

Throughout the ages inquisitors have sided with Aristotle rather than Dostoyevsky on this sentiment. The result is that, although not all metaphysics have been violent, I would say that all violent people of great dimensions have been metaphysical. If Hitler only hated the Jews of his particular neighborhood, he might have burned up their homes. But how much more dangerous he was because at a certain point he theorized about the general nature of all Jews and thus felt justified in his efforts to exterminate them all. I do not think it is that difficult to understand this. Nietzsche is very explicit in this sense. According to him, metaphysics is itself an act of violence because it wants to appropriate the "most fertile regions," hence of the first principles, in order to dominate and control. The first lines from Aristotle's *Metaphysics* more or less confirm this when he says that the wise is the one who knows all. The wise knows all by knowing its first cause and is thereby thought able to control and determine all its effects. Our tradition is dominated by the idea that if we only had a stable foundation we could move and act more freely. But philosophical foundationalism does not promote freedom. Rather, it is for the purpose of obtaining some desired effect or of consolidating some authority. When someone wants to tell me the absolute truth it is because he wants to put me under his control, under his command. Is it any wonder, then, that we hear the refrain "Be a man" or "Do your duty" whenever it is those who are in power send others off to war?

Where is this discourse going with regard to Christianity? Recently I participated in a debate in Turin on Gadamer, who had died only one year before. Many years ago Gadamer was my teacher. Some have said that in recent years Gadamer had developed some sort of religious hermeneutical attitude. This was seen in his frequent dialogues on religion and between religious traditions. In addition, he spoke increasingly about goodness. This religious turn in his philosophy was fundamentally a result of his hermeneutics. That is to say, if there is no objective truth given to someone once and for all, a truth around which we must all (for good or bad, willingly or unwillingly) gather, then truth happens in dialogue. The truth Christ came to teach the church is not an already accomplished truth. Its message grows with history. Similarly, you cannot read Plato without taking into consideration the whole history of interpretation of Plato. What seems natural is in fact historical. After all, is it any surprise that when a middle school student sits down to write poetry his poems sound just like those of Giovanni Pascoli?[9] Here is where Nietzsche's hermeneutics of suspicion is helpful: if there is anything that appears to you to be absolutely self-evident, you must distrust it. It is probably some joke that has been inserted in your brain. You can be certain of everything besides your most treasured certainties, because it was probably your aunts, grandparents, churches, authorities, and media that taught them to you and remain most invested in keeping you from second-guessing.

As I see it, Christianity is moving in a direction that cannot but lighten or weaken its moral load in favor of its practical-moral charity. And not only the weakening of its moral-metaphysical assumptions, but, by this transformation, charity will eventually replace truth. After all, are Catholics really supposed to fight, first with the Protestants because they do not accept the

Vatican's authority, then eventually with the Buddhist and the Hindus because they do not believe that God is three persons in one? Are we really expected to believe that when the Pope meets up with the Dalai Lama he worries that the Dalai Lama will end up in hell because he is not Catholic? No, they discuss how to mutually advance the spiritual dimension in human life, and they probably make deals on many things.

The future of Christianity, and also of the Church, is to become a religion of pure love, always more purified. There is a church hymn that states this succinctly and that also helps us see how far off we are from realizing this promise: "Where there is love, there is also God." As this hymn shows, my reading of Christianity is really not that strange or unorthodox. As Christ states: "When two or more of you are gathered in my name" (I cannot help but wonder whether, when Christ says in "my name," he might just as well mean charity), "I am with them." Charity is the presence of God. It is difficult to imagine that at the end some will be damned because they are Buddhist and others Muslims, etc. I say, on the contrary, that we will be damned—or more precisely, we damn ourselves on earth—when we clash against one another, each believing that they have the one true god.

By saying this, I am not putting forth the usual message of tolerance. Instead, I am speaking of the ideal development of human society, hence the progressive reduction of all rigid categories that lead to opposition, including those of property, blood, family, along with the excesses of absolutism. The truth that shall set us free is true precisely because it frees us. If it does not free us, we ought to throw it away. Hence I refuse to admit that this (weak thought, with everything it means) is only a specious kind of preaching (as, in part, it is—I'm after all an interpreter) tolerance. It is much more than that, as a future project that contributes to the progressive elimination of walls (e.g., wall of Berlin, natural laws configured as a wall that limits the freedom of individuals, the self-interested law of corporations that erects a wall between its success and the social good).

By recovering this message of charity, it allows for the lightening of the dogmatic burden and a new spirit of ecumenism to fill the church. Of course, this is also the message of hermeneutics, of Gadamer, and of so much of contemporary philosophy—all of which have come to be reasonably well accepted. Now it is time for Christianity to realize this nonreligious destiny, which is its own.

Spectral Hermeneutics

On the Weakness of God and the Theology of the Event

JOHN D. CAPUTO

A Theology of the Event

Events

One way to put what postmodernism means is to say that it is a philosophy of the event, and one way to put what a radical or postmodern theology means is to say it is a theology of the event. Obviously, then, on such an accounting, everything depends upon what we mean by an event, which, for the sake of simplicity, I describe as follows. 1. An event is not precisely what happens, which is what the word suggests in English, but something going on *in* what happens, something that is being expressed or realized or given shape in what happens; it is not something present, but something seeking to make itself felt in what is present. 2. Accordingly, I would distinguish between a *name* and the event that is astir or that transpires in a name. The name is a kind of provisional formulation of an event, a relatively stable if evolving structure, while the event is ever restless, on the move, seeking new forms to assume, seeking to get expressed in still unexpressed ways. Names are historical, contingent, provisional expressions in natural languages, while events are what names are trying to form or formulate, nominate or denominate. 3. An event is not a *thing* but something astir in a thing. Events get realized in things, take on actuality and presence there, but always in a way that is provisional and revisable, while the restlessness and flux of things is explained by the events they harbor. 4. What happens, be it a thing or a word, is always *deconstructible* just in virtue of events, which are not deconstructible. That does not mean that events are eternally true like a Platonic *eidos*; far from being eternally true or present, events are never present, never finished or formed, realized or constructed, whereas only what is constructed is deconstructible. Words and things are deconstructible, but events, if there are any such things (*s'il y en a*), are not deconstructible. 5. In terms of their temporality, events, never being present, solicit us from afar, draw us on, draw us out into the future, calling us hither. Events are provocations and promises, and they have the structure of what Derrida calls the unforeseeable "to come" (*à venir*). Or else they call us back, recall us to all that has flowed by into the irremissible past, which is why they form the basis of what Johann Baptist Metz calls "dangerous memories" of the injustice suffered by those long dead, or not so long, a revocation that constitutes another provocation. Events call and recall.[1]

Events are what Žižek calls the "fragile absolute"—when Žižek leaves off abusing postmodern theories he often serves up excellent postmodern goods—fragile because they are delicate and absolute because they are precious.[2] Events are tender shoots and saplings, the most vulnerable growths, a nascent and incipient stirring, which postmodern thinking must exert every effort to cultivate and keep safe. Postmodernism is the gardening of the event, the thinking of the event, offering events shelter and safe harbor. Events are menaced by great monsters who feed on their tender pulp, by large and overarching theories that would catch them in their sweep, organize them, make them march in step to some metaphysical tune or other, right or left, theistic or atheistic, idealist or materialist, realist or antirealist. Events, on the other hand, travel close to the surface of what happens, lying low on the plane of immanence, far beneath the radar of big theories like the history of the Absolute Spirit or the Destiny of Being (*Seinsgeschick*). Events are little gifts, and postmodern thinking seeks to keep them free of big deals, which would sell them out.

On my accounting, things take a *theological turn* in postmodernism when what we mean by the event shifts to God. Or, alternately, things take a *postmodern turn* in theology when the meditation upon *theos* or *theios*, God or the divine, is shifted to events, when the location of God or what is divine about God is shifted from what happens, from constituted words and things, to the plane of events. When events take on the specific look or sound or feel of the sacred, when the sparks we experience in words and things are sacred sparks, divine promptings, or holy intensities, then we have stepped upon the terrain of postmodern theology.[3] Think of the event as a fire, a flame, even as what Deleuze does not hesitate to call its "eternal truth"! Fire, flames, and sparks have from time out of mind been figures of the divine. To cite but one very famous example, Meister Eckhart said there is a little spark in the soul (*ein Seelenfünklein*), which is the point where God and the soul touch. In postmodern theology the event lends things, we might say, a kind of divine glow, what Deleuze calls a brightness and splendor, "the splendor of Being." Theology keeps its ear close to the heart of the pulses or pulsations of the divine in things.

However postmodern, a theology of the event has an ancient pedigree, going back to a famous narrative about a very seminal event indeed, whose punch line was that life glows with the "good" that Elohim pronounced upon creation—six times, the final time emphasizing the point in case we missed it: *very good*. For if we look closely at just what Elohim did in the first creation story in Genesis, we will quickly notice that it did not consist in drawing being out of nothing, as the metaphysical theologians would have us think, but in putting the glow of life and light upon what was dark and lifeless, charging it, sparking it, lighting it up, we might say with the splendor and brightness of life. It was as if the great elements—the womblike deep (*tehom*), the formless void (*tohu wa bohu*), and the wind (*ruach*) were sleeping, and Elohim's word was a call to them to awaken and glow with life. On this alternate account of creation, what Elohim did was to release the events that stirred within these great sleeping elements.

We might even say, to put all this in a bold and simple stroke, that in postmodern theology what happens to us is God, which is why we call it postmodern *theo*logy. Or, to couch it in a slightly more cautious terms, in postmodern theology what happens to us is the *event* that is harbored in the name of God, which is why we want to cultivate the resources in this name, to nurture and shelter them, and to let us ourselves be nourished by their force, made warm by their glow, charged by their intensities.[4] The crucial move lies in treating the event as something that is going on *in* words and things, as a potency that stirs within them and makes them restless with the event. Deleuze says that to will the event means more precisely to will "not exactly what occurs but something *in* that which occurs, something yet to come which would be consistent with what occurs." "The event is not what occurs (an accident), it is rather inside what occurs, the purely expressed. It signals and awaits us."[5] That is to head in a more Derridean direction where willing the event means to "affirm" the event, to say "*oui, oui*" (Amen!) not to what is present but to *what is coming*, to what stirs within things, within words and things, to what is *promised* by them.

Then events assume a more messianic or even a ghostly look, for in postmodern theology we believe in ghosts, very holy if slightly pale ghosts called events, which are the stuff of what I am calling here a spectral hermeneutics. Then one has turned one's face to the future and one is haunted by the possibilities harbored in events—by the fragile "perhaps" in things—which promise a new life, a new being, a new creation. We replace *amor fati*, which is one of those big stories that threatens to quash the fragile absolute of the event, with an *amor venturi*, a love or affirmation of what is to come, which makes more sense.[6] For all of us, everyone from Deleuze to evangelical Bible-thumpers, want to be born again.[7] For Deleuze, the event is a kind of anonymous impulse, a prepersonal transcendental field, a nomad that moves freely across the border that separates words and things, essence and existence, or else it is the very "surface" that joins and separates them. The event constitutes a transcendental archi-sense (which Deleuze somewhat misleadingly calls non-sense) that makes garden variety sense and non-sense both possible and impossible. If so, then what is distinctive about postmodern theology is that this prepersonal, prehuman field is taken to be a domain of the divine, a sacred surface that is lined with divine strings of force or sparked by divine impulses or charged with divine intensities.[8]

A Postmodern Covenant

In thinking of radical theology as a theology of the event, the stress is on the event as an irreducible possibility, a potentiality that can assume various forms of expression and instantiation. The event is not reducible to the actual, but stirs as a simmering potentiality within the name or the state of affairs, incessantly seeking an outlet, constantly pressing for expression in words and things. The event is irreducible; indeed, I am inclined to say that it is the very form of irreducibility itself. For what is irreducible is what resists contraction into some finite form or other, what seeks to twist free from the finite containers in which it finds itself deposited, what cannot be contained—which is what we *mean* by the event. Whenever we encounter an occurrence like a word or a thing, a proposition or a state of affairs, a belief or a practice, a discourse or an institution that cannot contain what it contains, that is because of the event it contains, because it is astir with the event, because it has been shocked, shaken, and disturbed by the event, which is seeking to twist free from its present confinement. Indeed, that is also how I would put deconstruction in a nutshell. For what else is deconstruction but the work of analyzing phenomena that contain what they cannot contain in order to release the event they (cannot) contain?

The event is not so much something present as something coming, something stirring, something signaling us from afar, something waiting for us to catch up, something inviting, promising, provoking, and, let us say, for this is a word that packs a special punch in theology, something *promised*. When Derrida speaks of the "democracy to come," that phrase refers to the event of something coming that is presently astir in the word *democracy*, something that invites and calls us in this word, which is the least bad word we have at present for something given to us now only by an anticipated grace, that is, in our prayers and tears. This is how the event is capable of taking a religious form and just why it provides the stuff of a theology of the event. For the event constitutes a kind of *covenant* that has been cut with us, which makes us the people of the promise, of the covenant, of the cut. *Religion* is the covenant that has been made—by whom we cannot quite say—between the event and us. So beyond—or perhaps *within*—the Jewish and the Christian Covenants, let us dream of a postmodern covenant, where we are the people of the event, the ones called together by the event.

Still, by speaking of the "religious" form taken by the event, have I not endangered this tender sapling by exposing it to the Monster or Master Narrative of Religion, whose history in the

West is one of violence and bloodshed? Have I not baldly betrayed the irreducible event by reducing it to the religions of the
Book, the ones constituted by the Covenant that has been cut
between God and his chosen people, which are famous for their
monotheistic exclusivism and jealousy? I will be your God and
you will be my people, and we will not allow any foreign gods
or infidels to disturb this intimacy of this private relation. It is
for this reason that I insist that the event is not what occurs but
something *in* what occurs, something stirring, something still
to come. The idea behind a postmodern theology is to *release
the event* that stirs in the famous covenantal scenes and not allow it to be contracted to any present form or constricted by
its local conditions.[9] The event is the *unconditional* that is astir
in these local conditions, what is undeconstructible in any historical construction or discursive practice. If I take "religion" in
its most radical sense as a covenant cut between the event and
its people, my intention is to avail the event of the most flexible form available to safeguard its irreducibility. To say that the
event has a religious sense is to underline something crucial in
it, which is the *unconditional passion* or the *passion for the unconditional* that the event engenders. In the Scriptures the covenant
is a promise or a covenant cut by *God*—that is why I speak un-
abashedly of *theology*—where the name of God is the name of
an event, of something that stirs within that name, something
I know not what, some sacred spark or fire. The name of God
shelters an event, and the task of thinking about or meditating
upon this name is to safeguard that event and release what is stirring there. The name of God is very simply the most famous and
richest name we have to signify both an open-ended excess and
an inaccessible mystery. That is why I insist I do not "reduce"
the event to religion when I speak of a theology of the event
but on the contrary find a place to safeguard its irreducibility
and unconditionality. The name of God is the name of one of

humanity's most famous fires, one that has inflamed humankind from time immemorial—which explains why, like every fire, it is also so dangerous. Affirming the eternal flame of the event that burns within the name of God is also a way to flag the consuming violence that is stored up in this name.

The name of God is one of the names that Derrida has in mind when he meditates upon the phrase *sauf le nom*, "safe the name," an expression that for Derrida means both: let us keep this name safe, let us save it, but also: God is everything save (*sauf*/except) the name, save or except what the name names explicitly, everything except the excess that exceeds what is explicitly named. The name of God names everything save the event that is sheltered by this name, which is an event that solicits and invites, calls and signals us, but is never finally named.[10]

The affirmation of the event is less an agency than a responsiveness, less a subjectivistic decisionism than accepting the terms of a covenant. For what else can the affirmation of the event be but the response of a subject to a visitation by something that overtakes it? What else can such an affirmation be but the responsibility by which the subject is organized or galvanized into a subject of the event? What else is the event than the fire that inflames the movement of the subject or what Derrida calls the decision of the other in me? To affirm the name of God is to say yes to the forces that work their way through that name and traverse our hearts and bodies. For the event is what calls us and we are the people of the call, the people of the event who want to make themselves worthy of the call.

Prayers and Tears

Religion begins and ends with prayer; where there is prayer, there is religion; where there is religion, there is prayer. Now the event is the stuff of which prayers and tears are made, that by which we are always already solicited, invited, called. The event is always already ahead of us, always provoking and soliciting us, eternally luring us on with its promise. The truth of the event is its promise to come true. Events make promises that are never kept by any actual occasion. That is also what I have been calling the irreducibility of the event. The event can never be held captive by any particular instance of the event, never reduced to any present form or instantiation. It would be the height of injustice, not to say of arrogance, to say that justice is finally realized in some existing form, in some present person or state. The unconditional event is only conditionally realized in any time or place, in any word or proposition or discursive formation, in any ontic realization or actualization. The irreducible event is what reduces us to tears, to prayers and tears, for its coming. The event is what destabilizes all such relatively stable structures as attempt to house it, making them restless with the future, teeming with hope and promise, even as it is in virtue of the event that things are haunted by the past, made an occasion of dangerous memories, which are no less unnerving and destabilizing. The eternal truth of the event is its nomadism, its restless journey across barren deserts, or perhaps its venturing upon uncharted seas, in any case, its discontent with more sedimented, sedentary formations, even as the ancient charge that is laid upon us by the nomad is hospitality, to throw wide the door of welcome to its coming. Not only to welcome its coming but to pray and weep over its arrival.

Theology is a place where the energies of the event may be nurtured and released, its intensities cultivated and affirmed, built up and discharged—free from all the constraints of what exists. *Alice in Wonderland* and the stories of Borges suffer very little disadvantage from having to do with nonexistent entities, a point that Deleuze makes throughout *The Logic of Sense*, which on my reading is also a bit of a cryptotheologic of sense.[11] Nor does prayer, as we do not pray for what already exists, unless we are praying for it to go away and exist no more. Indeed, such inexistence is the condition of the range and power of literature and prayer, of sense itself. Literature and theology are places where we dream of what is coming, where we pray and weep for something that eye has not yet beheld nor ear heard, where we venture upon the plane of what does not exist and wonder indeed why not. I think that on the whole such inexistence constitutes a very upbeat and affirmative definition of theology; every genuine affirmation of God must pass through a dark night and mandatory atheism. Whenever Derrida speaks of the event, which turns on what is undeconstructible, he adds the precaution *s'il y en a*, "if there is any"! For if whatever exists is deconstructible, then the event, which is undeconstructible, lies just beyond the reach and across the borders of what exists, which is the special province of a postmodern theology.

Indeed, there is even something of a classical ring, a paradoxically Anselmian tonality in this formula. The name of God is the name of an event that is greater than anything that exists.[12] If anything does exist, that is not what is named by the name of God, or, rather, it is not the event that is harbored or contained within the name of God. For the very meaning of the event is to prevent the name or the thing from blocking or containing the intensity of the event within. When something happens that contains an event, it contains precisely what it cannot contain. To exist would mean to exhaust the event, which means the event that is named in or under the name of God can never take final form, can never exist and exhaust itself on the ontical or ontological plane, neither in some highest being up above nor even in Being itself, even as it can never be conceived in some logically adequate expression or concept. The event that stirs within the name of God is always soliciting us and inviting us, calling and signaling us. We do not properly say of this event that it exists but that it solicits and calls to us from within what exists, which is why events are a matter of prayers and tears. Prayer is not a transaction or interaction with some hyperbeing in the sky, a communication with some ultrareality behind the scenes, the invocation or appeasement of a magical power of supernatural intervention from on high. Prayer has to do with hearing, heeding, and hearkening to a provocation that draws us out of ourselves.[13]

The Desire for God

To speak of our prayers and tears is but another way to speak of our desire, and to speak of our desire is to enter a never-never land more outlandish than anything Alice ever ran into down that rabbit hole, for desire is situated in the space between, or perhaps it is the very spacing between, what exists and what does not exist. Desire is nourished and fed by what does not exist, by the power of what does not exist to solicit and disturb us, which is why desire has ultimately to do with events. To speak of desire is to address all that we are and are not, all that we know and do not know, which means an enigma wrapped in a secret so deep that it can never be known by us or by anyone else, which is why Derrida calls it the absolute secret. Because desire has to do with the event, we do not know what we desire, but this nonknowing is what keeps desire alive. If the event would be exhausted by existence, by existing in full, it would be exterminated by the white light of knowledge.

We should never give up on our desire, as Lacan says, upon which Badiou comments, "For desire is constitutive of the subject of the unconscious; it is thus the non-known *par excellence*, such that 'do not give up on your desire' rightly means: 'do not give up on that part of yourself that you do not know.'"[14] I would put the same idea by saying that our desire is for the Messiah who never shows up, which is what keeps desire going. Unless in a futile attempt to get some peace and quiet we give up. But if we give up on desire, that will succeed only in making us miserable. For then one part of us, the part of us that we know, gives up while the other part, the part of us that we do not know, has not given up. That will not bring us inner peace but the inner illness of the sickness unto death.

From time immemorial the name of God has been the name of what we desire, with a desire beyond desire, so one way to try to give up altogether is to give up on God—or to try. The name of God is not precisely the name of what we desire but the name of the event that occurs *in* what we desire that keeps desire alive. Whenever we desire this or that determinate thing, it is true that that indeed is what we desire. But that is not the whole truth; it is not the final form in which our desire can take shape. For were the thing that we desire delivered, that would only feed desire all the more, and were, God forbid, that thing or person dashed, that would not, or need not, dash our desire, for desire can never be reduced to that determinate occasion. Our desire is irreducible because the event, which is what we desire, is irreducible. To speak of making ourselves worthy of the event means that we spend our lives, or so we should, trying to make ourselves worthy of what we desire. We spend our lives, or so we should, hoping, dreaming, sighing for the event, praying and weeping over the event, praying for the coming of the event. For the event does not quite, never does exactly—*exist*. If theology is the science of nonexistent entities, it is because theology is born in the space between what exists and the event, which means that theology is born in prayer. That is its great dignity, its glorious body, which pulses through and animates the language of Saint Augustine's *Confessions*. The name of God is as old and venerable and hoary a name as we have for desire, for our desire beyond desire. "Inquietum est cor nostrum," our heart is made restless with this desire, "donec requiescat in te," and our heart will not rest until it rests in you, in the event that this "you" embodies.

What do I desire? Who or what is desiring within me? That, by the very terms of what we mean by desire and event, cannot finally be formulated. Of course, this is only the half of it. For the issue of our inability to give our desire any *final* formulation is a steady flow of provisional formulations.[15] We are all along in the dark about what we desire, about what is desiring us, about what is desiring *in* us. But this darkness keeps desire safe from the withering sun of knowledge. "Quid ergo amo, cum deum meum amo?" Derrida asks with Augustine (*Conf.* 10:6–7). What do I love when I love my God? What do I desire when I desire God? What is the event of desire that takes place in me, that makes its place in me, here in this place where I say "I." What is the event of desire, which is always the desire for the event, that occurs in theology?

The Weakness of God

The event jolts the world, disturbs, disrupts, and skews the sedimented course of things, exposing the alternate possibilities that course their nomadic way through the normalized quotidian paths that things routinely follow. That is one reason we read literature, and that is why Deleuze takes so much joy in the works of Lewis Carroll, and well he should. I am only puzzled—well, not really puzzled, but disappointed—that he did not notice another literature—and here he differs from Derrida—no less anarchical and chaosmic, an anarchy no less crowned, but this time with a sacred crown, the sacred anarchy of the "Kingdom of God." I am disappointed that he did not pursue the fountain of events that issues in the mad, paradoxical, parabolical, upside down, topsy-turvy world that is to be found in the Scriptures. For if postmodern thinking is intent on following the movements of the events by which words and things are inwardly disturbed, by which they are even driven slightly mad, we theologians of the event are here to insist that madness is of many kinds. To the bright and witty giddiness of Alice of Wonderland and the dark pain of schizophrenia mapped by Deleuze we add a third: the divine madness of the Kingdom of God described in the New Testament, where the event provokes the most sublime effects, a veritable "sacred anarchy," whose parables and paradoxes are easily the match of any of the tales told by Lewis Carroll. It is precisely this impossible circulation of such divine events that gives rise to a story like the wedding feast that is every bit as odd as a party thrown by a Mad Hatter.

Deleuze should have suspected an event there. He should have wondered whether the zany reversals and astonishing paradoxes in the New Testament were any less the offspring of an event than is the tale of a tardy rabbit darting down a hole. What marvelous stream of events has left its traces on this surface and marked this surface with such vivid and unforgettable figures? But, for the most part, the New Testament remained for him a missed opportunity, and he allowed himself to be waylaid by the received institutional reading of the text and discouraged by the high wall of ecclesiastical power by which it is surrounded. So one way for a postmodern theology to proceed—and there are several; I make no claim to have a corner on the market—is to feel about for the event that has so disturbed the surface of these stories. What intensities, what nomadic bit of nonsense or archi-sense there throws everything into reverse? What flow of forces issues in such unforgettable madness, in such sacred foolishness, where people make themselves fools for the Kingdom of God?

Sacred Anarchy

My thesis is twofold. 1. In the Scriptures the odd phenomena constituting the "Kingdom of God" are the offspring of the shock that is delivered by the name of God to what is there called the "world," resulting in what I call a "sacred anarchy." Consider but a sampling of its more saliant features. In the Kingdom, the last are first and first are last, a strategically perverted system of privileging, so that the advantage is given not to beautiful Athenian bodies that house a love of wisdom, but to lepers, deaf mutes, the blind, epileptics, and the paralyzed. The favor of the Kingdom falls not on men of practical wisdom, of *arete*, of experts in *phronesis*, but on tax collectors and prostitutes, who enjoy preferential treatment over the upright and well behaved. In addition, in the Kingdom the way to be arrayed with all the glory of God is to neither sow nor reap but to behave like the lilies of the field. If you try to save your life you will lose it, but if you lose it you will be saved. In the Kingdom one should hate one's father and mother but love one's enemies, and if a man strikes you you should offer him the other cheek. There, if you are rich, you have a very fine needle indeed to thread to get into the Kingdom. If you would want to become rich with the treasures offered by this Kingdom, you should sell all that you have and give it to the poor. Moreover, you should give to the poor not only what you can afford but even what you need for yourself. If one of your sheep is lost, then you should not worry about endangering the other ninety-nine but go out and search for the lost one, which is an unaccountably odd way to count. If you host a party—even a wedding for one of your children—you should go out into the streets and welcome in the passers by. There bodies pass easily through solid walls, rise from the dead, traverse the surface of water without sinking, glow with a blinding whiteness, and pass instantly from one state, like water, into another, like wine.

Cripples are made straight, lepers are cured, and the dead rise from their grave. All these bodily metamorphoses are in turn figures of a personal transformation best described as *metanoia*, which might be retranslated from "repentance" to "being of a new mind and heart," being tuned and attuned to the new being that comes of belonging to the Kingdom.

2. The event that shocks the world is not a strong but a weak force. Underlying, or arching over, all these famous paradoxes, there is, on my hypothesis, a thesis about God, or about the event that is harbored in the name of God, one that is contrary to the powers that be in theology and the church, a startling thesis found in what Paul calls "the weakness of God."[16] Saint Paul puts this thesis about weakness very powerfully, even paradigmatically, in a veritably Deleuzian discourse on the "logos of the cross (*logos tou staurou*)," the mark of which Paul identifies as "foolishness." Here, in a virtuoso performance of the interweaving of sense and non-sense, of a *logos* that is the offspring of *moria*, Paul spells out the way this weakness jolts the world: God chose the foolish ones in the world to shame the wise, and what is weak to shame the strong, and what is the low down in the world, the ones who "are not" (*ta me onta*), to shame the men of *ousia*, men of substance, the powers that be. The "weakness of God," Paul says, is stronger than human strength (I Cor. 1:25).[17]

A Postmodern Theology of the Cross

A good deal of what is going on in these texts comes back to a certain event, to a disturbing experience of God as a "weak force," and it is this crucial paradox that incites such a riot of reversals and paradoxes in its narratives. This crucial event is paradigmatically expressed in the Cross, where Jesus is subjected to an excruciating and humiliating execution as a common criminal, defeated by Roman power, deserted by the disciples and even forsaken by God.[18] Jesus was crucified, not freely, but against his will, against the will of everything that is good and just, human or divine. Jesus was the spokesman of a message about the coming of the Kingdom, which delivered the shock of the event to the world, for which the world made him pay with his blood. Blood is the coin of the realm in the world, not in the Kingdom. Blood is how things are done in the world, for the ways of the world are the ways of power. When Peter raises his sword to prevent Jesus from being taken by the Roman guards in the Garden, Jesus tells him to put it down, for that is not how things happen in the Kingdom. If we take from this that Jesus could, with a wave of his hand or a wink of his eye, demolish these Roman soldiers but freely chose not to exert his omnipotence because he was on a divine mission, then we would concede that he merely seems, *docet*, to be a helpless and innocent victim of this power. But that is what he was in truth. The radical uprooting of the heresy of Docetism demands that we locate the divinity of this scene of misery and defeat, the sacredness of its memory, not in some hidden divine power play or long-term investment in a divine economy of salvation. The sacredness lies in the cries of protest that rise up from the scene. The event to be willed here is the depth of outrage at the injustice of imperial power, of the crushing of the Kingdom by worldly forces. The divinity lies in the identification of the name of God, for Jesus was the *eikon* of God, not with Roman power but with an innocent victim of that power, not with retribution but with the act of *forgiveness* that is attributed to Jesus by the evangelists. The ways of a father in the Kingdom are illustrated by the story of another father, the one who was prodigal with his love of his prodigal son. Those are the ways of the Kingdom. In the world, violence is met with counterviolence; in the Kingdom it is met with forgiveness. In the world, betrayal is concealed with a kiss; in the Kingdom, betrayal is healed by a kiss.

The event harbored by the name of God in this scene, the eventful paradox or paradoxical event whose tremors can be felt throughout the New Testament, is that of the power of power-lessness or of something "unconditional without sovereignty," of a "weak force," to take up a discussion that Derrida was developing in his final writings.[19] The majesty or glory of the name of God does not lie in the power of a strong force but in something "unconditional," undeconstructible, but without an army, without actual force, real or physical power. It is the name more of a potency than a power, a restive possibility that makes the world restless with hope for justice and impatient with injustice, while the actuality or the realization is assigned *to us*, as Bonhoeffer claimed. The transcendence or majesty of God lies in the un-conditionality of the claim that is made upon us by God, by the name of God, in the name of God. And when it comes to claims, realization depends upon the response, even as events require actualization and we are required to make ourselves worthy of events. Claims, which are events, depend upon us to respond, to realize or actualize them, to make them happen, which here means to make *God* happen, to give God body and embodiment, force and actuality. Deleuze puts the event that (we are saying) takes place in the name of God very nicely when he says "To the extent that events are actualized in us, they wait for us and invite us in. . . . It is a question of attaining this will that the event cre-ates in us; of becoming the quasi-cause of what is produced in us."[20] Of becoming worthy of the events that happen to us.

Religion is what is happening to us in the name of God. Re-ligion means to make God happen in the world and make our-selves worthy of what happens to us. We are functionaries of this event, sent into the world to serve it, to respond to it, to realize it and make it happen, missionaries of its emissions. But this event, like any event, is not reducible to *someone* or *something* with the power to makes things right. Rather it takes the form of a call, an address, or solicitation, of a force that lays claim to us, addressing us unconditionally, but without the benefit of either a terrestrial army or arsenal of weapons or of some celestial metaphysical power base in the heavens. It would be magic, supernaturalism, fetishism, reification, idolatry to confine this event within a name, to constrict it to a being, even the Being of beings, to try to contain the event within the confines of some sort of superentity that can outthink, outwill, outpower, and generally outdo anything we mortals here below can come up with. God is not a cosmic force, a worldly power, a physical or metaphysical energy or power source that supplies energy to the world, who designs it, starts it up and keeps it going, and who occasionally intervenes here and there with strategic course corrections, a tsunami averted here, a cancerous tumor there, a bloody war quieted over there.[21]

The very idea of this event, to come back to what Anselm saw within the confines of a medieval metaphysical imagination, was that whoever or whatever bears the name that contains this event cannot contain what it contains. Anything that bears this name, anything that so presents itself, is deconstructible, while the event itself, *s'il y en a*, is not deconstructible. The name of God is the name not of a *res* but of a *realissimum*. The name of a God is not the name of an abstract logical possibility but of a *dynamis* that pulses through things (*rei*), urging them, soliciting them, to be what they can be, and it is in that sense what is most real about them. The name of God is not the name of the most real thing but of what is most real *in* things. The name of God is not the name of something that happens or occurs, but of something *in* what happens or occurs, which solicits what is best in them. In my slightly postmodern version of Anselm, God is the *ens realissimum* not exactly as such, but as the *realissimum* in any *res* or *ens* that urges that being beyond itself, like a kind of hyperreal inching it beyond its present reality.

I am proposing a postmodern theology of the Cross in which I ask, what is happening on the Cross? What is happening to us? What events pulsate through that unforgettable scene? Of what are we to make ourselves worthy? It is a mystification to think that there is some celestial transaction going on here, some settling of accounts between the divinity and humanity, as if this death is the amortization of a debt of long standing and staggering dimensions. If anything, no debt is lifted from us in this scene but a responsibility imposed upon us. For we are laid claim to by this spectacle, by the cry against unjust persecution that issues from the dangerous memory of this scene, by the astonishing spectacle of greeting hatred with love, of answering persecution not with retribution but with forgiveness. The crucified body of Jesus is a site—one among many—of divine eventiveness, through which there courses a stream of events that traverse our bodies and shock the world under the name of the weakness of God, and we are to make ourselves worthy of this event.

The Death of God

To propose a postmodern theology of the Cross, to meditate the event that transpires in the death of Jesus, is to try to think a certain death of God, the death of the *ens supremum et deus omnipotens*, the death of the God of power, in order to release the event of the unconditional claim lacking worldly sovereignty that issues from the Cross. I am not satisfied by the death of God announced by Nietzsche, who was too unguardedly in love in with power and hierarchy and struggle, nor even with the beautiful mystical death of God in apophatic theology, which is trying to affirm the still higher being of a hypereminent *hyperousios*.

I would press further to a more pressing and important death, the death of the *deus omnipotens* of classical theology, and this in order to nourish the life of the event that stirs within the name of God, which is the stuff of our rebirth. The death of the God of power gives birth to what Sallie McFague calls the "body of God," to God's suffering body, which rises up in unconditional protest against needless and unjust suffering. Insofar as there is any philosophical life left in this increasingly dated expression, the death of God, it refers to an ongoing and never finished project of deconstructing the God of ontotheologic, which is for me above all the God of sovereign power. I am always interested in loosening up the events that stir within beliefs and practices that have gained too much grip on us, whose prestige threatens to intimidate us, which have grown into big theories and big stories, big deals and big pains, which bring along with themselves a history of intimidation, oppression, and violence. And, God help us, that is certainly true of the name of God. The more some people use the word *God* the more I find myself praying to God for the death of God, asking God to rid us of God, to cite a very famous mystic. There is surely something to be gained from undertaking a deconstruction of the name of God precisely under the auspices of a "death" of God. To this campaign I make modest annual contributions, just so long as this is understood to be a way of affirming the event that lives within the name of God. For with Deleuze and Saint Paul—and the Bible-thumpers—I too want to be born again, at least once before I die. The work of burning off the old metaphysics of omnipotence, which can never cease, must always be a way to fan the flame or build the fire of the event that transpires in the name of God. Mark Taylor's famously downbeat description of deconstruction as "a hermeneutic of the death of God" is but a moment in a more upbeat description of the theology of the event as a "hermeneutics of the desire for God."[22]

Indeed, I am happy to countersign the striking improvement Mark Taylor has made over the earlier versions of the death of God to be found years ago in the group that formed around T.J.J. Altizer in the 1960s. Although articulated in Nietzschean terms, Altizer rejected the central sense that the death of God had for Nietzsche, which is to announce the end or withering away of the "ascetic ideal," of some absolute center or metaphysical foundation. In Altizer the death of God primarily meant that the absolute center had shifted its residence from transcendence to immanence by means of a metaphysics of *kenosis*, by which the full presence of a transcendent God was transported to the plane of immanence. Altizer merrily danced in the street over the metaphysics of immanent presence, nay, over "total presence," brought about as the dialectical offspring of "total absence" or negation. Taylor incisively plied apart this and any metaphysical theology, classical or Hegelian, with the stylus tip of deconstruction. At that interment I will certainly be in attendance dressed in my best black. But Taylor's own "deconstructive a/theology" is for me less an affirmation of the event that stirs within the name of a God than a dissipation of the force of this name under the guise of a dissemination. Taylor's *Erring* leads to an affirmation of the world—*oui, oui*—but in such a way as to leave one wondering if we are not left unclaimed by anything, unresponsible to anything, unsolicited and unprovoked, as if nothing has happened to us, as if there were no events. If it is certainly true that Taylor is not dancing in the streets over the metaphysics of presence, one sometimes wonders if he is not just dancing in the streets, *simpliciter*. He hardly observes the "/" in his a/theology, the undecidable fluctuation of the event that stirs within the name of God, but allows the *theos* to dissipate into thin air; it is atheology, not a/theology, decisive death, not undecidability.

My lingering worry is that the death of God theologies are themselves thinly disguised *grands récits*. They are theologies of history that tell the big story of how we go from the religion of the Father in Judaism, to the religion of the Son in the New Testament, to the religion of the Spirit in modernity (Altizer) or in postmodernity (Taylor), which is the Final Story. Despite the fact that Taylor is telling us deconstruction spells the end of the Book and of History, he does not resist this schema. Indeed he completes or perfects it. When he describes deconstruction as "the hermeneutics of the death of God," he means that it is the *final* version of the death of God, the postmetaphysical completion of the story, the *decisive* way to uproot the metaphysical residue that clings to Altizer's patently metaphysical version of the death of God. This is quite a Tall Tale to be telling in the name of deconstruction, a story of how consciousness or history traverses from transcendence to immanence, from alienation to homecoming, in which Judaism, as the religion of the Father or of alienation, plays the bad guy. Death of God theologies tend to be *Christian* theologies—I do not object to that; so is my own "postmodern theology of the Cross"—but ones that present *kenosis* as a zero-sum game in which the transfer of being is made at the expense of the "religion of the Father" and to the advantage of his local incarnation. God overcomes his alienated condition (= Judaism) in order to pitch his tent right here in Christian Prussia, or Christian Europe, or, let us say, more generally and more generously, the Christian West. Deconstruction, which is much more distrustful of these periodizing and incarnational schemata, has been sent into the world (if I may be so ironic) to break up such illusions[23] and to dispel gospels of economic exchange in the name of the gift.

Nonetheless, I will always want to preserve the work of thinking the death of the God of power, which belongs to the infinite task of the critique of idols. Indeed, by distinguishing between the name and the event, between the name of God and the event that transpires there, I have laid myself open to the possibility that this event, or stream of events, can twist free from this name and that we might then find ourselves out in the desert, in a khoral place of namelessness and the desire for new names. If we release the event that is harbored by the name of God, we might end up having to release that name itself, in the sense of letting it go, letting go of it. The event of solicitation that is issued in the name of God stands on its own, calls and solicits us on its own, whether or not someone named God is the author of that solicitation, in which case the death of the author, which would be here the death of God, is the condition of hearing this solicitation. In the desire for God, it is not God but the event that stirs within that name that is undeconstructible, and it would always be possible for that desire to take other forms, to find other formulations, now or in times to come. So my theology of the event is prepared to concede, if not exactly the death of God,[24] at least the mortality or historical contingency of the name of God, the separability in principle of the event from the name, like a spirit leaving a lifeless body behind. For, however precious and prestigious it may be, the name of God remains a historical name and, as such, a contingent formation or unity of meaning. I myself have no inside information to pass along about how well this name will flourish in the future, whether it will live or die, which means how well it will shelter the event with which it is entrusted and by which it is inwardly disturbed.

On Radicalizing the Hermeneutical Turn: In Dialogue with Vattimo

Weak Theology and Vattimo's Weakness Theorem

This brings me directly to the work of Gianni Vattimo and to his provocative notion of weak thinking, which is one resource for what I call by a certain analogy weak theology, which turns on the weakness of God that is expressed for me in the death of Jesus. There are other ways to do what I am doing here, but mine is confessedly Christian, and it is the point at which my theology of the event converges with the thought of Vattimo.

I have an inner sympathy with Vattimo's work on more than one count.

Like Vattimo, I am a Catholic and an Italian—well, a weak Italian, a quasi-Italian, a simulacrum of an Italian, an Italian American who does not speak Italian, two generations removed from the ancestral city of Napoli, and no doubt an even weaker Catholic. As such, I share with him a common intellectual culture and a common education in the great medieval metaphysical theologies. Like Vattimo, Jacques Maritain was an early hero for me, and I was from the start suspicious of modernist dogmas. When I first read *Being and Time*, I thought, here is what I am looking form, a way to critique modernity which is not a narrow-minded antimodern Catholicism but the very latest thing in European phenomenology! Like Vattimo, I feel a common outrage at the pontifical authoritarianism and "fundamentalism"[25] of John Paul II and I would be astonished if anything different emerged from Benedict XVI. If the late pope was a lovely man who lent a hand in bringing down the reign of terror in Communist east Europe, he was also an administrator who installed his own form of terror within the Roman Catholic Church. John Paul II virtually extinguished every trace of the notion of the "people of God" that was the hallmark of the Second Vatican Council and thoroughly betrayed the spirit of that great council. He set back the legitimate aspirations of women in the Church a generation, intimidated Catholic scholars and free speech with inquisitorial violence, and left behind a Church in which it is impossible to imagine that its dangerous and reactionary teachings on birth control and homosexuality will be corrected in the foreseeable future. He suppressed open discussion in the Church of the legitimate civil rights of men and women in secular society to decide these and other matters, like abortion rights, without ecclesiastical intimidation. He contradicted the spirit of Jesus, who risked his own life by defying the very authoritarianism practiced in his name by the Vatican. This pope helped align the Church with right-wing and reactionary political causes in Europe and the United States that have shrunk the Christian message to opposition to abortion rights and homosexuality. Jesus took his stand with the poor who are oppressed by the political forces with which the Catholic Church is today aligned.

Like Vattimo, I too first made my way beyond a conventional Catholicism into postmodernism by way of Heidegger, Nietzsche, and Gadamer, although later on Derrida would become my principal ghostwriter. Like him, I have not given up on the word *hermeneutics* but have tried instead to save or rehabilitate this word in a more postmodern modality, to save the event harbored within this word, which I have practiced by way of a campaign of long standing to defend what I called radical hermeneutics.[26] By this I mean a view that takes interpretation to be radically inescapable, which is something all of us have learned from Gadamer, but with the special twist of trying to help hermeneutics itself escape from metaphysics, especially from a version of Hegelian metaphysics by which it seems particularly menaced. If I had convened a conference on the Isle of Capri to talk about religion, I too would have wanted to see both Derrida and Gadamer at the same table. I have long dreamt of setting such a table, for my idea has been for some time now to hold the feet of hermeneutics to the fire of deconstruction. I affirm the inescapability of interpretation less because of Heidegger and more because of the play of *différance*, a misspelling that spells the end of overarching, ahistorical uninterpreted facts of the matter.

Like Vattimo, I have found a way to reinscribe, or reinvent, or reaffirm, my Christian beginnings within a framework that I do not know how to describe except as a certain Christianity, a Christianity of a certain sort, focused on the image of weakness in the New Testament and the death of Jesus on the Cross. Like his, my Christianity has laid aside the trappings of modernist certitudes and, as Vattimo puts its so perfectly, at best I believe that I believe. Like Vattimo, I am interested in a certain postmodern version of religion and have found it necessary to "weaken" metaphysical objectivism in order to make room for faith. For the effect of the various revolutions that shook twentieth-century philosophy, which we might too hastily summarize under the names of the linguistic turn and the hermeneutic turn, in fact showed the door to reductionism and made it possible for religious discourse and religious faith to be seen once again in public.

Like Vattimo, I too have tried to sing a postmodern theological and slightly Italian love song to the God of love, to the hermeneutics of charity. Above all, I am inclined today to organize everything I think about postmodern thought and about postmodern theology in particular around the figure of weakness, a figure forever associated with Vattimo's brilliant articulation of what he calls weak thinking (*pensiero debole*). On an analogy with Vattimo's weak thought, I speak of a weak theology. Such an expression, which is also to be found in Jeffrey Robbins and the Dominican theologian Ulrich Engel,[27] does not refer to intellectual spinelessness but, in the first place, to a weakening of the militant dogmatic tendencies of the confessional theologies, which in modernity fused in a lethal way with the Cartesian paradigm of certitude. As Engel points out, were the great religions of the Book to look to their own teachings about humility and to their traditions of mystical theology, which stressed that the truly divine God is the Godhead that eludes our comprehension, it would give them pause to so militantly pursue their purposes. As with Engel, my hope too is that "a rediscovery of this moment of 'weak,' ambiguous theology" could perhaps curb their tendencies to violence.[28] But, beyond that, my interest in a weak theology presses past the weakness of thought to the very weakness of God, which I discussed above.

The Secularization Theorem

Vattimo undertakes a two-pronged process of weakening. The first process is the weakening of Being, from an objective meta-physical structure into interpretation ("event" in the Heidegge-rian sense) or, as he sometimes says, into the "world as picture" (Heidegger's *Weltbild*). This is described in the Nietzschean lan-guage of "nihilism," which means the historical process in which the objectivistic pretensions of metaphysics, of locating an abso-lute foundation, have withered or become incredible (or "noth-ing"), that is, have emptied or weakened and been replaced by "perspectives" or interpretive schemata. The second process is the weakening of God into the world, which is described in the Pauline language of emptying (*kenosis*), which is paradigmati-cally expressed in the Christian doctrine of the Incarnation, the birth but also the death of Jesus. Kenosis is not a one-time-only event occurring in the life and death and Jesus but the ongoing history or tradition inaugurated by this event. This process Vat-timo calls "secularization," which means not the abandonment or dissolution of God but the "transcription" of God into time and history (the *saeculum*),[29] thus a successor form of death of God theology.[30] The two processes, nihilism and kenosis, are strictly parallel. Nihilism is the emptying of Being into interpre-tive structure; kenosis is the becoming nothing of God as a tran-scendent deity. The two processes of weakening, of Being and of God, are the correlates of what Vattimo calls weak thought (*pen-*

siero debole). Kenosis, as the transcription, translation, or transmission of God into the world, means establishing the kingdom
of God on earth. This is an idea whose political correlate is a
nonauthoritarian democracy and whose epistemic correlate is
a Gadamerian vision of dialogue and horizon-fusion, where,
as Gadamer says, "Being that is understood is language"—and
conversation. Weakening then is Vattimo's more radical version
of hermeneutics.

The Christian church should accordingly reconsider its critique of an increasingly secular culture, and, instead of lament-
ing defeat at the hands of secularization, it should declare victory
and march home in triumph. For what else is Western culture
than the translation of otherworldly Christianity into terrestrial
structures, the conversion of its celestial currency into the coin
of the more benign ethical, social, political, and even economic institutions of the Western world? The weakening of Being
(Heidegger) has made "Christianity" once again a legible, cred-
ible story, one that we can take seriously, and secularization has
transcribed that story from unreadable myth into legible history.
In secular culture the old religious narratives are published in
a new edition, translated into the secular vernacular in an af-
fordable paperback. There they are no longer tales told about
transcendent transactions in eternity but stories about the *saeculum*, the historical time in which real people live. There is thus
a "family resemblance" between the weakening of Being and the
rebirth of religion, an essential correlation.[31] With the withering away of metaphysics, which was given ample opportunity to
prove its worth and whose only result was an arid and reifying
rationality that turned the world and human life into objects for
instrumental reason, we are free to return for nourishment to
the old religious narratives.

For example, for Vattimo, the commonplace complaint that
the secular world has taken the Christ out of Christmas and

transcribed it into "Happy Holidays" is to be viewed as still another success on Christianity's part. For now the Incarnation, a theological doctrine accepted in a strong or robust form only within confessional limits, has been translated into a popular secular holiday in the West, in which the spirit of generosity and goodwill among all people prevails. During the "holidays" this attenuated if wispy "spirit" of love becomes general among humankind, which is what in fact this doctrine actually "means," its application in the concrete reality of lived experience. The tolerant, nonauthoritarian and pluralistic democratic societies in the West are the translation into real political structures of the Christian doctrine of neighbor love. When the transcendent God is "weakened"—or emptied—into the world, it assumes the living form of Western cultural life. Vattimo shows that this schema, which modernity first learned from Hegel and Schelling, and was deployed by Altizer and the 1960s movement, is found in its earliest form in Joachim of Fiora's millennialist doctrine of the "three ages," that of the Father (Judaism), the Son (the New Testament), and the Spirit, which is the unfolding of the Kingdom of God on earth from the year 1000 on. Western history for Vattimo is the *Wirkungsgeschichte* of a "classic" in the Gadamerian sense, of the New Testament, its unfolding life and application, its developing revelation and realization, translation and transcription.[32] But in Vattimo the age of the Spirit is not a version of metaphysics, not the biography of the Absolute in time, as it is in Joachim, Hegel, and Altizer, which is strong thinking, but an interpretive schema, a way to put the realization that we have always to do with conflicting interpretations whose only measure is love without measure.

The task of intellectuals today is therefore twofold. On the hand, they must move beyond the old reductionism and objectivisms of the nineteenth century and take the hermeneutic turn. In such a world the old religious narratives have once again to be taken seriously as irreducible language games or forms of life that uniquely instruct us about the meaning of our lives. On the other, the task of the intellectual is firefighting, that is, to see that while the flame of such religious narratives is kept alive it does not burn out of control. While the stories are to be taken seriously, they are not to be taken literally, which would issue in the worst sort of fundamentalism, the worst hardening of theology into authoritarianism and dogma, as opposed to its weakening into pluralism and hospitality.[33]

"The West or Christianity"

While I am full of admiration for Vattimo's bracing and embracing hermeneutics, I have certain reservations that turn on the privilege "Christianity" enjoys in his work, as when he boldly uses the "provocative" expression "the West or Christianity," which he takes as an inclusive not an exclusive disjunction,[34] as if to thwart the way Heidegger tended to see the "West" as "the Greeks" and to treat "Christianity" as a fall from the authentically Greek. It is a generalization of Weber's thesis that capitalism grows out of the spirit of Protestantism; capitalism and democracy, science and technology are the applied or secularized truth of "Christianity,"[35] ways of "achieving our religion," to adapt the title of a book by Richard Rorty, Vattimo's recent dialogue companion. What Vattimo and Rorty mean by achieving our country or achieving our religion (Christianity), is realizing the universal ideals that each emblematize. Christianity is to be superseded as a particular sect and taken as a (privileged) stand-in for universal hospitality to the stranger; the United States is to be taken not as a unilateral player in the power games of world politics but as standing for the ideals affirmed in the Declaration of Independence and the Constitution. Up to now, Vattimo says,

Christianity has been part of the problem, but if it would under-stand itself correctly it would become the basis of the solution,[36] because Christianity means love, and if love, then hospitality and pluralism. My concern is that there is an unguardedness in talk like this, considering that each time different people use these expressions, like "our" country or religion, they mean differ-ent countries and different religions. While it is productive to frame things that way in an in-house debate among Americans or among Christians, in order to make sure that the doors of hospitality are held open, it is riskier business to talk this way on a global stage, in the international community, where many countries and religions are in play.

But, beyond the rhetorical limitations, there is a substantive problem: Judaism gets *aufgehoben* in this expression, absorbed and assimilated into "Christianity," which is asked to do service for Judaism, asked to remember all the specific contributions of the Jewish in "Christianity," or in the "Judaeo-Christian," deploying the famous "hypen" that was the subject of Lyotard's book. I do not think that Jews will be reassured by this strategy any more than feminists would be reassured by a male philosopher who would assure them that every time he said the "rights of man" he was also including women. Why not either make one's discourse more complicated or even, in a gesture of strategic reversal, let *women* or *Jews* serve as the universal emblem—as in "Athens and Jerusalem"—something that Vattimo could do if he is invok-ing a broadly biblical tradition, if what he ultimately means is the translation of God into neighbor love. But the problem is substantive, not rhetorical. It lies in Vattimo's implication that this schema cannot be worked out in a Jewish context, which I think is a mistake. He is a critic of the transcendence of God in Levinas, but he does not observe that in Levinas, every time we attempt to direct our glance to God on high it is "deflect-ed" by God to the face of the neighbor here below. The pragmatic meaning of the transcendence of the *tout autre* in Levinas is service to the neighbor. Levinas's Jewish deflection does the work of Vattimo's Christian kenosis. The very transcendence of God as *tout autre* of which Vattimo complains is *transcribed* into neighborly love: it is precisely because the face of God is transcendent that the only form in which you will ever find the face of God is in the face of the neighbor, which is where you should direct all your attention. Indeed, given that Jesus was a Jew attempting to renew Judaism and with no intention of starting a new religion, that is almost certainly what was behind Jesus's own sayings about neighbor love. But if Vattimo's privileging of Christianity poses a problems for Jews, it does so a fortiori for Islam, where the question of a simmering religious war is even more acute. For the Arab nations the hyphen in *Judeo-Christian* is the name of an ominous political alliance between the state of Israel and the United States. At that point, Vattimo's talk of "Christianity" as the bearer of world hospitality becomes still more questionable—even as it takes a great deal of crust and nose holding to use the words *United States* as the emblem of international hospitality, when it is in fact the emblem of the wasteful overconsumption of the world's resources and the hegemonic exercise of national sovereignty.

This bring us back to the problem that I pointed out above with the death of God theologies—and there is a deep family resemblance between Vattimo's secularization thesis and the death of God theologies. For, however radical they may be, these are theologies with a *Christian* pedigree that turn on the doctrines of the Trinity and the Incarnation. They tend toward a schema that inevitably casts Judaism in a bad light and hence restages what Derrida calls the "duel between Christian and Jew."[37] From Joachim of Fiora through Hegel, Schelling, and Feuerbach up to the contemporary death of God thinkers, these theologies always plot the transition from transcendence to immanence, from alienation and estrangement to homecoming, from God as a distant and severe Father to God first as Son and sibling and then as the spirit of love. Somebody has to play the bad guy ("the religion of the Father") in this story, and that is inevitably Judaism.[38] The death of God is a *grand récit* all its own that is complicitous with Hegel's story about the Jews and a certain quick reading of Saint Paul on the Jews. That is a supersessionist story of the transition from the alienated Old Law of the Pharisees to the benign New Law of love and the gift, from the dead letter of literalism to the living Spirit, from the legalism of slaves to the religion of the children and friends of God, from an eye-for-an-eye economy to the gift, etc. The hint of Marcion is never far from this story, however much it is resisted and revised.

To be reminded of the violence implicit in this schema one need only read Hegel's *Spirit of Christianity*, which manages to say the most hateful things about Jews in the course of defining Christianity as the religion of love. Hegel's metaphysics of the alienated Jews is as much a metaphysics of hate as a metaphysics of love, and it is upon this metaphysics of love/hate that Derrida descends in *Glas*. That is why, rather than serving as its "hermeneutics," deconstruction does well to keep a safe distance from the death of God theologies. Deconstruction is something more of a Jewish science, that is, a deconstruction of idols that, while affirming flesh and the body—the Jewish Scriptures are all about land and children—is constantly worried about divine incarnations, because incarnations are always *local* occurrences. Deconstruction would always worry about a divine kenosis that resulted in filling up someone's pocket with the transferred goods of divinity. Because the death of God takes place in a particular time and place, in a particular people and language, it raises the problem of privileged theological access and pits those among whom God has pitched his tent against their Jewish predecessors. Jewish alienation is overcome by a kenotic process conceived as a zero-sum economy that empties out the Jewish account and transfers its funds to Christian holdings. So difficult is it for this schema to stay clear of this implication of supersessionism that it even shows up in completely secular, atheistic neo-Marxists like Žižek and Badiou when they start singing the praises of love and grace in Saint Paul over the Law, which is death.

Vattimo criticizes what he variously calls existential, tragic, or apocalyptic Christianity. In this version of Christianity, he says, secular history is devalued as senseless and violent and is seen to require an in-breaking revelation from God as *tout autre* to redeem it. Such a view of Christianity is inspired by the "Old Testament faith" or a "theology of the first age"[39] and "undervalues" Christ's incarnation; it goes hand in hand with a "Judaic religiosity" that is "affirmed at the expense of any recognition of novelty in the Christian event."[40] The very idea of God as "wholly other," which has played a leading role in the renewed philosophical interest in religion that has come about because of Levinas and Derrida, he says, is an alienated one, estranged from the genuine sense of kenosis according to which God, instead of maintaining his holiness or separation from the world, empties himself into the world. I do agree with Vattimo's aim of disarming the metaphysics of apocalypticism, the dualism of two worlds, one immanent, lost, and secular, the other in-breaking, salvific, holy, and wholly other. Like him, like all death of God theology generally, I do affirm the one and only world we know, the one that Elohim declared good five times, then adding, for good measure, "very good." But I want to preserve the salvific effects of distance, of the shock or trauma of an "unconditional claim" that disrupts the human-all-too-human course of the "world." I want to preserve not the metaphysics of apocalypticism but the ethicoreligious sense or schema of the event. For the event is not what happens but what is going on *in* what happens that makes it restless with the future. Thus instead of opposing two worlds, or of opposing God and the world as if these were two realms of being, I distinguish between the world and the event by which the world is disturbed, the unconditional claim that solicits the world from within, that interrupts and summons it, which is what I think deconstruction is (if it *is*). I do not distinguish two different worlds but two different logics, the logic of the mundane constituted economies and the logic of the event that disturbs them, and I see in Jesus of Nazareth an exemplary embodiment of the logic or paralogic of the gift, who told paradoxical parables about and who was himself a parable of the kingdom of God, which he opposed to the economy of the "world." The event that transpired in Jesus knocked Paul from his horse and delivered a shock to the world. And if I do not pit a supersensible world against a sensible one, neither do I pit Jesus against Judaism. On the contrary, on this point Jesus could not be more Jewish; he does everything he does in the name not of Judaism's supersession but a renewal of the living doctrine (*Torah*) of neighbor love, which is also found in Levinas's notion of deflection and still more inclusively in Derrida's *tout autre est tout autre*.

That is why I cast the theology of the event in terms of a structural analysis of the distinction between the name and the event, or the thing and the event, or between the pure messianic and the concrete messianisms. I do not cast my views in terms of the death of God, or even in terms of the secularization thesis, and I keep a safe distance from the historical periodization in which these theologies are caught up. I object to them on two grounds. First of all, I do not see how it is possible to decontaminate these schemata from supersessionist theories that cast Judaism as a religion of the father and hence as theater of alienation and cruelty, even if one's personal intentions are certainly not antisemitic.[41] Second, they tend to become grand narratives, overarching a priori histories that are selling us another metaphysical bill of goods under the name of demythologization. That is why they suffer embarrassment and consternation under the hand of the empirical facts, of the course that history actually takes. The suggestion that traditional orthodox faith in God is somehow on the wane in the United States, which hit the streets in the 1960s as both a sociological and theological thesis, could only be made today by someone who has been in deep coma for the last quarter of a century. I dare say that faith in the supernatural, angels, a six-thousand-year-old world fashioned in six days, and a human race descended from two parentless and naked people in a garden somewhere in ancient Mesopotamia who were tricked by a snake into eating a piece of forbidden fruit has never been as lively as it is today.

Spectral Hermeneutics

My own version of weak theology is the offspring of a spectral hermeneutics, of what I have been calling for some time now radical hermeneutics, as distinct from Vattimo's, in whom I do find, I repeat, a kindred spirit. If in my weak theology everything turns on the distinction between the name and event, the hesitations I feel about Vattimo center around how "strong" the names of Christianity and the Incarnation remain in his thought, where such strength comes at the cost of the event, whose most important effect is to weaken any such names. Accordingly, I wonder if Vattimo's weak thinking is too strong and if his version of radical hermeneutics, because it has not truly eradicated this strength, is not sufficiently hauntological—and radical.

When all is said and done, my hesitation about Vattimo is that there is no counterpart in his work to what Derrida calls *khora*. This is the figure that Derrida borrows from Plato's *Timaeus*, although it is also linked by Derrida to the figure of a desert, of an archi-desert within the biblical desert, to emblematize the elemental spacing in which all our natural languages and historical institutions are inscribed. The effect of this figure in Derrida is to underline the sense of the contingency and deconstructibility—the weakness—of the names that are inscribed in this desert space and hence the deep and intractable secret in which our lives are inscribed. But *khora* is also used by Derrida affirmatively, as the quasi condition of the im/possibility of prayer, as a way to describe a scene of messianic hope in the coming of someone, of a Messiah whose figure I cannot describe and hence a scene of desert prayers and tears and of desert hospitality. Since Vattimo has no counterpart to *khora*, the figures of the Christian Incarnation and more generally of incarnation itself go unchecked. Christianity is made the privileged figure of love and hospitality, which are made out to be distinctively Christian notions, a gesture that corresponds quite directly to the idea of a final revelation in Tillich. For all of Tillich's talk of the symbolic character of our language about God, his theory—like Gadamer's and Vattimo's—is situated within a Hegelian view of history as the transcription, transmission, and translation of a more robust and holy Spirit. But, for me, events are inscribed in the weaker, more ghostly play of *différance*. Events are haunted by a paler ghost in a more hauntological hermeneutics.

In a similar way, Vattimo's hermeneutics is less a weak hermeneutics of prayers and tears for some coming figure whose lines I cannot make out and more a robust hermeneutics of the application, realization, and translation into the secular world of the already given and authoritative figure of the Christian Incarnation. In my notion of a weak theology such an authoritative figure is far too strong. In the end, Vattimo offers us a hermeneutics of "application" in the Gadamerian mode, where the hermeneutic task is a matter of the application of an authoritative figure or "classic." I am concerned that Vattimo's hermeneutics is another example of something I have worried about in the past: when hermeneutics is too closely aligned with Gadamer, it comes under the spell of Hegel and of some version of the metaphysical siren song that history is the way the absolute works itself out.[42] Does that not here take the form of the thesis that Christianity is a classic truth that needs an updated application in the postmodern or secularized order?

But should it not be the work of weak thinking to weaken the force of such metaphysical tendencies, including the metaphysical distinction between an inexhaustible classic and its current application? When weak thinking works its way into its own story, when it finds a big story in which to tell a tall tale about the passage from strong metaphysical thinking to weak, from an alienated God to an incarnate God here on earth, and from orthodox Christian dogma to the contemporary secularized truth of Christianity in the postmodern world, then weak thinking has grown a little too strong. It is guided by a too authoritative and particular figure of truth and it proceeds on the basis of too strong an idea of truth as a classic that must find its contemporary realization.

Is not a truly radical hermeneutics a little more lost in the desert, a little more *destinerrant*?

Is not a radical theology less a matter of asking how do I apply and translate this authoritative figure of the God of Christianity to the contemporary world and more a matter of asking what do I love when I love my God?—where the name of God is the name of the event that is transpiring in the name of God?

Is not a radical hermeneutics a voice of one crying in the desert, praying and weeping in the desert?

Is not a radically weak theology a theology of the desert?

II

A Prayer for Silence

Dialogue with Gianni Vattimo

To start things off, could you briefly explain how you see the philosophical significance of the death of God?

For myself, there are complementary meanings of the death of God. In terms of Nietzsche, the anthropological meaning to the death of God is most clear. It is the idea that mankind has killed God because they recognize he is no longer a necessity. God was born into human consciousness to provide some security against the dangers of natural life. In this sense Nietzsche is similar to Giambattista Vico, who describes the condition of primitive man as somebody who sought in everything and every natural event the work of a god. In many senses this is the same in Nietzsche. The origins of God, therefore, lie in the natural processes through which we pray to God in order to protect ourselves from natural forces. As such, this primitive state of consciousness must be deconstructed. In addition, because humanity started to believe in God, it also started to have rules. The rules organized a sort of rational society that became another source of our security in this world. Science and technology developed in this vein as well. And that is why at a certain point God was no longer a necessity. Nietzsche sometimes expresses this in these terms. Humanity also discovered that God was a lie. And if God had ordered them not to lie, God therefore negates himself. The idea is that in a civilized condition we no longer need such an extreme assurance, such a guarantee of our security.

This is the literal interpretation of the death of God, which I studied mainly in Nietzsche's works and in Heidegger's essay of 1943, "The Word of Nietzsche: 'God is Dead,'" and his lectures on Nietzsche published in two volumes. But the other, nonliteral, interpretation seems to me to be more convincing and not so strongly Nietzschean. I would say it this way: the death of God about which Nietzsche speaks is the death of Christ on the cross. Why? Because it is exactly after Christianity, or the event of Christianity, that it becomes possible to no longer believe in the classical, rational gods of the Greeks.

There is an important idea from Dilthey, *Einfuehrung in die Geisteswissenshaften*, that says, above all, metaphysics was killed by Christianity because Christianity turned the attention of man inward so that philosophy became subjective, more Cartesian. This, by the way, is very important for Heidegger: remember that Heidegger in *Being and Time* said that what he wanted to do was simply make more understandable and clear to the people of his time the teachings of Dilthey. That is the case even though Heidegger himself never developed a specific commentary on Dilthey.

Of course, Dilthey also asked the question why metaphysics lasted so long given the fact that Christianity began two thousand years ago. There are complementary processes that Dilthey sees between the one and the other. At the end of the Roman Empire the bishops were almost the only authorities still in existence around the ancient world. For example, Augustine was both a philosopher and a bishop. On the one hand, as a philosopher he calls the people to come back to themselves by inhabiting the mind within. On the other hand, as a bishop he had to organize a community, to take cover and protect the structures of the ancient world. This is more or less a popularized version of the idea from Dilthey—that is, the Church has the possibility to completely renew a community founded on the event of Christianity that puts an end to metaphysics. But they did not do that because they still were very strongly engaged in secular culture. So only after a lot of revolutions did Christianity realize that the core idea of Christianity was the negation of a necessarily objective rational (i.e., eternal) structure of the world. This takes time, of course, and it can occur only in a Protestant world. At any rate, the ethical Christianity under development involves the dissolution of the faith in the metaphysical structure of the world. This is historicism in many senses, which corresponds to the history of salvation and so on.

Now, when Nietzsche says that God is dead, as a matter of fact he is only developing this extreme point introduced to the world by Christianity of the historicity of history. In other words, no structure, no objective or eternal God, just as Christianity has always said. So I would say that this connection between my thought and Nietzsche and the idea of secularization, etc., is that Nietzsche realized the occurrence of the death of God that corresponds to the idea of the dissolution of metaphysics. We don't believe in the Greek metaphysical God as the rational structure of the world. This God obviously has nothing to do with the Christian God.

What is the connection between your idea of "weak thought" or the "weakening of being" with the theological image of the death of God?

I must confess that the theological movement of the death of God is not something I've studied intensely. While there are many important authors such as G. Vahanian, W. Hamilton, T.

Altizer, J. Robinson, H. Cox, and V. Buren who have escaped the natural intentions of traditional theology and who have successfully articulated a theology without God, they could never have done this work without Luther or Nietzsche, for example. Also, my use of the death of God depends very much on the history of Being as connected to the problem of ontotheology. In this more philosophical context, the theology of the death of God has a great deal of current resonance and force. It becomes part of a much larger effort that speaks not only of the death of God but also of the end of metaphysics and the end of truth. So, in answer to your question, I would say that my notion of weak thought can actually help the death of God theologies better understand their origins in Nietzsche's and Heidegger's philosophy and in the broader context of the end of metaphysics.

In After Christianity, *you write that "the end of metaphysics and the death of the moral God have liquidated the philosophical basis of atheism."[1] Why is it, according to your understanding, that the death of God does not necessarily eventuate in atheism?*

There is an Italian saying that I sometimes make reference to: "Thank God I'm an atheist." Of course, this is referring to the God of the philosophers. God can only be propped up or demonstrated by reason or rational argument for so long. Yet this effort to demonstrate the rationality of belief is still something the Catholic Church feels very strongly about. Why? Partly, it is a matter of remaining faithful to the medieval tradition. After all, it is only natural that the Church assumes that the real, true human culture was the period when the Church had the most power. So in many senses there is a sort of historical imprinting in the Church, like they would like to go back to the Middle Ages if they could. But there is also the matter of power. As long as the Church can depend on some natural, rational ethical structure, they can try to enforce this ethics not only on the believers but on everybody. The examples in Italy are many. For instance, they have tried to keep the law against divorce in Italy. In addition, more recently, under the strong leadership of Cardinal Camillo Ruini, the pope's vicar in Rome and president of the Italian bishops' conference, and with the explicit support of Pope Benedict, the Church mobilized at all levels to persuade Italians to stay away from the ballot box, with the goal of keeping turnout lower than 50 percent and thereby invalidating the referendum on medically assisted procreation. They do this not on the basis that it is an aspect of Christian law but rather that it is an aspect of natural law. Now they are arguing the same thing with regard to various facets of bioethics.

This corresponds very well to my idea of metaphysics, which I define as the violent imposition of an order that is declared objective and natural and therefore cannot be violated and is no longer an object of discussion. By the way, this is also why we can believe that Heidegger was against metaphysics for exactly the same reason. If you admit there is a first principle that can be grasped and known in a definite way, you prevent anybody from ever asking again. So, on this basis, I have developed the following theory with regard to violence. As I have explained in *Nihilism and Emancipation*,[2] violence is the fact of shutting down, silencing, breaking off the dialogue of questions and answers. This is what ultimate foundations do; they impose themselves as impervious to further questions as objects of contemplation and *amor dei intellectualis*.

When I say that, it seems as though it is exaggerated. Why? Think about war, for example,: as Pascal observed, if you kill someone on this side of the river, you are declared a hero, but on the other side you are an assassin. What about euthanasia? Once more, the reason the Church doesn't want to speak about this is because they believe there is an objective violence in killing. Yes, but what about God? If there is an objective violence to killing somebody, then it would follow that God is the biggest murderer of all. Violence, then, is the fact of no longer permitting the other to ask questions. Now, the Church, on one side, pretends that they very much respect human nature, human reason, and things like that, but, on the other side, the very core of this is that they want to impose their view of the natural essence of man, reason, etc., which involves a certain authoritarian posture.

Building on this comment you made about violence being the fact of shutting down, silencing, or breaking off the dialogue, this violent imposition of power is quite apparent throughout the city of Rome. Being here in Rome, one cannot help but notice the contrast between the ruins of imperial Rome and the Church triumphant. This cityscape seems to me to be an apt visual for your idea about the dissolution of metaphysics.

Yes, we grew up with the idea that the magnificence of the Church continues without any interruption from the history of the Roman times. In many senses, this idea is more natural for us than for you Americans. But, of course, somebody might also wonder about the signs indicating that the Church is no longer so alive. Even when the Church insists on doctrinal conformity and engages in various inquisitions—this reveals a certain confessional weakness because it promotes in a conceptual way the idea of the Church as an army. An army regiments your sexual life, for instance, enforcing rigid conformity and discipline. In many senses, the insistence of the Catholic Church on these points is a way of training an army that is supposed to be ready for a new war, a new world. Otherwise it makes no sense to insist so much on their position on prophylactics. When I try to understand why Pope John Paul II was so strongly engaged in reproduction politics, I wonder whether he was afraid of social change, such as the reduction of the birthrate or the influx of immigration of other religions. Does the Pope wish to increase the number of immigrants who are notoriously more prolific? It seems to me that the most reactionary part of the Catholic Church can count upon the development of the third world churches. These churches are much worse than ours from a theological view. For one, many are part of minority communities, so they are strongly communitarian, going back to primitive Christianity. They are also dogmatic; they believe in wonders, etc. If that is the case, then we secular Europeans are faced with some very difficult days ahead.

I want to talk about that a bit, specifically about the future of the Church, because your book with Jacques Derrida, On Religion, *is credited by many with bringing the return of religion to the attention of philosophers. But when we talk about the return of religion—at least in your work—we are also talking about the process of secularization. So can you explain the connection between the return of religion, which is often violent and as you say in the third world often primitive, with the simultaneous process of secularization, which is associated with modernity and the West?*

The connection has many meanings in my mind. In one sense, it is exactly because of the loss of a unified religious authority that there is a sort of rebirth of religiosity. Real religiosity relies on secularization because religion is no longer single or uniform and there is no longer a central religious authority. On the other hand, secularization and the new religiosity are also related by a sort of therapeutic connection because if I am ready to accept literally the return of religion in Italy, I would say that this religiosity tends again to be a sort of resecularized religiosity—that is, a religiosity that lives only as a consequence of secularization. For example, Pope John Paul II made great use of the media, his message was communicated via television, and, as his death

showed so well, he was a legitimate global media star. There is a
sort of false universalism promoted by the media, which is very
contradictory. People are more interested in the religious show
than they are in religious engagement.

One of my favorite examples of this comes from the Roman
Catholic Church's celebration of the Year of the Jubilee in 2000.
Many young people came to Rome to see and hear from the
pope. This was perceived by many as an example of the rise in
religiosity among today's youth. But, after they had left and when
it came time to clean up the area where the youth had spent the
night, they found three hundred thousand condoms.

The number I heard was actually twenty thousand.

No, there were more. Of course, there is difficulty in the
counting. Maybe many were thrown away out of respect for the
pope. [*Laughter*] The point is that there are many contradictions.
The threat is that, with the means of the mythologies created by
television, we reconstruct a sort of primitive religiosity, a form
of superstition—a religious show in contrast to devotion. Now
with the new pope we seem to have a new situation, although it's
too soon to come to any conclusions. Benedict XVI seems, for
the moment, to be more interested in philosophical questions
such as "relativism" rather than prophylactics. I think this is a
good thing because he is leaving people freer to live their faith
without restrictions. Now it is quite possible that this is a decision the Vatican has taken in order to begin to attract all those
people who left the Church because of the dogmatic preaching
of Pope John Paul II. And although I still haven't heard about
the number of condoms left after World Youth Day in Cologne,
I did read about a controversy that arose over plans for police
to distribute condoms at World Youth Day. The church tried
to halt plans to distribute them, according to the spokeswoman

of the German police unions (the union commonly distributes them at large public gatherings to protect the public).

I met Ratzinger in Paris at the Sorbonne many years ago for a debate and I must confess he is distinguished as a theologian. But, then again, let's see what will happen now that he is inside the metaphysical structure of the Church. Not much has changed as of yet. What I would like from Benedict XVI is silence! I would like a pope who talked less, because Wojtyla talked about everything everywhere. People want to hear the pope preach about the gospels, not about the "right" or "natural" constitution of the family. This is also the thesis I put forward with Richard Rorty and Santiago Zabala in *The Future of Religion*. In that book we tried to "save the church from itself" by demonstrating that the future of religion depends on the future of the Church.

In this sense philosophy is important for secularization. It is important because it helps again and again to repeat new possibilities for religion, which depend exactly on secularization. For instance, it is precisely because the God of Greek philosophy is dead that it is possible to listen to the Bible again. There are no longer strong, rational reasons for being an atheist. This is a consequence of secularization, not the consequence of desecularization. This is also very important philosophically. I would say that religion can have a religious meaning only with the help of philosophy—that is, with the help of a theory of secularization that recognizes in many traits of the modern world the basic features of Christianity. When we think of the Enlightenment period, we could say that Voltaire was more religious than the Jesuits were religious because the Jesuits were becoming the guardians of the traditional order of society, while Voltaire was leading the case for the society of man. In many senses, then, what seemed to be "less Christian" was actually "more Christian."

So you would disagree with those who say that we are living in a post-secular or desecularized world; or those who say that the return of religion disproves the secularization thesis, that the secularization thesis was yesterday's incorrect vision of the future?

I don't know what a desecularized world would be. As for the postsecular, it is a definition that takes into account the mass phenomenon of religiosity, like the great attention for the pope. But these are not so characteristic, because if Pope John Paul II, who died in Rome some months ago, had not been such a pop star, promoted so strongly by TV, then things would have been very different. After all, many people watch TV, but not so many attend church. If you go to a church in Italy on Sunday morning, you don't see an enormous crowd.

So, yes, I would say there is a sort of religious content in the humanitarian interests we have, but that, again, is negated by the media. After all, does the media portray the poor children in Rwanda on a daily basis? In many senses, this widespread interest in religion is the positive meaning of secularization. It has infused Christianity with a sense of trying to accept the problems of the world, but this is an ambiguous problem. I believe that the truth of Christianity is not the pope but democratic society. The consequences of Christianity are the modernization of society, less violent relationships within society, and so on. And the problem is that this is precisely what the Church tends to deny. This is real secularization, a sort of desacralization of the Christian message in the sense of ethics, less violent politics, shared power, and so on. On the other hand, this is still ambiguous because if real Christianity is revealed in modern democracy, then what about the Church's teachings on things such as eternal life, life after death, the authority of the Church, etc.? I would say that real Christianity is the secularized theory that belongs to charity. On the other hand, I would say that there is a sort of discord that is preserved.

In the end, what is Christianity? Is it the belief that God is one in three persons? Take the credo in the mass: If I stopped at each proposition from the confession, there is not even one article I could literally believe. For instance, Jesus is sitting at the right hand of the father. Why the right? Why the father and not the mother? There are so many literalisms that are passing away. But, on the other hand, I still believe that the power and truth of Christianity is the event of an intervention of God in history. This need not be tied to the historical existence of Jesus. What I believe in is the Christ of the gospels. I still believe in the mystery of creation. Not the creationism that is taught in the schools of the American South. Rather, I am interested in a theologian like Pierre Teilhard de Chardin, who is friendlier to evolutionism and also to the idea that God need not be omnipotent now, though he may be omnipotent at the end.

This sounds reminiscent of Rudolf Bultmann, as well, who famously declared that even if we were to find the bones of Jesus, that would in no way change the truth of Christianity.

Yes, of course, there is this shared concern with hermeneutics and the problem of biblical literalism. Literalism seems to me to wipe itself out or discredit itself by being beholden to an interpretation of the Bible that becomes only a sort of repository for stories of the type of *The Da Vinci Code*, for instance. If you take the Bible literally, then you find a lot of sources for conspiracies. Even the story of Job—this is a story of an absolute God who makes a bet with Satan. OK. But, along the way, people are killed. For what? Just for a bet against the devil. All that—whether the conspiracy theories or the co-opting of science by theology—is a product, or, better, the trash or refuse of the literal interpretation of the Bible.

Staying with this ambiguity some, I want to ask a more critical question—specifically about how you employ Christianity with regard to such things as democracy, secularization, modernization, and so on. You have written that modernity is "unthinkable" apart from the Christian heritage and, further, that the task of secularization is not only the message of the New Testament but also constitutes the very destiny of the West. Finally, you have said that it is not possible to have a non-Christian philosophy. My question is how this privileging of the Christian heritage does not lead us back to the very form of religious triumphalism you are trying to avoid.

Once again I would say that the problem of Christian triumphalism is based on a sort of literal reading of the Bible. I see modernity as a dissolution of the sacred distance between God and the world. So if I understand modernity in these terms, then I understand that I cannot think of modernity without this origin or basis in Christian incarnationalism. But also, as I mentioned before, I can also make the confession "Thank God I'm an atheist." Only because of the event of Christianity can we be modern and no longer believe in a sacrificial God, as René Girard has said, or in a literal God. This is the path described by Joachim of Fiore—who, by the way, I have a great difficulty understanding—when he speaks of the age of the spirit. My view of the future of religion and of Christianity is based exactly on his idea of the intense spiritualization of the Holy Scriptures, which means no longer taking even the primacy of the pope literally. This relativization or spiritualization of religious authority can be seen in the dispute that exists among biblical scholars about which is the first of the gospels. Most scholars say Mark, but the Church prefers to say it was Matthew because that is where the statement about Peter being the rock upon which Christ will build the Church is found. So it is a matter of what I prefer the Church to be.

Getting back to this question about the Christian meaning of secularization and Christianity having a meaning today only through secularization, it raises the critical issue about the role of the Church in today's world. What do we do with the Church? My answer is that we have to invent another meaning of the teaching of the Church, one that does not rest on the Church's efforts at concentrating power in the Vatican. What I would say is that if the Church believes that it is best to go on concentrating its authority and insisting on certain literal readings of the Bible, how long can it last? This is not simply a hermeneutical or philosophical problem, it is practical as well. Take, for example, the question of women priests. We don't have many priests as it is, so if a woman wants to become a priest, then OK. Same with the issue of condoms, as we've already discussed. These are all things that John Cornwell explained very well in his book, *Breaking Faith: The Pope, the People, and the Fate of Catholicism*. Of course, this touches on the matter of the authority of the Church itself. If the Church still preaches something that appears to be lacking in credibility, that is utterly absent in meaning, then the only way would be for the Church to gradually ease its doctrine bit by bit. Imagine if I were pope and tomorrow announced that everything was permissible—obviously that would spell the Church's destruction. But, at the same time, in order to be preserved, the Church has to change.

Following your interpretation, then, couldn't one just as easily talk about the idea that there can be no philosophy without its Islamic transmission through the Middle Ages? Or, as your friend Umberto Eco writes in his wonderfully imaginative novels, he is always picking up these alternative strands within the historic tradition to somehow question or unbalance the dominant or prevailing tradition. My question is whether you might be caught in a contradiction, since it is not only that there can be no philosophy apart from Christianity, because, first of all, Christianity itself is not a single or uniform tradition and, second of all, regardless of how Christian is the character of the Western philosophical tradition, it might very well have been lost or forgotten without the benefit of Islam.

Yes, I understand, and I admit that maybe it was expressed a little too strongly. Let me say first that philosophy is a European product. This includes Greek, Jewish, and Islamic contributions, to be sure. But, at the same time, I do not want to reduce the Islamic tradition to a strictly instrumental role. Perhaps what I should say instead is that we could not have had philosophy and modern science without the Bible, without this relation to the book, which doesn't mean any essential privilege for this tradition. There is no modern philosophy today that exists without any possible reference to the Bible or, more specifically, that is not born out of the struggles surrounding the meaning of the Bible. I'm thinking here of Martin Luther and his struggles with the Church authorities over the right of interpretation. So that when I say I believe in God, what I mean is that, without the Bible, I couldn't think about myself. The terminology I use is inextricably beholden to the Bible.

That does not mean that this is the only way for religion. I would say that the event of Christianity does not deny mythologies, but has, in effect, authorized the different mythologies and religious traditions. Because if God has become a man, he could also have become a sacred cat or a sacred cow. So there is another way of seeing the incarnation. Incarnation is an event that doesn't say that everything that came before is false or that any other mythology is false, only that we have another relation to this tradition.

This is my favorite example to explain this point. Imagine that, after the pope has had a meeting with the Dalai Lama, afterward he goes to his private chapel and prays for this poor man who is damned because he is not converted. What kind of fantasy this would be! Most probably the pope and the Dalai Lama agree on many things. They exchange spiritual experiences. And that is what should be done between religions.

*Moving then from the dialogue between religions and religious lead-
ers to the present exchange between you and John Caputo, the two of
you the leading proponents of what he calls radical hermeneutics. You
have also both become two of the leading voices defining the nature
of postmodern religiosity. His radical hermeneutics is very much tied
to Derrida's deconstructive philosophy and rests on a certain epistemic
undecidability. At the same time, Caputo is careful to distinguish this
radical hermeneutics from nihilism—for him, the one does not and
should not lead to the other. His talk of religion is also deeply influenced
by Derrida, specifically what he has identified as the affirmative religious passion that drives Derrida's work. This leads Caputo to his talk
of "religion without religion," wherein he affirms the desire for, and
love of, God, but remains critical, if not suspicious, of the historic faiths.
Finally, with regard to the nature of the postmodern condition, Caputo
has identified postmodernism with the postsecular. Could you please
comment on how you understand and would distinguish your work in
hermeneutics and postmodern religiosity from his?*

First, I would not identify myself too closely with the "radical" of his radical hermeneutics. Also, my use of hermeneutics is not so much bound to Derrida as his. It is true that the
philosophers with whom I feel most affiliated are only Derrida
and Rorty, but not because we share the same idea of hermeneutics but rather because we share the necessity to overcome metaphysics. Also, and this must be the greatest difference between
Caputo and myself, regarding nihilism: I would say not only
that hermeneutics leads to nihilism, but nihilism appears only
thanks to the work of hermeneutics. This is the meaning of my
book *Nihilism and Emancipation*, where hermeneutics corresponds
politically to democracy, but only as long as they recognize their
nihilistic vocation. I think that Caputo would not agree that in
order to overcome metaphysics we would need to recognize the
nihilistic vocation of hermeneutics. This is all explained in my
Beyond Interpretation.

Changing directions a bit, I want to ask you about your impressions of faith and politics in the context of the United States. Two questions about this: First, to what extent do you see today's global political conflict driven by religious interests? I'm thinking here about what you would say about the notion of the so-called clash of civilizations, specifically, the role religion might play in this conflict. Second, much attention has been paid to President Bush's faith and the integral role the evangelical right played in his reelection campaign in 2004. My question here is to what extent do you think this apparent politicization of religion should be an item of concern or alarm.

For the first question, with this situation it becomes clearer and clearer that Marx was right about the ideological function of religion. The notion of the clash of civilizations was developed under the influence of general political ideology. It is true that even under Saddam Hussein there were clashes of religious groups within Iraq. Of course, this was aggravated by the fact that the West had created the conditions for the boundaries of the state. Iraq was a state in which people of different ethnic origins and religious traditions were put together only in order to create unstable conditions, thus necessitating the intervention of the West. But also, again paradoxically, the apparent clash of civilizations is powered by the proliferation of the media as we see when Al Qaeda uses Al Jazeera for communicating its message. There is a mixture between modern technology and real or pretended religious belongings.

Abdelwahab Meddeb wrote an insightful book on the relation between modern technology and religious fundamentalism, *The Malady of Islam*, in which he starts by explaining that if fanaticism was the sickness in Catholicism and Nazism was the sickness in Germany, then surely fundamentalism is the sickness in Islam. Meddeb believes that if the politicians who govern our world had intervened to save the Buddhas from the destruction of the colossi of Bamiyan on March 9, 2001 (the Taliban did announce they were going to destroy them a few days earlier), New York would have escaped the loss of its twin towers: they are after all two acts of destructions that belong to one single tragedy. Through his erudite and historical analysis Meddeb shows how the rise of fundamentalism has its roots in European colonization and American neocolonial domination of the Islamic world. Until the baroque and classical periods, Islamic civilization kept pace with European cultures and their developments in science and art. This progress was suddenly disrupted because of the progressive loss of international commerce. Islam had established its greatness at the very moment when Europe had fallen into lethargy (from the eighth to the eleventh century). One of the effects of the Crusades—which lasted two centuries, from 1099 to 1270—was the reestablishment of the dynamism of the Italian city-states (Genoa, Pisa, Venice), which broke the Islamic monopoly on Mediterranean commerce. This is also why, for example, in the Middle Ages we had the Crusades. The Crusades were clearly preached in religious terms and encouraged by religious authorities, but they were also about the redistribution of power and the conquering of new markets. The Italian Middle Ages were developed precisely by these means. The primitive bourgeoisie were those who reaped the advantages from these expanded markets and travels.

So I would say beware of discounting a Marxian analysis too quickly. After all, concerning Bush's war in Iraq, Marx is absolutely right. It is just a matter of ideological masking. The logic is as follows—we are in this war first because we are believers. As believers, we want to expand democracy. If they will not accept our democracy, then we will bomb them. Then, at the end of the journey, there is, of course, oil. But, after all, Americans such as Noam Chomsky and Michael Moore have marvelously explained this dynamic, which has become increasingly apparent to everyone.

With that in mind, clearly there would be a great advantage to demythologizing the religious component in this struggle because many of the factors are not religious in nature but ideological. On the other hand, if there are some who still believe we are struggling in Iraq against the devil, this would be a way to educate them, to show them otherwise. It is like modernization; modernization is in many senses desacralizing. What Christianity should do in our world is to be a little more materialistic, to show that God is not involved in our struggles; rather, our struggles are about oil, domination, power, and so on.

It is also a matter of conversion. Only through conversion can people start to understand Marx. As a good Christian, I have to understand that God is not on my side in a war or somehow aligned with one side in the so-called clash of civilizations. This is exactly what a Marxist would say. If someone still believes that God is on his side in war, then he has to be demythologized. Even President Bush. But with Bush—does he believe or not? When I think that he truly believes, I imagine that his conversion was an absolute misfortune for the world. But then, this is not a question about Bush but a matter of a certain logic of the military-industrial complex instead.

Then, with regard to this second question about whether this politicization of religion should be of concern, you would say that it needs to be demythologized?

Philosophy has to be a modernity discourse, that is, a secularizing discourse. For instance, today, in France, when they say there is a struggle about the integration of Muslims into French culture, it is also a matter about the material conditions of life. This is obviously the case with many of our problems today. If a rich Saudi buys an apartment in my neighborhood, do I feel like I am in a clash of civilizations? No, because he is rich. The only thing is that it leads to an increased property value in my neighborhood. But if I have a thousand Moroccan immigrants around my home justifiably begging every morning for food and money since the Italian government doesn't do anything to help them, then I would probably become a sort of anti-Arab. Is this a matter of religion? No, it is just a matter of material conditions of existence. Even the Israeli-Palestinian struggle is like this. What I see today is that if you visit a refugee camp in the Middle East or in Africa, then you see that this is an impossible existence. These refugees have nothing to lose. If they are led to believe that their sacrifice might serve the liberation of their people, then they would do that. It is very easy to understand. But one can only understand this if the media would show us these camps, but this, of course, never happens.

All this then is the responsibility of the chiefs of the great religions—Muslim, Jewish, Catholic, and Protestant. Religion can become a way of understanding one another instead of ex-acerbating our differences. When you think that even Catholics and Anglicans are still divided, which was just a matter of Henry VIII wanting a divorce, it is horrible. That is also why, when it comes to religion, I say that truth does not matter. It is morals, ethics, and charity that count.

Staying with this notion that religion becomes an ideological cloak hiding the actual material conditions of our lives together, I want to read to you a quote from Antonio Negri and Michael Hardt from Empire *in which they criticize postmodern discourses like your own that emphasize oscillation and plurality: "Simplifying a great deal, one could argue that postmodernist discourses appeal primarily to the winners in the process of globalization and fundamentalist discourses to the losers. In other words, the current global tendencies toward increased mobility, indeterminacy, and hybridity are experienced by some as a kind of liberation, but for others as an exacerbation of their suffering." How do you respond to this analysis of postmodernist discourse?*

This is my suspicion too. It is true that postmodernism involves this idea of mobility and hybridity—imagine the picture of a yuppie. But I am not sure that I could describe what the poor in this situation would actually desire. Negri, like many post-Marxist-Leninists, believes that he represents these people. But, after all, he is a yuppie. He knows personally all the members of the establishment. As a matter of fact, this is a mistake that many revolutionaries make. The mistake they make is that they always believe that they represent the people without a voice. It is like the Church pretending to represent the rights of the embryo.

But, to answer the question, I realize that the problem of postmodernism is a sort of a privileged position. But the university education in past centuries was a privileged position as well. This was not a reason to reject the efforts to provide a university education for everybody. Now it is possible that in the postmodern world this problem is compounded by its easing of communications, making populism more and more attractive as the ambiguous identification with the rich by the poor. After all, many poor people in Italy voted for Berlusconi. But, again, I have to ask the poor. If the poor voted for Berlusconi, how can I decide that I speak in their real interests? I do try to persuade them not to vote for Berlusconi, but surely not by saying that I know their real interests.

Finally, then, I would say that this is an indication of the ideological rigidity of Tony Negri. Regarding Hardt and Negri's entire project, I have the same objection Noam Chomsky had of it—namely, why did they need to say in a complicated way what you can say in an easier way? I have the feeling that not only do they not represent the so-called multitude but neither do they want to be understood by them if they make their book so complicated. This is an old game that intellectuals play to gain prestige and power. In contrast to this approach, Santiago Zabala and I are currently at work on a book on politics, to be

entitled *From Within*, in which we hope to show how socialism is what you get when one starts to criticize the inequalities
of capitalism. In the meantime, I would recommend Richard
Rorty's *Achieving Our Country: Leftist Thought in Twentieth-Century America* as the best instrument for progressives in America
who are interested in changing the direction of their country.
This is a book that can promote serious democratic initiatives
instead of Negri's intellectual discussions on metaphysical es-
sences such as "empire" or "multitude" that are quite useless for
political activism.

As Zabala describes in his introduction to your philosophy in Weakening Philosophy, *the origins of your concern with "weak ontology" and
"weak thought" was your effort to speak to the new democratic left and
your concern with how many young, radical, revolutionary Leninists
on the left were still beholden to strong metaphysical assumptions. In
this way your political philosophy has always been concerned with the
connection between violence and metaphysics and, further, the permanent potential of terrorism. How, if at all, has your thinking on these
matters changed or developed through the years?*

Yes, what Zabala explained in the introduction is a very important factor in explaining the meaning and origin of weak
thought. With my teacher, Luigi Pareyson, the most important
philosopher since Croce in Italy, we were always telling each
other that we were much more revolutionary than the student
revolution of '68. That is because we were reading Heidegger,
hence reading a philosopher who tried to overcome objective
metaphysics, which so often gives rise to violence. Weak thought
became not only a response to the violence of terrorism but also
an unveiling—to the extent that I was even threatened by many
of the revolutionaries. Of course, today the situation is a little
different, but I do still believe that weak thought is the best response we can give to violence and discrimination.

In my conversation with John Caputo, he discusses the promise of a democracy to come. Caputo states that the promise of democracy is that it is self-correcting or auto-deconstructing. And, when talking about the democracy to come, he borrows from a comment first made by Derrida, in which Derrida stated, "Maybe in the expression 'the democracy to come' the 'to come' is more important than the 'democracy.'" One reason for this is that there are no "existing democracies" but only the "dream" of democracy. How would you respond to this statement that Caputo draws from Derrida? Specifically, do you think this futural, almost messianic tone is appropriate for political philosophy, and does it provide an adequate philosophical base for political activism?

This is a difficult question because I cannot understand why Caputo put more emphasis on the "to come" rather than "democracy." Perhaps it is because of his Heideggerian background, indicating the fact that he remains very much conditioned by him.

But there is also a sense in which I agree with the emphasis put on the "to come"—namely, the fact that democracy seem to me a permanent future more than a constitutional status. This is visible above all if we consider the existing democracies or so-called democracies. The frequently repeated question about whether or not democracy will prohibit antidemocratic parties—thus contradicting itself—shows that it can never be considered a given reality. It is always a program, a value. I feel in democracy an accent of Heideggerian "projectuality," and it seems to me that the current crisis of democratic societies depends on the fact that citizens don't accept this projectuality. We can never think that democracy is actual; hence the many implications for political participation. What Roberto Mangabeira Unger has called a "high potential democracy" looks far more similar to what had been planned to be the soviets—the popular counsels that had to determine the political decisions (and existed only for a while at the beginning of the Russian revolution), than to our formal electoral democracies (which are, by the way, full of corruption and strongly dependent on big money).

But, getting back to Derrida's expression, I think both expressions must be read together, and neither of the two should be emphasized more than the other because they could fall into metaphysics too easily. If we only talk about the future, then we may never accomplish what we want and, on the other hand, if we only describe how democracy should be, then we might forget that it is something constituted in such a way as to be modified through time. In *Nihilism and Emancipation* I give a complete account of what I understand by democracy in chapters 7 and 8.

Final question. Returning to Negri and Hardt, and adding Giorgio Agamben to the discussion, they have expressed grave concerns for the future of democracy. Hardt and Negri's Multitude *begins with a critical analysis of the permanent state of war that has become a standard feature of the current international order as dominated by the United States. Similarly, Agamben has written extensively about the "state of exception" that threatens to transform democracies into totalitarian states. Speaking from your dual expertise as a philosopher combined with your experience as an actual politician as a former member of the European Parliament, do you agree that this state of exception has become the new working paradigm of government? If so, then what can be done?*

If I believed that this had become the paradigm, then the simple answer to the last question would be that there is nothing that can be done. On the basis of my experience in the European Parliament, I feel very strongly that the logic of war is becoming the logic of everyday life. We speak more and more explicitly in war terms. It is also the game of power. For example, while I would not say that Bush provoked 9/11, surely he has exploited it very, very well, to the point that books such as *Before and*

After by Phyllis Bennis or documentaries such as *Loose Change* by Dylan Avery make us all wonder if such exploitation has any limits. The repercussions of this become tragically evident when his government proved too slow in responding to Hurricane Katrina, which utterly devastated the city of New Orleans, exposing the finite resources the government has in hand and the fragile balance of a society still haunted by its legacy of racism. Many criticized Bush for responding too late and devoting so much of the nation's resources to the war of choice in Iraq when his own country remains in such grave need.

But, returning to Negri and Agamben, my problem, as I suggested earlier, is that they are both guilty of too much ideological rigidity. By interpreting the state of exception in absolute terms, everything fits together quite reasonably. The only possibility for democracy in our current situation is to exploit the holes, the margins, which was, by the way, the idea in the 1970s behind something Tony Negri called *autonomie*, the effort to construe or build autonomous communities—not try to take the power, but try to construe peripheral powers. If people around the world protest the war in Iraq, for example, it doesn't mean taking control of Windsor Palace or the White House, but, nevertheless, it eases and slows down the wheels of power.

At the beginning of the nineteenth and twentieth century, philosophy was very suspicious of technology. This has changed. The only possibility today is not to categorically reject the machinery of power but to slow down the process of the reproduction of capital. How can this be done? There are the hackers and the saboteurs, of course. But imagine, for instance, how Italians could ruin Berlusconi if we all decided to boycott any merchant who advertised on his many television stations. But we don't do it. Why? Because we are not yet so poor, so angry. But when that comes, we cannot oppose the logic of power with weapons because they would kill us. But we can try to extend the replication of autonomous centers. I believe in that. After all, there is nothing better to believe in. Isn't this the very idea of the multitude? Having many communities working—not necessarily together in the sense of a coordinated effort—but simply working against.

That is why I sometimes call myself an anarchist. I have proposed in the conclusion to one of my recent papers that we take seriously the idea from a book by Reiner Schürmann on Heidegger (*On Being and Acting: From Principles to Anarchy*). Schürmann emphasized how Heidegger had preached the end of the epoch dominated by an arché, by the principle, so that we now live in an anarchic age. But now I would say we have to interpret this a little more literally. We have to be outside. This is a postmodern idea. The idea is that I must subtract myself from the game of power. For instance, it was important for me to no longer be elected as a member of parliament. I discovered I could do something without too many engagements vis-à-vis a party. I discovered that when you get into power, it is not because you have conquered the power, but because the power has conquered you.

The Power of the Powerless
Dialogue with John D. Caputo

Let's begin with a biographical question. Tracing a genealogy of your thought through your published writings, one could say that you have come full circle as a philosopher of religion—from your early interest in the mystical element in Heidegger's thought, to a radical hermeneutics of demythologization, to Derrida and your present interest in religion without religion. Could you please explain how you understand the evolution (or is it a revolution?) of your thought, and reflect on what, if any, common thread runs throughout these developing interests of yours?

The consistency is that I have always been interested in the space between philosophy and religion. In one way or another, I have always been reflecting on philosophical questions by exposing them to theological and religious resources. At the same time, and perhaps this is at bottom the same thing, I have always been interested in the question of the limits of philosophy. My first serious philosophical project, *The Mystical Element in Heidegger's Thought*, was a study of Heidegger's delimitation of philosophical rationality—or metaphysical reason, or ontotheology—by way of establishing the relationships between mysticism, which mainly meant Meister Eckhart, metaphysics, and what Heidegger calls thinking.

My interest in mysticism was stimulated by my Catholic starting point. While the mystical tradition pervades the Christian Middle Ages, it acquires a certain ascendency at the end, in the twilight of the great scholastic systems when philosophical rationality was beginning to decline. A certain skepticism emerges about metaphysics accompanied by a turn to the mystical. My interest in the mystical is rooted in the fact that it positions itself at the limits of metaphysical reason. One of the books that I cherished as an undergraduate was Jacques Maritain's *The Degrees of Knowledge*, which described a sort of ladder of ascent of the soul to God—from metaphysical reason, through faith, to mysticism. Maritain places mysticism at the peak, while faith itself remains still in the dark.

So I have always been addressing the question of the limits of philosophy by way of its exposure to religious discourse. In a certain way it has always been the same question, but in the first half of my work I tended to see the mystical, and also what Heidegger called thinking, as a kind of crowning perfection that superseded rationality. With Heidegger, the notion of the experience of thought is deeper than metaphysical reason, even as mystical union crowns what metaphysical theology seeks. But with my turn to Derrida—my real confrontation with Derrida began in the early 1980s—I began to see not so much a *crowning* but the *delimitation* of reason. At the same time, my sense of the religious became a lot less mystical and a lot more prophetic or ethicopolitical, and I became a little skeptical about the very idea of something "deeper." In deconstruction the delimitation of rationality is not made in the name of something deeper, but in the name of something other or new or novel, of an event rather than an abyss of Being. The stress is not upon nonknowing in the classical mystical sense, where that implies an even deeper, "learned" nonknowing, but rather nonknowing in the sense that we really don't know! Nonknowing is not an expression of a deeper truth;

it means that we really don't know! So, in that sense, there's a genuine continuity in these books, but there is also a real turn, and the occasion of the turn is Derrida. I blame everything on Derrida. [*Laughter*] Whenever I get in trouble, I blame Derrida.

Would you say that your skepticism is now directed at both metaphysics and mysticism?

Yes, but not in such a way as to say there's something bogus about mysticism or that we can dismiss metaphysics. My skepticism has to do with the interpretations that are given to mystical experience, including those of the mystics themselves. Clearly mystical experience is important and life transforming, but like every experience—this is what we mean by hermeneutics—it requires interpretation. Something very important is happening, but the question is what. What kinds of words do we give to what's happening? And then, in that regard, I'm a bit skeptical. We must admit that these experiences could mean many things, including even certain pathological things. So, in my more orthodox Catholic youth, I would have said that in mystical experience we are touched by . . .

Revelation?

Yes, and even beyond revelation—by God, directly, immediately, wordlessly, whereas Revelation is always given in words. Whereas now I stress that we are touched by something I know not what.

We'll return to the subject of the death of God later, but could you equate this nonknowing, this radical turn in your own thought, as a moment of the death of God?

Yes. For the death of God certainly means the dying off not only of ontotheology and of classical metaphysical theology but also of this notion of a supervening mystical unity conceived as the fulfillment or the crowning of metaphysical theology. The death of God entails the deconstruction not only of the *ousia* of classical metaphysics but also the *hyperousios* of Neoplatonic mysticism. The value of the notion of the death of God is that it gives a provocative name to an ancient and venerable tradition, the ongoing work of the critique of idols, one of which is certainly the idol of some naked prelinguistic ineffable given, which is pretty much what the *hyperousios* comes down to in classical mysticism. Mystics often claim to speak from within the heart of God, with a kind of absolute knowledge or absolute point of view. I value mysticism as an expression of our nonknowing, but my skepticism has to do with reaching this absolute point of view. One important thing we mean by the death of God is the death of the absolute center, of inhabiting an absolute point of view. That's the point of Derrida's critique of negative theology—which he calls hyperousiology—which is also why deconstruction is not negative theology.

In the face of this epistemological uncertainty, or in the wake of it, what then is the task or the point of philosophical and religious thought? What is its effect?

Well, on the one hand, serious philosophy and theology involve a work of ceaseless critique of our capacity to deceive ourselves. They remind us that everyone is on the same footing, that no one enjoys privileged access. This has a salutary ethical and political import because it shows us that we're all in this together and that nobody is hardwired up to the Secret. That produces a desirable ethical, political, and religious effect—an egalitarian effect.

But I think that philosophical and theological thinking have to be—beyond critique and uncertainty—affirmative. If all there is to thinking is critique and delimitation, skepticism and doubt, then it will not inspire us. It will simply be disruptive and negative. So I think that philosophy is always looking for a way to articulate what we love, what we desire, what drives us. That is the Augustinian side of my work, which is emblematized by what Augustine calls at the beginning of the *Confessions* the *cor inquietum*—the restless heart. We write with both hands. Radical critique and delimitation is the left hand, but the right hand is the affirmation of something that we desire with a desire beyond desire, which is the sum and substance of my argument in *Prayers and Tears*, which conceives of praying and weeping in a deeply affirmative way. Something can be affirmative—we can say yes to it, for that is what we love—without being positive. That is to say, we may lack a positive formula for what we affirm. Whenever someone erects a positive content, making our affirmation into a determinate object, that can always be deconstructed. Whatever is constructed can be deconstructed, otherwise it is a menace or an idol. But the affirmation itself is irreducible. So I would say philosophy—philosophical and theological thinking, really any kind of thinking at all—has to be driven by a radically affirmative energy, by a desire for what is undeconstructible.

Could you give us an example of the difference between this affirmative energy and something that has a positive content? What exactly is the difference?

The positive can be located as soon as the affirmation is contracted to some ontical and historically constructed form. These forms are the inescapable materials and circumstance of our lives, the things that time and place have put at our disposal. They are the things we know, the historically determinate forms in which our desires take shape. For instance, the great monotheistic religions are all ways of giving determinate positive content to our desire for God, and even more fundamentally to our desire *tout court*. The great philosophical systems or constructions of Hegel and Kant and even Heidegger do the same thing. But in my view what they say, the positive programs of both the philosophers and the theologians, must be regarded with a certain ironic distance. These are beautiful and powerful constructions, but they are, as such, deconstructible. They have positive and determinate content, having been constructed out of historical, social, political materials. But they're deconstructible. Whatever has been constructed, whatever exists, whatever is present, is deconstructible. What we affirm is the event these programs contain, which is not deconstructible. That doesn't mean that one thing is as good as another.

It seems to me that the nonknowing, the skepticism, and the irony would have a debilitating effect on anyone's affirmations or desires. Anything that I affirm is also deconstructible. Are my desires also in a sense deconstructible? I wonder what there is besides that which is deconstructible, and what to do about the potentially debilitating aspect of deconstruction?

That is why I distinguish between the construction and the event that the construction contains. I think that there is something irrepressible and irreducible, an event that is undeconstructible, a promise that animates these various deconstructible structures. Things start with the event of a promise. What we love and what we desire is the promise, what is promised. But this is also frustrating because promises are never completely delivered on and we are always being sold short. Still, we're driven or energized by something that stirs within these contingent objects of desire. Of course, you're right. I do think that the endless deconstructibility of the things we love poses a challenge. It is discouraging. But then having courage is precisely what's required in the face of what's discouraging. After all, that's what courage is.

I agree about what you say about our desires and what we love—that there's a sense in which we never get there. I understand how desire is always defeated, or always deferred, and that we never get there. But, in another sense, we at least partially get there. So, for example, if we think about a relationship with a child or with a spouse or a friend, there's a sense in which that relationship can never live up to its full promise or at least all that we might desire for that relationship. Nevertheless, it's a valuable relationship. Similarly with my relationship with God, or with religious experience, whether in church or whatever, the experience may not be everything that I'd hoped it would be. Nevertheless, there's something valuable there. So although it's fair to say that my desire isn't entirely fulfilled, still I wouldn't simply want to say that it wasn't everything that it could be. After all, it was still valuable. And there's something affirmative about that.

I think that's true. If it were not, we really would be defeated. If every value had become utterly valueless, as Nietzsche says, then we would be defeated. But the fact of the matter is that we are continually solicited and addressed and gifted with all sorts of provocations that draw us out of ourselves, that elicit these affirmations from us. They are real and we have to respond to them. It is up to us to make these promises come true. They have to be realized in the things we experience to the extent possible, otherwise we really would be defeated, but then again they never are realized, and we live in the space between what is possible and what is impossible.

The clearest example of the promise that Derrida gives is his analysis of democracy. Democracy is a promise that is so imperfectly realized that he can say there are no democrats, no democracies. What calls itself democracy is not democracy. But, on the other hand, the word *democracy* is not arbitrarily chosen. He doesn't find himself praying and weeping for a National Socialism to come or an oligarchy to come or a monarchy to come, but a democracy to come. The democracies that we do know, that presently exist, cannot be dismissed out of hand or regarded with pure cynicism, because it is precisely these political structures rather than others that contain the promise.

The link between *democracy* and the promise is that democracy is self-correcting or, as he says, "auto-deconstructing." A democracy allows for its own revision or deconstruction, its own repeatability and revisability. It builds the future into itself so that—this is the hope—it doesn't freeze over. It doesn't take itself to be the last word. Therefore, the primacy of democracy will be that it is the most promising, however badly flawed. Today democracy has become just another name for capitalism. Sometimes it's just another name for imperialism or consumerism. It's a name for everything—all the evils you can think of get practiced under democracy. But that doesn't mean that democracy is nothing. That doesn't mean that democracy is not to be preferred to its alternative, which means that it shelters the promise in a way that the alternatives do not.

That also raises the question of Heidegger. One of the things that happened in the 1980s, when I really encountered Derrida, was that I reached my limit with Heidegger and I found it necessary, as Levinas put it, to leave the climate of his philosophy. Long after the war, in the *Der Spiegel* interview he gave in 1966, Heidegger was still saying that Stalinism and fascism and democracy were all "essentially the same." I reached a point where I could not stand this "essential thinking" anymore. When it comes to politics, essential thinking is essentially stupidity. There are important differences among these structures, and if essential thinking has reached a philosophical point of view that erases those differences then so much the worse for what he calls thinking, which seems to me quite thoughtless.

But how then does Derrida or Derridean deconstruction account for its preference for democracy?

This comes back to this idea of autodeconstructibility. Democracy is a system that provides for its own correction. It proceeds from the idea that we have always to do with contingent structures, revisable unities of meaning that are essentially de-constructible. At the same time, it's driven by an aspiration. It's not merely a system of self-criticism. It's driven by an aspiration for invention and plurivocity, for diversity and difference, for singularity. Were a democracy to come—and it cannot come, that would not be possible for it to actually come—it would not be a place in which there is pure harmony or perfect "peace." It would be a place in which there would be endless and irreconcil-able differences, a profusion of differences that would be adjudi-cated without killing one another. I do not think that in decon-struction democracy means moving in unison or harmony; it's a notion aimed at maximizing difference and endless reinvention. The dream of democracy—let's say it's prayer—is the dream of a world in which we would endlessly be able to reinvent ourselves, in which there would be a profusion of difference rather than fusion or playing in harmony.

Well, we can see that that world will never come.

The very nature of living, of being alive in time and history, means that what we affirm, what we desire, will never come.

But is the point to try to make the world that we do live in as much like that world as we can?

Yes, the point would be to make the impossible possible. My only proviso in saying this is that, in a theory as radically anti-es-sentialist as this, we should not think in terms of an ideal essence that we are trying to reach asymptotically. The promise is radi-cally unforeseeable. The religious expression of this sentiment is to say that I do not know what I love when I love my God. So this word *democracy* is a placeholder, a stand-in, an anteced-ent state for something unforeseeable. We call it democracy, but I don't know what lies ahead or what it will be like. Further-more, it might turn into a monster. It might become a disaster.

It might be awful. It might be worse than what we've got now. Every promise is also a threat. Once Derrida was asked, "If you talk about the democracy to come as unforeseeable, how do you know it'll be called democracy?" He answered that in the expression "the democracy to come" the "to come" is more important than the "democracy." I think that's right. It's the "to come," which is the structure of hope and expectation, that is the very nature of the promise that requires faith and love and hope. This is why I think the whole thing has a religious dimension. Deconstruction is structured like a religion, but not of the orthodox, classical variety.

I can imagine critics saying that this all sounds very ephemeral.

Well, in an important sense that would be true. The democracy to come is a specter. It has a ghostly, spectral "hauntological" dimension that keeps us up at night. I agree with you that we're dreaming now, dreaming out loud, but I think that dreaming is important, that it is essential. Still, during the waking day, these dreams would have to be linked to most detailed analyses of concrete institutions and structures. And that's why when people dream their dreams should always be accompanied by very careful, close, and rigorous analyses. We need trained political and legal theorists who understand political structures and economics and the law and who can do concrete scientific work, but who are inspired by this dream, by this kind of understanding. I am thinking of theorists like Drucilla Cornell, who has put the dreams of Derrida to work in a concrete way in radical legal theory, or Ernesto Laclau and Chantal Mouffe, in political theory, or Peter Eisenmann, in architecture, and the list goes on. These people do real work that is acknowledged by their peers. They meet the protocols of their discipline. But they also dream these kinds of dreams. So it is true. What we're doing—what I'm doing—is a dream. But the dream is important. What I and many others have been trying to do is to bring these dreams to bear upon theological and religious analyses, to find a way to talk about the Church and theology and God. It impacts upon religion and architecture, in principle upon everything—deconstruction is not a body of doctrines but a way to think and question—but it impacts upon them all as a dream of something to come.

The idea of the democracy to come is especially interesting in light of the thinking and work of Gianni Vattimo. As you know, Vattimo has not only written a great deal about political philosophy but also, at least for time, he was an actual politician serving in the European Parliament. He has been critical of various currents in contemporary political philosophy because of either its ideological rigidity or its impracticality. In this way he has aligned himself with the neo-pragmatism of someone like Richard Rorty. How does your understanding of democracy to come and this Derridian imperative to dream compare?

I am very sympathetic with Rorty and Vattimo. Like them, I too have lost my patience with high political theory and I too look for more determinate ways to effect the democracy to come. Take the case of Badiou and Žižek. They complain about our inability to imagine anything other than capitalism, but there is no better example of this inability than these two noneconomists, Badiou and Žižek themselves, who do not offer the least realistic advice as to how to generate wealth differently, even as the whole world, including even China in its own way, has begun to adopt a market economy. They have abandoned a good deal of classical Marxism but they offer no real economic alternative to capitalism. As for myself, I would be perfectly happy if the far left politicians in the United States were able to reform the system by providing universal health care, effectively redistributing wealth more equitably with a revised IRS code, effectively restricting campaign financing, enfranchising all voters, treating migrant workers humanely, and effecting a multilateral foreign policy that would integrate American power within the international community, etc., i.e., intervene upon capitalism by means of serious and far-reaching reforms. And to do that piecemeal over twenty-five years, the way the right wing has managed to do exactly the opposite. If after doing all that Badiou and Žižek complained that some Monster called Capitalism still stalks us, I would be inclined to greet that Monster with a yawn. Their idea of a "revolution" seems to me vacuous. I think deconstruction is implemented in a series of specific interventions, in concrete circumstances, and I think that is quite consonant with what Rorty calls neo-pragmatism and with Vattimo's hermeneutics. My biggest and quite Derridean reservation regarding Rorty and Vattimo is a certain innocence in the way they put all this, which leads to a latent, or not so latent, chauvinism. Rorty is too inclined to call this program of intervention "achieving our country," by which he means realizing the ideals of the United States, which for me does not put enough distance between the existing democracy we have here and the democracy to come. Vattimo is too inclined to say that this all comes down to achieving our religion, that is, transcribing or realizing "Christianity," which is the West, which does not put enough distance between one of the concrete messianisms and the pure messianic hope. I think they both need a larger measure of the hermeneutics of suspicion, to put more distance between themselves and the United States or Christianity, to stay more on their toes about what Levinas and Derrida call the *tout autre*.

I want to stay with the political dimension of deconstruction for a minute. You once wrote of your solemn duty to "dispel the idea that Derrida is not an anarchist, a relativist, or a nihilist." It strikes me this is perhaps the greatest accomplishment of your Prayers and Tears—*that is, the compelling case you made that Derridean deconstruction is driven by an affirmative, even a religious, passion, and thus proving, once and for all, that Derrida is not a "nut." Once again, these are your words, not mine.*

Did I say "nut"? [*Laughter*]

Yes. However, as you yourself confess, in making deconstruction look respectable, there is always the danger of domestication, of making Derrida and deconstruction safe. How have you negotiated between these twin dangers of, on the one hand, what you call the "axiomatics of indignation" in which critics automatically project onto Derrida their worst fears and, on the other, what we might called the "axiomatics of piety" in which religious advocates of Derrida project onto him their most treasured and heartfelt pieties? Or, more simply, how do you speak of the affirmative nature of deconstruction without stripping it of its critical edge?

Well, after just speaking of the need for a hermeneutics of suspicion, that's a good question, especially for me, because I am more exposed to this second danger of making it "good," of becoming pious. I don't want to make deconstruction good or pious or to domesticate deconstruction. If it turns out to be good, then that would be awful. I need, we all need critics, people who get after me and keep me on my toes about the words that I love, like *love*. So, for example, as you well know, Gregg Lambert has lambasted me, as I said, about using the word *love*, which is a very pious word.[1] It is perhaps the most venerable and sentimental word in our vocabulary. And so it is very dangerous to talk about love and to describe deconstruction as love. Derrida talks like this himself, but that does not make it safe. So, when I am attacked like that, I regard that as being kept on guard about what I do. That is the danger that menaces what I do. Everything is dangerous, but this risk is what Levinas calls a beautiful risk; it's a danger that is worth risking, because it is an even bigger risk to avoid love. After I wrote the response to Gregg, I came upon a sentence of Lacan's cited by Žižek, "les non-dupes errent," those who are too smart to be duped by love outsmart themselves; those who do not want to be led astray by love are led astray. Love believes all things, but love is not deceived, which is the line from Saint Paul that Kierkegaard elaborates in *Works of Love*. That is why Derrida thought that deconstruction cannot proceed without love. So we must do exactly what you say, "negotiate" between these "twin dangers."

It also helps to consider the sort of religion—the "good" dimension—I am identifying in deconstruction. This religion is a nightmare to orthodoxy, which is very unhappy with it. That is something I experience fairly often. For some reason or another, I get invited to Christian colleges with evangelical cultures to talk about deconstruction and religion. I don't know why they do this. There are other people who are a little more up for that sort of thing than I am, but they invite me. And so I often get into a situation where I'm talking about the radical deconstructibility, the historical relativity, of Christianity, and then I get attacked and people say that this is destructive, this is awful, this is terrifying, this is a monster. Once a young woman looked me straight in the eye and said that I had been sent to her campus by the devil to test her faith. And that's good! Because then I'm being bad, and that's what I'm supposed to be. [*Laughter*] Deconstruction should be bad in order to avoid this danger you point out.

Is it important to you that deconstruction be either good or bad?

Not if that means everything is either black or white. But it is important to keep the tension alive between affirmation and critique, the possible and the impossible. I am always saying that, no matter how much it is critique, deconstruction is affirmation, that is, describing the difficult, even the impossible, conditions under which affirmation is made. In that sense it must be always be "bad," perhaps like the Michael Jackson song "Bad."' In order to avoid piety it must be scary and unnerving, and that would be good, because my constant claim is that we get the best results from facing up to the worst. In *Radical Hermeneutics* I said that by the title of this book I meant restoring life to its genuine difficulty and disarming the illusions we are always constructing. Describing in an honest way, insofar as we can be honest—if we could really be honest and explain or admit to ourselves the utter contingency and deconstructibility of the things we believe—that would be the beginning. If we could admit how bad things are, that would be the beginning of something good, of a kind of radical honesty with ourselves. That would inspire a certain compassion for one another because we would understand that we're all in the same boat, all shipwrecked. To confess the wounded, fractured condition of our lives—that is who we are! And that would be the beginning of wisdom in deconstruction, of something good. If everyone actually believed that, if everybody acted on that, there would be better political processes and better relationships. If people actually believed that they really don't know in some deep way what is true, we would have more modest and tolerant and humane institutions.

We could say that about anything. If everyone actually believed Karl Marx, the world would be a simpler place. If everyone were an evangelical Christian, the world would be a simpler place. But everyone's not going to believe the same thing.

Yes, that would be simpler, but in that case simplicity would mean uniformity.

Yeah, well, we'd believe the same things, right?

What I want everyone to believe is that there is no one thing for everyone to believe. I want everyone to acknowledge the deeply contingent and historicized character of what they believe. Then, instead of everybody believing the same thing, everybody would affirm the same right to be different. I mean something like Deleuze's univocity of being: what all things have in common is the singularity of their difference. There would be a flowering of differences, and we would all recognize that we don't know the Secret, what's true in some deep sense.

Of course, many are skeptical of such a position. There are people like Derrida—people like you—who can live comfortably with that kind of contingency. But, for a lot of people, that kind of radical contingency would be not only deeply frightening, but it might also approach what we might describe as a kind of psychosis. And I can imagine that one description of this psychosis would be schizophrenia. This sudden experience of radical contingency when everything becomes unfastened and nothing is predictable or secure.

So now we are back to negotiating between piety and scepticism. Without recommending pathological suffering and endorsing mental illness, I think that what Heidegger and Kierkegaard said about "being ready for anxiety" (*Angstbereit*) is right and liberating.

I mean, I think that's partly why your evangelical audiences respond as they do to you and to Derrida. Because they do understand what we're saying and it scares them.

I think that part of genuine mental health is to recognize a certain phenomenological psychosis, a certain nonpathological madness or instability. I often find myself struck by people who are able to live stably inside of a single worldview from beginning to end—from birth to death—and it's never broken. Maybe they've really questioned it and they've held on to it and not lost it. And then we eulogize them and we say that they're good and faithful servants. And I think, "that would be good!" I can admire that, but, as an intellectual, I cannot identify with it, and, at least for me, it represents a closed frame of mind.

The deconstruction you're speaking of . . . are you saying it's not a choice?
  What do you mean?

You didn't choose to question your worldview. You didn't choose to grow uncomfortable in your given tradition. It's something that happened to you.
  We make choices that get ourselves into this situation. Choosing to be an intellectual means that you set a course in a certain direction that is going to be risky and dangerous. You set a course that will make things questionable and it would have been more comfortable simply not to worry about those things. But intellectuals worry about everything; that's their business. They trouble themselves about presuppositions. Especially us. Especially people who are working in philosophy and religion. And there is a certain loss and there is something unnerving about it. But I think that then there's a kind of second level of joy or affirmation in which you recognize what you affirm and love, which is not finally reducible to these determinate finite structures. What I affirm survives the death of any given construction and has a more radical irreducibility.
  But I agree that one can launch an intellectual career and hold on to a determinate, inherited faith. That happens all the time. Intellectuals are committed to Christianity, albeit in a more sophisticated way than the people in the pews are committed to it. I admire that, even if I am not quite there. On this point I follow Saint Paul: If God is God, God is not partial. And if God is not partial, there can't be any advantage to having been born a Christian that God would give to Christians and that God would withhold from others born in another time and place outside the reach of Christianity. The problem of religious pluralism is constantly getting radically honest theologians into trouble with the powers that be. Roger Haight is a good example in the Catholic tradition. There is something profound and important about the

Christian tradition, but there are a lot of traditions, and there is a lot of violence in the Christian tradition to other traditions. So when I speak to young people in evangelical colleges and I say, look—suppose you were born at a different time in a different place and you'd never heard the name of Jesus, then what? That aporia seems to me inescapable. Sometimes they say to me, "God's ways are mysterious and I would be damned." And I say, well, look—think about that some more. I'm here to ask you to think about that. But that's really what they think.

And there's a certain integrity to that.
    Certainly.

Just as there is to your response to Derrida. Your response to Derrida seems inescapable to you because when you confront his writing it feels right. It describes your intellectual experience in a certain way. Whereas someone like John Searle or Noam Chomsky—when they confront Derrida's writing they don't have that same experience, right? And it's not that they're locked into an evangelical Christian worldview, it's that they're locked into . . . or, locked is the wrong word—that they're in a very different intellectual framework.
    I think we must always be in an intellectual framework, while recognizing that we are also not within it. But what you say about Derrida is also true. Deconstruction has a nicety about it, an ability to move among frameworks, that allows it to be attacked not only from the right but also from a classical liberal left standpoint that wants firm Enlightenment foundations, in which deconstruction is taken as a form of relativism. So there is a critique of Derrida that comes from the left—you see this in the *New York Review of Books*—just as there is a critique from the Christian right. He is a man of the left, certainly, and not of the right, but he is opposed to the axiomatics and the certitudes of the Enlightenment.

If that is the case, then how do you make sense of Derrida's own claim that his project is an extension of the Enlightenment?

When Derrida says that deconstruction means the right to say anything or to question anything, that democracy is deconstruction because they both mean the right to ask any question, he is saying that deconstruction is a continuation of the Enlightenment but by another means. It is a more critical continuation of the Enlightenment, one with the same aspirations for emancipation and freedom of thought and democratic freedoms. But its aim is to be enlightened about the Enlightenment and critical of its idea of pure critique and pure reason. The Enlightenment goes back to a notion of rational certitude and universality that does not hold up under the very kind of critique for which Derrida is known. If Enlightenment means the right to ask any question, then it is the right to make the Enlightenment questionable.

So you would also agree with Heidegger that the quest for metaphysics comes to an end with Nietzsche?

Like Derrida, I am suspicious of the periodization involved in talking like that. There are texts in which even Heidegger would tend to back off from that talk a little bit. Derrida doesn't think that modernity is over and now there's something that comes after it. For instance, the biannual conferences I hosted at Villanova, which Derrida headed up, were called "Religion and Postmodernism." Derrida objected to the word *postmodernism* (and he was not very comfortable with *religion* either, so it is a wonder that he showed up). He disliked the word *postmodernity* because he doesn't think that modernity is something that ended, and he thinks of himself as a modern philosopher who is continuing the Enlightenment project under the name of a *new Enlightenment*. By the same token, I don't want to dissociate myself from the Enlightenment—from its aspirations—from what is promised by the Enlightenment. The promises of the Enlightenment are the promises with which we still identify. They constitute us. Freedom from authority, from hierarchy, and from social immobility where one is condemned to some form of life because of the circumstances of birth, gender, and class—who does not want such freedom? So, whether we speak of a poststructural post-Enlightenment or an Enlightenment without Enlightenment, the idea is to find a more open-ended, questioning enlightenment. The ultimate failure of the Enlightenment I think is its reductionism, its reductionistic notions that the world is "nothing other than" Reason or "nothing other than" the progress of the Spirit or of science, etc. That shuts questioning down. That's ultimately an uncritical position because a critique launched from the point of view of an absolute principle cannot be critically sustained. So we criticize that critique; we are postcritical.

The thing that intellectuals didn't see coming is the way this opened the door to the postsecular. Modernity was secularizing, and this critique of modernity opened the door to something beyond secularist reductionism. When Nietzsche says "God is dead," he's saying that there is no center, no single, overarching principle that explains things. There's just a multiplicity of fictions or interpretations. Well, if there's no single overarching principle, that means science is also one more interpretation, and it doesn't have an exclusive right to absolute truth. But, if that's true, then nonscientific ways of thinking about the world, including religious ways, resurface. The idea of some kind of postsecular moment emerges precisely from what Nietzsche calls "the death of God" because it's the death of any version of monism or reductionism, including secularism. Nietzsche fancied himself a prophetic voice, but he didn't see that coming.

Before moving on to a fuller discussion of postmodernism, I wanted to point out one more danger with interpreting Derrida, which has to do with the nature of his work as being occasional rather than systematic.

Are you afraid that by systematizing Derrida's work—does that then turn Derrida into an academic commodity? How do you yourself caution against that?

I think everything is ambiguous and dangerous and we are always negotiating. So whenever you dispel one problem, you create some other opportunity for trouble. I like to say, look, Derrida is not crazy—he's not systematic, he's an avant-garde writer, but he's not crazy—and here's what he's saying, in a nutshell, in a coherent and accessible form. This is something he himself was very good at doing, by the way, in his spontaneous responses to questions in various roundtables; that's where I got the idea. If I do this, I've dispelled a danger—a perfidious one—but then I've created a new one, and now there are new perils and new monsters to worry about. So, whatever you do, it will be dangerous. There isn't any nondangerous answer to serious questions. It's just that some dangers threaten more destruction than others, and the one that says Derrida is irresponsible is a particularly egregious one. It undoes all the good that deconstruction does for thinking because deconstruction opens things up in a way that I think is fruitful and promising, freeing and productive. So to denounce it in those terms—which is inspired in no small part by an old Anglo-American bias against continental things—is destructive. So maybe I've created another problem and maybe someone else will come along after I retire and maybe they'll make Derrida look more dangerous. Or they'll forget about Derrida and there'll be somebody else.

Let's move from Derrida to Caputo, if such a thing is possible. As you know, in his review of your Prayers and Tears, *the late Charles Winquist, following on your lead, played on the names* Jack, Jacques, *and* Jackie, *implying not only a slippage in language but also a slippage of and between identities.² And, indeed, in spite of your obvious differences, at times it is difficult to distinguish between you and Derrida or at least, when reading your work on and about Derrida, of identifying where the one ends and the other begins. So how do you make this distinction in your own mind? Where, if at all, does Derrida's thought end and yours begin?*

Jacques is a muse who inspires me and, as I said in several places, he has loosened my tongue. If you look at the first couple of books I wrote, they're absolutely cold sober, nothing whimsical about them at all. Both *The Mystical Element in Heidegger's Thought* and *Heidegger and Aquinas* were absolutely straight academic exercises. Then I began to seriously wrestle with Derrida and he freed me up to speak in my own voice. Of course, it did not hurt that I had by then been granted tenure and promoted to full professor and was feeling a little more secure. Derrida cites a line from Lacan that I like a lot, "To give a gift is to give something that you don't have." That is what Derrida did; he gave me something that he doesn't have—myself! He gave me back to myself because he enabled me to find my voice. It is interesting that this was something that did not happen when I was under the spell of Heidegger. I worked on Heidegger for twenty years, from the middle sixties when I first started graduate school to the middle eighties, and I am grateful to Heidegger for helping me break the grip of dogmatic Catholicism and leading me into the contemporary philosophical world. I have a much more historical way of looking at my Catholicism because of Heidegger. But I realized through Derrida that Heidegger was also telling another big story, a metanarrative about the beginning of the West. Then, in the middle eighties, when it also became unmistakably clear how deeply entrenched his thinking was with National Socialism, the spell was broken. Heidegger casts a spell over people, and for me the spell was broken by Derrida. People who do not like Heidegger or Derrida try to run them together, but I think they are very different. I was liberated from Heidegger by Derrida.

I do not think Derrida is just a new spell! On the contrary, I began to write in my own name in a way that I had never done before. Like the Bible-thumpers, I can name the hour when I was born again: it happened in 1984 (a fateful date!), when I was writing the last three chapters of *Radical Hermeneutics*. That is when I found my voice. I kept staring at the manuscript, realizing that the book was not over, that something was missing, when I realized that what was missing was what *I* wanted to say, and those three chapters sketched the course of all my subsequent writings. I have been writing and rewriting those three chapters ever since. They prefigure *Against Ethics* and then, well, really everything, but especially *Prayers and Tears*, which really is "a game of Jacks." Even I don't know who is who in that book. Perhaps I should say that I am inspired by Derrida, but I go where he does not go. He's not interested in religion in the same way that I am. We're really very different people. He's an Algerian Jew; I am the American grandchild of Italian Catholic immigrants. He rightly passes as an atheist; I rightly pass as a Christian. He was a world-famous intellectual, I am—well, enough of this.

I feel I instinctively know what he's getting at when I read him—that I have the same kind of impulse. But I deploy my impulses on different materials. He thinks of me as a theologian. In this book that Mark Dooley edited where Mark interviewed Derrida about *Prayers and Tears*, throughout the interview, every time he referred to me, he referred to me as an American theologian. So I go in a direction that he doesn't go and I pursue questions about Christianity that he doesn't pursue and I am more deeply implicated in the "concrete messianism" that is Christianity.

One other difference between me and him is that I don't put the same stock that he does in psychoanalysis. When I apply deconstruction to psychoanalysis, it just comes out as one more big story. I think that the idea of the unconscious is a crucial critical resource to have in your toolbox, but I don't put much stock in the details of any theory of the unconscious, which seem to me to produce fantastic unverifiable mythological clouds. I think that psychoanalysis is a deeply historically discourse, constituted by the literature that it draws upon—the figures of Greek mythology, for example—and that it is extremely dubious as an empirical science. Derrida is French and he gives psychoanalysis more credence than I do, whereas I have a more American attitude toward it. I think that it's largely what Rorty calls a "form of writing"—interesting speculation—but I put no stock in its specifics, as you can tell from the scarcity of references to it in my texts. It is read by people in comparative literature and religion departments, but rarely by people trained in natural and medical science.

I want to come back to the point of the name. When I found out that his name was Jackie, it was just this absolutely felicitous thing, like a grace. Jacques is a pseudonym. Beneath Jacques is Jackie, which is the name on his passport, the name by which he is called by his family, etc. It was very touching for me. He's a kind of very distant soul mate for me, and because of him, because of this other, I write in my own name. Although that is something you can only do in the later part of your academic career. It's not a good idea to start out writing the way I do now. You can get yourself into trouble. [*Laughter*] I could never have written *Against Ethics*, for example, if *Radical Hermeneutics* hadn't been a success and bought me some leverage. So then I thought, in the spirit of Jackie, I'm just going to let it all out. I'm just going to write what Jack is thinking.

That must have been very liberating.

Exhilarating. Incidentally, there is another figure here that we're not talking about who is also really important for me—I mean Kierkegaard. More pseudonyms.

Kierkegaard of the aesthetic literature is the model for the way that I write—which is, again, another difference between me and Derrida. Derrida is a subtle, elusive, playful, and avant-garde writer. I'm a playful writer, but not like Derrida, who is very difficult to read. I've been reading Derrida for years, but whenever I get a new text from him I always have to work through it slowly. It's always difficult. I don't write like that. I don't even try. The person who inspires me as a writer is the Kierkegaard of the pseudonymous literature. But what Kierkegaard and Derrida have in common—and what I find in both of them—is this: Kierkegaard has this deep, grave, serious, churchyard sensibility—his name means churchyard, graveyard—that is expressed in a brilliant humor. Derrida has this too, but Kierkegaard is a more accessible stylist. Kierkegaard is also the most consistent influence on me. From the time I was eighteen years old, when I first discovered him, Kierkegaard has been my hero. Unbroken. All the time I was studying Saint Thomas and, later on, Heidegger and then Derrida—at no matter what point in my life—Kierkegaard has always been my hero as a writer. What I try to cultivate, what I have learned from both Derrida and Kierkegaard, is this power of laughing through your tears, which distinguishes both from Heidegger. As Johannes Climacus says, humor serves as the incognito of the religious.

Has Derrida changed the way that you read or think about Kierkegaard?

Yes. I have consciously run them together. I will sometimes quip about something I call Danish deconstruction. I write in a space marked off by the proximity or congeniality of deconstruction and Kierkegaard. They are neighbors, siblings of a certain sort, although Kierkegaard is a Christian and religious in a way that Derrida is not. But it was Kierkegaard who helped me understand Derrida. Once, when we were together in a conference in Italy that I used to go to in the eighties, Derrida was there lecturing on undecidability. That was when I first heard him say that undecidability is not the opposite of a decision, it is the condition of possibility of a decision. When I said to him, "That's *Fear and Trembling*!" Derrida said, "Of course it is!" And that was where *Against Ethics* came from. I decided then and there to present a Derridean reconstruction of *Fear and Trembling* (just as *Radical Hermeneutics* was a kind of reconstruction of *Repetition*!). Then a funny but frightening thing happened. At the same time that *Against Ethics* appeared, Derrida published *Donner la mort*, which, of course, I would not have had a chance to read. So I read Derrida's book with a little fear and trembling that my prediction of a Derridean reading of *Fear and Trembling* would be contradicted by its actual appearance! But I think it was not. Derrida is always saying how difficult it is to make a decision, how undecidable the situation is, how you can never economize on anxiety when you make a decision, and that is what a real decision is. From a certain point of view, that's what deconstruction is, what it's about. Derrida will emphasize the mirror play of complications that beset a decision, but Derrida is telling you what *Fear and Trembling* tells you, that at a certain point deliberation must cease and you must decide.

Then I saw clearly what a bad take it was on deconstruction to view it as aestheticism, as antireligious or ethically irresponsible. Decidability means that there's a formal decision procedure for a decision, that a course of action or a decision can be formally derived, that it's formally decidable, programmable. But what interests Derrida is situations that are formally undecidable, which is what Kierkegaard is all about, too. That is also what interested Aristotle, who was the first one to really see that making ethical choices, which requires *phronesis*, is not formalizable.

Some of Derrida's more recent critics have linked this notion of undecidability with the political philosopher Carl Schmitt.

That objection is useful for bringing out something important. Schmitt's decisionism is a kind of hyperbolic version of subjectivity where the essence of the decision is subjective discharge. But Derrida will always say that decision is the decision of the other in me, the move I make in response to the other. To decide something is to respond to what is asked of me, what is addressing me from this other, this unique, singular situation which requires everything. It's a far more radically "responsible" view than a decisionistic one. A lot of "existentialist" talk is decisionistic, but, if you go back to Kierkegaard himself, you will see that he too has a notion of responding to the Other who comes over me. He saw Abraham's faith as *hineni, me voici*, which is a model for Levinas and Derrida.

On this link with Derrida and Kierkegaard, when you discuss Derrida's deconstruction as a "Jewish science," you say that Derrida has been engaged in a certain "reinvention of Judaism." Similarly, one might say that your reading of Derrida and deconstruction in conjunction with Augustine and Kierkegaard is a certain reinvention of Christianity. Do you see it that way? And, if so, would it be fair to call this a recovery of a distinctly Jewish Christianity in that case?

That is what I would like to have done, and it would be flattering for me to think that I've reinvented Christianity, or a version of Christianity—reproduced it in some new and different form that gives it new life, extends it, one that recognizes its Jewishness. To have actually done that would be a dream, and to have done so by avoiding supersessionism, by maintaining the Jewishness of Jesus, of Yeshuah, as I called him in *Against Ethics*. Of course, I have learned this from the best New Testament scholars; they see Jesus in continuity with the prophets and with the Jewish tradition of neighbor love, which he meant to reaffirm and deepen. In the interview with Richard Kearney, Derrida says that the prophets are never far away from deconstruction. I see that prophetic stream in connection with the Augustine of the *Confessions*, so that all of this flows together in the—for me—paradigmatic figure of the man of "prayers and tears," which means the desire for God, and the question of what I love when I love my God. In this sense Christianity too is a Jewish science or Jewish practice. I see deconstruction touching a nerve—a messianic-prophetic nerve—that runs from the prophets through Jesus to a prophetic Christianity.

Of course, as we said earlier on, we must avoid heaping up too much piety and making things too simple. When I say "the prophetic," as a kind of shorthand, I tend to condense into one everything that's good and just and true, Martin Luther King and Dietrich Bonhoeffer, without making note of how much violence and hierarchy there is even in the prophets. I say somewhere Amos said he wants a religion without religion, but that's not quite true. He just wants religion to clean up its act. So, I must avoid a certain tendency to present a kind of distilled, simplified picture of the prophetic and then call that Judaism and then call deconstruction Jewish and then present Christianity as extending this pristine virtue. Religion is much more violent and complicated than that.

But I would always be engaged in some kind of reinvention of biblical religion in dialogue with deconstruction. That's what I do for a living. Philosophers annoy me when they try to insulate themselves against the biblical tradition, when they are dismissive and even contemptuous of it. Even when continental philosophers speak in the name of exposing philosophy to its "other"—by the other they usually mean literature or psychoanalysis! They don't mean the Scriptures (or the natural sciences), even if you tell them that the Scriptures are literature! They don't mean that. So I want to make philosophy vulnerable to religion and I want to expose religion to the resources of philosophical critique, to occupy the space between them. At

Syracuse University I have the opportunity to work in a religion department, so I don't have to keep explaining what I'm doing all the time. People in a religion department are already interested in religion! And it's the space between religion and philosophy that actually interests me. Perhaps there is no such a thing as "religion" or "philosophy." Perhaps they're both very contingent ways we in the West have of formulating what Tillich called matters of ultimate concern or what we deconstructionists might call the affirmation of the unconditional or the affirmation of the impossible.

I guess I'll turn to the question about the theological turn of contemporary philosophy since that's where our conversation has led us. While some have been extremely critical of the so-called theological turn of phenomenology in particular, and philosophy in general, you have been on the forefront of establishing and growing this burgeoning field of continental philosophy of religion. A few questions in regard to that: First, traditionally, a distinction has been made between theology and philosophy of religion. What is the distinction? You said earlier that you objected to Derrida calling you a theologian. Why? In your mind what is the difference in being a theologian and a philosopher of religion?

What we today are calling continental philosophy of religion, this theological turn in phenomenology and deconstruction, is a turn to phenomena that are staring us in the face and has been long overdue. Up to now, it has been mostly out of modesty that I myself declined the compliment of being called a theologian, the way Johannes Climacus declined to be called a Christian. I feel like I've never gotten as far as theology. I've never had the nerve to say that what I do is theology. For one thing, there is a disciplinary matter; my training is in the philosophers—in Kant and Husserl, not in Schleiermacher and Karl Barth. I am an "amateur," a lover, of theological things. I read them as much as I can, but I don't actually have that kind of disciplinary preparation. But it also seems to me that it requires enormous boldness or audacity to say that you do theology, that you have something to say about God. That has been my attitude until recently. But then, in *The Weakness of God*, I decided to cave in—or to come out of the closet. I decided maybe I could get away with calling myself a theologian if I put it not in the form of an audacious claim but in the form of a confession. "Comment ne pas parler?" I cannot not talk about God. I cannot talk about anything else. No matter where I start, I always end up at God in some way or another. And since that is really what the word—*theology*—means, then I confess, I own up to this. I do not write about the history of religion but about God. I am—*je suis*, I am, I follow—a philosophical theologian who is feeling about for the event that stirs within biblical religion, and especially within Christian religion, seeking what is unconditional in the conditional and historical actuality of Christianity.

The meaning of postmodernism is to weaken the classical difference between theology and philosophy. The distinction between faith and reason, for example, does not finally hold up for me. I take reason to be deeply structured by faith and I take any faith that is not simply madness to be obliged to be articulate about itself and, so, rational in that sense. Virtually all of contemporary philosophy is bent on showing the way in which to understand something is to operate within a horizon of understanding that has to remain tentatively in place for you to get anything done. That horizon of understanding is something like a faith. It's a presuppositional structure that is constantly getting tested, but it has to be in place.

By the same token, the natural/supernatural distinction also comes apart. To distinguish a natural order into which is injected some supernatural influx, some supernatural empowerment of our natural faculties, is, I think, to believe in magic. It's a good thing I retired from Villanova just as I was getting so heretical!

To think clearly about religion you have to clear your head of supernaturalism and magic. That is our permanent debt to Tillich. A religious faith is a historically inherited symbolic system, a hermeneutic, a symbolic way of looking at things that has been handed down to you by a cultural and literary tradition with which you have a built-in resonance.

So, there aren't any clean distinctions that you could make between philosophy and theology that I could not deconstruct, if you give me a computer and an hour and a half. The dispute between them is a lover's quarrel. Mostly it comes down to what extent you're willing to talk about God. When your discourse keeps returning again and again to God, and you cannot be cured of this, then you think, well, this must be theology. And that may be permitted so long as it a confession, not a self-congratulation.

I'm wondering how that distinction, though, breaks down after the death of God theologies of the 1960s. As postmodern theologians such as Mark C. Taylor and Charles Winquist have suggested, after the death of God even that distinction between confessional theology and the philosophical agnosticism of philosophy gets broken down. That is, it becomes increasingly difficult even to distinguish so-called God-talk from other forms of discourse.

I agree with you that the death of God also helps us to weaken this distinction. As Taylor says, "Religion is sometimes most interesting where it is least visible." I would simply add that however important a movement the "death of God" has been in this regard and others, it has not proved to be the last word, as we see from the very "theological turn" we are discussing, which I do not think would have been predicted by the death of God movement. The discourse about God, language about God, the emerging importance of the *Confessions* of Saint Augustine in secular figures like Lyotard and Derrida, of Saint Paul for Badiou, Agamben, and Žižek, all this must be a surprise to that movement. It means that the distinctive notion of God and of God talk remains lively and important and has reasserted itself. It makes little sense to describe Derrida's *Circumfession* in terms of the death of God. When Derrida filled that ballroom in Toronto at the 2002 A.A.R. with some fifteen hundred to two thousand people, these were not people who came to hear about the death of God. The "desire for God" would be much better. Of course, our discourse about God is a historically contingent language, and—who knows?—maybe one day we won't have this language anymore. Maybe the language will transform itself into something else. But at this moment after the death of God, it seems apparent that God is making a comeback. The name of God is not dead but the language of God is very haunting, and Derrida in particular has responded to it. I don't think that we're done with it yet. I don't think that the name of God will leave us alone—not for a while. We do not know how not to talk about God. I think that God is taunting us, haunting us. It's a "hauntology," but not a matter for morticians.

I am struck by the fact that theologians have something going for them that the philosophers do not—here perhaps is a way to distinguish them! When philosophers try to name the so-called matter of ultimate concern, or the thing that is the most deeply resonant for them, they have recourse to an invented vocabulary. They'll speak of *being* or *substance* or *monad* or employ some such construct. They erect a technical vocabulary. They produce a term of art. But theologians draw upon a word that is deeply imbedded in our conscious and unconscious life, in our everyday life and in our most sublime moments, at birth and death and everything in between. The philosophers have nothing to compete with this. The name of *God* is a name that we learn at our mothers' breast, a word that's deeply embedded in our language, something that comes out in Levinas's analysis of *adieu*. It's a word that saturates our experience and, for me, for deconstruction, I think it is endlessly, open-endedly analyzable. This is the event within it that invites us, waits for us, as Deleuze says. We seem never to get to the end of this word, never to finish probing this word and its work on us, what it's done to us. In that sense, this word contains a deeper provocation than anything else, and what it means always lies before us. That, I think, is what I don't like about the notion of the death of God. Apart from the fact that it's proven to be a sort of bad prediction, the discursive structure of the idea is to treat the name of God as something that we are putting behind us. The language is too decisive, as if henceforth this word is to be shut down and safely repackaged in some accessible, mundane form. It sounds like Hegel saying that art is a form that the Absolute has put behind itself. For me, the name of God is up ahead, the name of a provocation or solicitation, and it is undecidable.

This makes sense because, for many, the phrases "death of God," "secular theology," or "religion without religion" seem nonsensical almost, until you start to read the texts that they emerged from.

Yes. I think there is something intrinsically misleading about the language of the death of God that is cleared up when you study it. But it not only has a misleading rhetoric of death, more important, I think it follows a wrongheaded logic of transcription or transfer. To avoid misunderstanding it, to save the expression, it must always be reinscribed within a more affirmative context. I do not think the expression *religion without religion* is as misleading, but it too must be understood as an affirmation of something that is open-ended, ongoing, and futural, even if under a certain erasure. Religion passes through a kind of crucible of critique and delimitation—and this phase of critique one could certainly associate with the death of God—but it comes out the other end. Discursively, rhetorically, logically, the notion of the death of God suggests a finality and mortality that is too simple, too decisive. In the 1960s Derrida said, "I do not believe in the simple death of anything." He was talking in that context about the death of the book. For him, the dead have a specific way of living on. And then, of course, *Specters of Marx* is a hauntology, the logic of the specters that haunt us—not only Marx himself, but justice and the democracy to come, which are neither alive nor dead, neither being nor nonbeing. So, it's just when we say that something is dead that it is not dead, that it is continuing to haunt us. In the end, for me, I speak of the death of God in a restricted sense, in the sense of a critique of ontotheology, of the God of metaphysics, and, in particular, the God of sovereignty and power and omnipotence. But then I move on because for me to speak of the death of God in any final sense would be to speak of "the death of desire" or "the death of love" or "the death of affirmation." Now, of course, we must always and endlessly criticize the idols of ontotheology, endlessly practice a certain death of God, but always as part of a pact with a more open-ended project. In this regard, Anselm's description of God as that than which there is nothing greater is helpful here because this is an interestingly "autodeconstructive" notion: whatever it is that you say that God is, God is more. The very constitution of the idea is to deconstitute any such constitution. And that's built right into the idea. The very formula that describes God is that there is no formula with which God can be described.

I will always practice a certain strategic death of God theology, the death of some determinant idol, above all that of power. God should be undergoing a continual death in that sense. But it seems to me more productive and fruitful to think of God as the object of affirmation and desire. Then the question is not whether there is a God—no more than there is a question about whether there is desire—but the question is the one that Derrida picks out of Augustine's *Confessions*: "What do I love when I love my God?" God is the name—an endlessly translatable name—of what we love and desire and of affirmation and for me the question is, what is that? What do I desire? So the "death of God" is not a notion for which I have found much use. Of course, the name of God is historical, contingent, and it may be that for the love of God, and in the name of what we desire, we will have to give up this name. I have no inside information to pass on about that. It may be that this name will wither and give way to something completely unforeseeable. That would mean that a certain death of God can be accommodated by what I am calling the affirmation of this name. For, in the end, it is not the name of God that we affirm, but something—some "event"—that is being affirmed *in* our affirmation of the name of God.

You say that you do not have much use for the talk about the death of God. The idea of the death of God, however, still seems to play a central role in the philosophy of Gianni Vattimo. I wonder if his nuanced use of the talk of the death of God might be more acceptable to your understanding. For instance, in After Christianity, *instead of simply saying that God is dead, he uses the alternative phrase, "the God who is dead." In his book with Richard Rorty called* The Future of Religion, *he ironically repeats the saying, "Thank God I'm an atheist." And in our discussion with him for the present volume he discusses the important relation between weak ontology and the death of God when he says that there are "no longer any strong reasons for being an atheist." How do you interpret the significance of these various phrases from Vattimo, both for understanding Vattimo and in relation to your own work?*

I have a great deal of use for Vattimo and an inner sympathy with what you are describing. He is one of the heroes of the current recovery of religious discourse. I take Vattimo's project to be quite similar to mine: to radicalize the hermeneutic adventure, to push it to its extreme, and to do so in dialogue with Christianity. I also have great admiration for the thematic of "weakness" that he has almost single-handedly placed in the center of postmodernist philosophical discourse. Vattimo, along with Benjamin and Derrida—and Saint Paul—is one of the background figures in my own talk about the weakness of God and weak theology, and of my critique of the God of sovereign power, not to mention the power of the Vatican or of evangelical Christianity here in the United States. Even culturally, we have traversed a similar arc, from an ardent Catholicism in our early years, through Heidegger's critique of modernity and posing of the task of overcoming metaphysics, to a retrieval of our Christian beginnings in a postmodern mode. So we are united by far more than we are divided.

But, on one point at least, Vattimo is a good example of what concerns me. What I am uncomfortable with in his thought is tied up precisely with his recourse to the schema of the death of God. The matter is complicated, and I am being too simple here, but my reservation is this. To begin with, this schema unduly privileges Christianity and sets a trap for Judaism. It unavoidably casts Judaism as the religion of the Father, of alienation and the master/slave relationship, claiming that the substance of the Father must be transferred, transcribed, and emptied (*kenosis*) into the Son and finally the Spirit of Christianity, which is the plane of immanence, incarnation, homecoming, and love. It is not an accident that death of God theologies tend to be Christian, for they turn on an interpretation of the Incarnation and the Trinity, and they see history as this Big Story of Christianity's unfolding in time. For a weak thinking, this is very strong stuff. And, for a hermeneutics trying to be radical, this is to fail to uproot a fundamentally Gadamerian schema that takes the history of Being (weakening) or nihilism (the death of the old God) as at bottom the ongoing historical "application" of the deep truth of the "classic," which here is Christianity. Vattimo's hermeneutics lacks one thing that is necessary, the more radical idea of what Derrida calls the *khora*, according to which an inherited tradition like Christianity is more pitilessly historicized. Like all death of God schemata, it sees history through a rearview mirror; it looks back to the God who has come down to earth and is now transcribed into the pages of history. The name of God is the name of something that is behind us, and history is the process by which something that is behind us is now transcribed, applied, and transferred into time. The future is to become what we already are: a kind of realization or application, not a radical movement forward, a recollection, not a repetition forward. On my schema, which is a schema of desire and affirmation of the event that is harbored in the name of God, God is in front of us as the name of something that we desire with a desire behind desire, the name of an absolutely open-ended future, of an "event" that simmers as a certain "perhaps." Let me be clear. I do accept the critique of idolatry, above all the critique of sovereignty and omnipotence, implied by the idea of the "death of God." I accept its critique of two worlds, what Altizer calls the Gnosticism that has managed to cling to two thousand years of Christianity, and I too go back to Tillich in this regard. But I reject the periodization implicit in this schema (it has turned out to be a terrible sociological prediction, at least here in the United States). I reject the privileging of Christianity in which it is implicated. And I reject the way it puts the idea of God behind us. For me, the name of God is the name of an open-ended and unforeseeable future. For me, the work of theology is not a matter of transcription and application but a matter of prayers and tears, praying and weeping over what is to come.

Shifting directions a bit, I wanted to give you some opportunity to reflect on the political dimensions and the present global crisis we're facing in the world today and how your ideas about religion without religion relate to things like fundamentalism and terrorism. In your book, On Religion, *while explaining your notion of a religion without religion, you write that "the problem with religion is religious people" and, correlatively, you define fundamentalism as "religion gone mad." How would you expand this diagnosis when it comes to the present global threat of various forms of religious fundamentalism, the problem of religion and violence, and the continuing threat of terrorism? I realize that I'm asking a very big question, but please do with it what you will.*

Religion cannot wash its hands of this violence. Whenever historically constituted constructions take themselves to have ahistorical validity, to have dropped from the sky, then, from a theoretical point of view, that provides a basis for violence; it lends violence the hand of theory. Violence ensues for all sorts of reasons, but then religion itself is enlisted in its service and asked to make it plausible. If one adopted the deconstructive approach to religion that I'm advocating, you would neither fly aircraft into the side of tall buildings nor would you have launched this unjust war in Iraq; you would live in fear and trembling about the things that you believe and keep your fingers crossed that your beliefs will not harm anyone. The infinite resonance of the name of God also implies the violence of God—that so much violence can be perpetrated in the name of God. It's the flip side of the coin. Religion is so profound, it deals with matters of such gravity, that it is equally capable of radical violence and radical peace, and you cannot decontaminate it of this violence. In all of this violence there is a genuine passion. It's not precisely passion that we need to worry about, it's passion gone awry or passion gone mad. Fundamentalism is very difficult for me to understand because it really does seem to me to be perfectly crazy. [*Laughter*] You have to wonder how people can let things like that get inside their heads. It is a testimony to religion's depth or power that it's capable of this sort of extremism, but it is the perfect example of treating something that is inherently deconstructible as undeconstructible.

That being said, there are many other dimensions in politics in which religion is just simply drawn into the fire or used as a screen behind which other interests hide. Politics has to do with economic issues and ethnic issues and a lot of other things. I think, for example—take the example of Northern Ireland— there aren't very many theological issues at issue between those two sides. Catholicism and Protestantism are just flags for more entrenched rivalries, deeper conflicts, and older hatreds. What is truly interesting there is that, insofar as that conflict has begun to subside, what's winning the war—or winning the peace, I should say—is capitalism! That is, the folks in Northern Ireland are beginning to realize that they could make a lot more money if they stopped killing each other, because the bombings discourage tourism! The economy in the Republic of Ireland in the last twenty five years or so—the Celtic tiger—has boomed, and Northern Ireland has not failed to notice this. And so the sheer power of capitalism, the enormous success of Ireland as a booming national economy, has begun to silence the bombs in Belfast, which is now beginning its own economic renaissance. That does not mean that Catholicism has won the day. On the contrary, the once deeply Catholic Republic of Ireland is beginning to shed its Catholicism. There's actually a shortage of priests in Ireland; the Republic of Ireland is secularizing rapidly, and traditional Irish Catholicism is in crisis. What appeared to be a religious conflict was not just a religious conflict by any means, and it's being resolved in a completely unforeseen way by economic forces.

And yet fundamentalism is perfectly alive and well in the capitalistic United States.

That is astonishing, isn't it? If you've come to me for an explanation of that, you've come to the wrong person.

That's depressing . . . [Laughter] What, if anything, does that have to do with resurgent interest in religion and theology by contemporary philosophers? Are these two phenomena connected in any way?

They are parallel to one another, but one is on the left side of the center and the other on the right. The intellectuals, who are on the left, in a certain way, have caught up to the man on the street, who is on the right. Secularism and the death of God are phenomena known only in academic circles. Its academic theorists actually made the cover of *Time* magazine many years ago, but they have long since been forgotten, and there is no chance they will resurface again any time soon. People who do the sociology of religions, as you well know, will tell you that the only population group in which this extreme secularism is really widespread—even endemic—is academic culture. Virtually the rest of the population is very enthusiastic about religion. That's certainly true in the United States, and there is some evidence to show that it's actually true of Western Europe too. In Western Europe, as in the United States, you have a certain kind of disenchantment with organized religion, but not disenchantment with all religious practices or new age religion or spirituality. That's not just California. God never went away in the general population, and, in a certain sense, the intellectuals have finally caught up with this. In Wittgensteinian terms they have come to realize that God is an irreducible form of discourse. Religious discourse is an irreducible way we have of speaking and thinking about our lives, one of the irreducible ways in which we understand ourselves.

So intellectuals have two things to do. As the representatives of the left, they have the negative duty to criticize fundamentalist religion, which is a right-wing and reactionary movement, but they also have a corresponding positive duty to understand what is being affirmed in religion. Evidently, religion is not going to go away. That is the importance of thinkers like Wittgenstein, Heidegger, and Derrida, all of whom have important things to say about what is going on in language and hence in religious discourse. So if, in a sense, the intellectuals have finally caught up to ordinary people, still there's all the difference in the world between the intellectuals who understand these things with a kind of ironic distance and a more naive religious faith. I am fascinated by Derrida's recovery of the *Confessions* of Saint Augustine, but Derrida talks about Saint Augustine with a distance; he hardly identifies with Augustine. Nor do I. While I love the *Confessions*, there's not a lot in the *City of God* that I accept. *The City of God* represents a good deal of what is wrong with Western Christianity—for instance, the attitude toward sexuality and the body, the dichotomy of time and eternity, the distinction between this world and the next world. But there is no ironic distance in the religious faith of the fundamentalists. Their faith is direct, nonironic, and reactionary. And my own take on that is twofold. 1. They know something that the intellectuals have forgotten; they affirm something that we must understand. 2. At the same time, their faith is reactionary; it has been stampeded into a literalist extreme by the deracinating effects of modern technology and global capitalism. Their beliefs and practices are dangerous and uncritical and hence this allows their religion to be manipulated for nationalistic purposes, held captive by the worst forces, forces that contradict everything that Jesus and the prophets stand for.

Granted that, though, is it fair to say that, even if it's a perverse or dangerous form of it, is it a kind of form of the affirmation and desire you had talked about earlier?

Yes, certainly. That is its ambiguity; that is the aporia. I do not claim millions of devout practicing Christians or Muslims have not seized upon something authentic. It's religion! It's religion good and bad, for better and worse, and it is not all bad. That's why in *On Religion* I did that analysis of one of my favorite movies in this regard, Robert Duval's *The Apostle*, which I think is a marvelous account of the tossing and turning about of a genuine religious passion in an evangelical congregation. One of the more striking features of that film was the way it treated race. The Apostle E. F.'s congregation was largely black, and his evangelical passion erased that racial divide and made them all brothers and sisters. It was genuine, it was real religious passion. E. F. was also conflicted in the Pauline sense, "Doing the things I will not and willing the things I do not."

Of course, it was a little bit of an artifact because it prescinded from larger political questions, which never got into that film. It was just a portrait of an individual soul, like the *Confessions*. And it was a powerful, beautiful portrait of biblical passion. One image that really struck me from that movie was the scene in which E. F. lays the Book down in front of the racist figure played by Billy Bob Thornton, which just stops that big John Deere machine in its tracks. As a Catholic viewer, I don't quite have that thing about a book, The Book. It's very powerful scene, and who am I to say that what's being portrayed there is not real, not authentic, and not profound? It is. But when reading becomes literalism and when literalism becomes a politics, it becomes dangerous. When we cease to understand the contingency of our traditions vis-à-vis competing traditions, they become dangerous. Now the thing is, one could ask, and I always ask myself this—is it possible to inhabit a construction, understanding that it's a construction? Can you inhabit a tradition with ironic distance?

You can, I think. I think Derrida must have done something like that, right?

Something like that, although he says he rightly passes for an atheist, so his inhabiting was even more ironic than the believer's.

But I think that his formula "rightly passing for" is a good one for everybody, including believers. It builds the distance and the irony into the belief, which is what I treasure in it.

On the other hand, I don't think someone like Martin Luther King Jr. understood his Christianity as contingent.

King's affirmation of justice was unconditional. But we would have had to ask him whether the Christian and biblical formulations he gave to this affirmation were equally unconditional. I also wonder if Bonhoeffer's idea of a religionless Christianity may not have implied this sense of contingency. But that is something that you may know more about than I.

Perhaps. He certainly saw a certain phase of Christianity coming to an end, but that was also its recovery and rehabilitation, to use the word you used before. It seems that so long as you live with the contingency and the irony at the front of your consciousness—it seems to me that the possibilities of genuine political applicability are weakened.

Well, then, maybe instead of being held in the front of your consciousness, they need to be in the back of your mind. Maybe the name or the construction is in the front of our mind but the event is in the back. In any case, we need to distinguish the construction and the event. The name is the historically inherited form of life, what is handed down to us by the tradition. Then there is what is astir within this name, its inner energy or life, what I am calling the *event* within it. But my only means of access to it is in the construction that I've inherited. To that extent, that construction is very precious and needs to be preserved. Without the institutions of the West, we would not have preserved the memory of Jesus. That's why I said to you before that I wouldn't want to go the way of individualism versus community, because communities preserve traditions and they pass on memories. One way to put it is to say that I am trying to conceive of an absolute passion about something that's relative, that is, historically constituted. Kierkegaard tried to sort out an absolute passion for the absolute from a relative passion for the relative. In my Danish version of deconstruction I would rather speak of the affirmation of something unconditional, the event, that is always presenting itself under one condition or another, the construction.

By the unconditional I do not mean some supersensible being *up above*—that's what I share with death of God theology—but the event that stirs *within* the relative and contingent things around us. So I imagine a more porous situation in which we expend an absolute passion on what we know is relative or, more precisely, in which we affirm unconditionally the event that is always being given some relative conditioned expression. You always have to do with what you've inherited, your tradition and language. I know I'm white and male and a Christian and I know the situation in which I find myself, which provides me with my resources and my limits. I concede that, if I were born somewhere else in some other time, I would believe different things. But there's something that is soliciting me, something that is promised to me, something that provokes me, in what my traditions have handed down, about which I feel an unconditional response, to which I'm unconditionally committed. But the unconditional commitment is to something that is going on *in* the tradition, something that is happening, which I am calling the event, in the conditional structure. As Deleuze says, the event is not what happens but what is going on *in* what happens.

This idea of an absolute passion for the relative, it seems to me that's the definition of deconstruction. That deconstruction isn't something that happens from the zap of a deconstruction gun. Instead, you enter into something fully and, in doing that, you take it beyond its own limits or expose it to its own limitations.

Exactly. And it—this particular, inherited form of life—bursts under the strain of the unconditional event and is forced to reinvent itself anew. That is deconstruction in a nutshell. I'll have to add another chapter. [*Laughter*]

All right, to conclude with a wildly speculative question, in order to let you dream for a little bit: What do you believe the future holds for religion in general and Christianity in particular?

While I am eager to speak about the "to come" and the "promise," I am loathe to make predictions. The true future for me is the unforeseeable. The predictions of the death of God back in the sixties, like the positivist predictions of the nineteenth century that religion was coming to an end or the Marxist and Freudian critiques of the future of an illusion—all of those things have taught us to stop saying "God is dead" when that means "religion is over." Religious discourse, for the moment, seems to be an irreducible resource in our world. I don't see that either intellectuals or people of action will be able to do without it for the foreseeable future. It may be that it will dissipate. It may be that technology will so totally transform our existence in a hundred years or a thousand years that such things will be unrecognizable. And this kind of discourse will have evaporated. That could happen, but I must confess that I don't see that happening. Of course, that's exactly what one means by the absolute future: precisely what you don't see happening. So it could happen! I cannot imagine a future without religious discourse *and*, at the same time, that is what the absolute future means. Take the example of my own tradition. The Vatican is reassured that, despite the downward trend in vocations in Western Europe and the United States, vocations are flourishing in Africa and in Latin America. In the Western democracies it is in trouble, but, worldwide, Catholicism is doing fine. So, if your question means, do I think religion and Christianty have a future, then I say I cannot imagine an alternative. But was that your question? Or was your question, "what would the future look like?"

What would the future . . . how will they be transformed?

Well then, if we are not to succumb to pessimism, we need to dream, to release the deconstructive power of the "to come," which is the affirmative energy of deconstruction. We need to dream of a Christianity in which women will be recognized as equal members of the mystical body of Christ and in which the destructive effects of the neo-Platonism that crept into the tradition will dissipate. Christianity's dark views of sexuality and its reactionary views about the invention of new forms of marriage and the procreation of children, and about the reinvention of the meaning of marriage and of motherhood—these are radically reactionary views that, we can dream, will dissipate. We can dream of a truly non-Gnostic, nondualistic form of Christianity, which has abandoned the old idea of two worlds, which is not in flight from the body and incarnation, which will make itself into another way to affirm the world, the plane of immanence. We can dream of the Kingdom of God on earth, which means including those who are out—out of our power and out of luck—so that the real economic order would begin to reflect the sort of systematic reversals that define the Kingdom. Who belongs to the Kingdom? Precisely the ones who aren't invited to the banquet or to the wedding feast. The Kingdom is marked throughout by these radical reversals and privileging of the deprivileged.

To bring it all to a head, let us say that the greatest commentary on Christianity for me has been, ever since I first read it, the "Legend of the Grand Inquisitor." If Jesus came back, we would arrest him for meddling with the work of the Church. Jesus is powerless and he is denounced for interfering with the work of the Church, which is now correcting the mistakes made by Jesus, and, at the end of a long discourse, throughout which

Jesus is completely silent, he disarms the Grand Inquisitor with a kiss.

To me, it seems the great genius of Dostoyevsky there is that we are made to sympathize with the Grand Inquisitor. After all, Jesus is being arrested in a prison for all the right reasons.

That suggestion would make for an excellent discussion. What I am thinking about in saying this is not so much the question of bread and freedom but the parable of power. What is so much more compelling about Jesus than about institutional, ecclesiastical Christianity, Catholic or Protestant, is the figure of someone who was crucified not as part of a grand divine design but unjustly and against his will, and if he returns we would crucify him again for meddling in the affairs of the Church. The Christianity to come would recall the figure of a Jesus who is powerless and whose claim on us is unconditional even though he has no power. That is the event that stirs within the name of Jesus.

III

The Death of God

An Afterword

GABRIEL VAHANIAN

I A Maker of Words

As both a figure of speech and a method of interpretation, the death of God and deconstruction each equally burdens and un-burdens itself upon the other. Like two hands, they extend the body, and it is no longer the same again. Like the two lips of a mouth, they open the body to the call of language, embody-ing that word by which they are embodied. World without end. Word without end. And they are also like the two extreme panels of a triptych folded over its central one, covering and uncover-ing it. Or, again, they are like a TV screen—and, come to think of it, doesn't a triptych "act" like a screen, which it somehow anticipates, though in a manner similar to a car moving forward while its wheels turn backwards? But then, what do either the death of God or deconstruction *actually* show?

Language *shows*, and what it shows is only what folds in it, hides in it: words held on a leash and yet capable of unleashing language itself. Language is not this or that, but only happens or *works*. It works when, caught up in the web of words, it *de-mon-strates* what precisely it seems to demonstrate. It lies in the use of words, not in their magic. It points to the moon, or to God, and, like a fool, you're looking at the finger as though the moon were expelled from the horizon of language. Both construing and deconstructing itself, language has no beginning in and of itself and no end, either. It is as recusant of the idol as it is propitious to God, so far as God and idol can be kept apart, or at least so far as God is not caught in a name as in a lasso. A name as such is no event: that's why God has no name and, if not by antiphrasis, is not seldom referred to by way of a periphrasis—such as kingdom of God or ultimacy (Caputo) or church and intimacy (Vattimo). Only as a matter of words is God an event of language. So is silence, let alone its would-be deconstructive final vocabulary, the death of God. As Augustine says, we speak not in order to say something, but in order not to say nothing.

Deconstruction cannot be critical of Egypt and of Canaan without being critical of Israel; it cannot be critical of the religious metaphysics of presence without being critical of the death of its God. As Rorty would say, after the death of God we have no God's eye view of things any more than we seemed to previously—or think we do "after Christianity." Or, as Vattimo reminds us, the end of metaphysics has liquidated the philosophical basis for atheism. Call it deconstruction or by any other name, it must begin with itself, with an analysis of its own backyard, with a critique of its own background analysis.[1] Deconstruction cannot subvert God unless it also subverts itself together with the very idea of the death of God, a figure of speech after all more consonant with the presuppositions of a God taken for granted than with those of a world that can only take itself for granted and, serpentlike, bites its tail. Deconstruction is a matter of words—Derrida keeps reminding us—words that you don't find in nature or (if truth be told) in history. Only in language. In the light of which, your God being for me only an idol, mine, as soon as worshipped, by the same token, becomes one too.

Nietzsche is seldom wrong: like *God*, every other periphrasis of *God*—*kingdom of God* or *death of God*—is equally an event of language, though now only a fool can proclaim it. Having declassified the eventfulness of God, the fool shaves the name of God down to sheer facticity, or does he really? Nietzsche should know, shouldn't he? There are no facts, only words. Of which, like it or not, God once was the event, a word event, as naturally or historically valid as it would be were it only miraculously validated. Israel's liberation from Egypt is likewise a word event or else why would it take a miracle for them to cross the Red Sea? And why does it make no difference whether the oppressor is Egyptian or not—or whoever among one's own rulers identifies with the powers that be?

II   "God Spoken Here"

Yes, deconstruction deals with myths and fictions. Not with facts: facts are stubborn, they are two-faced. And deconstruction, never oblivious of its own ambivalence, must cope with a word and its inkling of a *God* that continues to figure in the dictionary as if nowhere. A dictionary is a mausoleum. Or an empty tomb—depending on the language, and, then, even that depends on the truth one stumbles on, a worn-out evidence or a new thing out of the clear blue sky of which one couldn't hear had it not been unheard of. Call it kingdom of God. Or death of God. The human ear is only receptive to periphrastic truth—a truth that is not always theologically correct.

From the patripassians of early Christianity to Luther and down to Hegel by way of Jean Paul, no one stumbled on a truth like that as did Nietzsche. A truth far from the theologically correct and no less, either, from the philosophically correct, not to mention today's harlot queen of the sciences, the sociologically correct, which ever since its inception has had no respite till it en-shrined in the Sacred what remained of God, dead or otherwise.

Nietzsche says three things about the death of God: 1. We killed him; 2. Things used to be that way, now they are this way; 3. All that is left after so many centuries of Christian theory is the Bible—and you can think of it as Beckett's Gogo and Didi do in *Waiting for Godot* when all that Gogo remembers of the Word of God are the maps of the Holy Land and the pale blue color of the Dead Sea he wished he were swimming in—not ex-actly an inkling of baptismal desire, but so what? How else could anyone deprived of language and reduced to the neotenic status of human beings not yet even biologically humanized, let alone existentially spoken for in and through language? Gogo can only remember the Dead Sea, as does Nietzsche, who remembers a dead book. A tomb. Or does he? Could this book possibly also stand for an empty tomb?

1. Vattimo and Caputo are right: there is something Christian and perhaps rather Jewish about the death of God (which affects the order of things), even as there is something Greek about dy-ing and rising Gods (which is indifferent to the nature of things). Amalgamating these two types of God, on the one hand, Chris-tianity further desacralizes Greek religion and thus accounts for a process which had already been initiated by Greek thought, as Augustine will retrospectively aver. On the other hand, Christi-anity further secularizes Jewish religion and thus remains within the orbit of the prophets' vision of a new world consonant with their condemnation of Israel's election as a national privilege rather than as a universal obligation. And yet the Jewish peri-phrastic God differs with idols that bear a name and would not qualify as idols were it not for that name. If idols are quasi gods, by contrast God is not God in name only or by sole refraction of a name, either, as seems to be the case with the many gods of the Greek mind that refract the oneness of God. Combining both

trends, Christianity is compelled to assert or confess that no sooner is God worshipped than this very God becomes an idol. There is "no other God," whether before or, for that matter, after God, before or after time or history or nature. God is not above and beyond time but strikes us with its timing, its *kairos*. In other words, the timing of that which, lasting forever, can and does only last once for all. Call it kingdom of God, which is all the more singular for being universal and all the more universal for being singular. Or call it word become flesh, a wording of God in and through the most local of all human-all-too-human idioms, through which being human is the task of a human being called to, spoken for, being neither the first nor the last, neither first Greek nor last Jew, and much less "man par excellence," but man *tout court*—eventuating in that language which, turning dogma into poetry, turns lips into words. Into event.

We don't always hear it (we don't always hear a tree falling in the middle of the forest either). But that's no reason to applaud with only one hand, only with half a brain, or altogether refrain from applauding with both hands, body and soul, flesh and spirit. With Caputo, I rejoice in his four-wheel-driven grammatological caval-cade riding in and out, processionlike, a theology of the event. For one thing, it does chase the taste of medical syrup that clings to his title, rather contrived. Like a trick which, by substituting depth of being for highest being, weakness for power, consists in dressing the wound differently, still in desperate need of healing. The so-called grace of God, pure and simple, is a matter neither of power nor of weakness; it is indifferent to both. It relies on its resilience to power and to weakness as well. And much less is its efficacy, confounding both, to be reduced to either. Caputo likes to quote Luther's *Hier stehe ich*, which, far from a stubborn matter of fact, does not even echo a matter of conviction so much as a conviction that matters regardless of either power or weakness and thus seals a matter of conscience—better still, of the unconscious suddenly coming into its own, eventuating in a language so far unheard-of, yet marking loud and clear a new dawning of the world to language, a new advent both to and of language, all previous hierarchic, authoritarian, premises to the contrary notwithstanding. We come into language as we come into the world—bare. And we come to God, or not, as we come to language. No language? No God. In the world's advent to language or of the unconscious to conscience, language, like the tower of Babel, is laid bare, so speechless it can only burst forth, at once recusant of the idol and propitious to God so far as God is no God, so far as no God is God, and God is beyond power and weakness, laying in a word as empty as a tomb on an Easter morning.

The word order that thus commands the Christian understanding of the world and its moral as well as social structure is no more theocratic than it is anarchic. Or it is both; depending on what is meant by each term, both imply that if power corrupts, as Lord Acton said, absolute power corrupts absolutely. In this respect, nothing is more anarchic than theocracy for which God is no *archè* and priesthood—or *sola scriptura* and its interpretation (pace Vattimo)—is no monopoly but an obligation that befalls all believers, especially if none pretends to being worthy of lording it over everybody else, aside from God. No God, no master—aside from a hardboiled unrepentant anarchist, even a theocrat could subscribe to this motto. No God? No master. Troeltsch hits the nail on the head when he suggests that Calvinistic theocracy is in fact a "Bibliocracy." It rests on the primacy of Scripture—not of *scripta* so much as of *scriptura*, not of that which is written but of that which is "a-writing." That is, it rests on the contingency of God's primacy or God's authority so long as God is a-wording in and through the worlding of the word become flesh. A process as symbolic as it is literal.

Nietzsche was right: it was time to bring an end to the positivism of ontotheism—that is, it was time for the death of God.

2. It used to be that way, he would also say. Now it's this way. From Galileo to Einstein by way of Darwin, Ptolemy has kept his prestige but his world has been replaced. Enchanting it, religion overshadowed the world. Disenchanted with religion, it is now the world that increasingly overshadows religion. At least during the Christian span of the West, what undeniably occurs is an entente between the religious and the secular, each enchanting the other, until the religious—failing to its own success, even spiteful—lets go of the secular. Recoiling from itself, religion, if it does not quite withdraw from the world, stops enchanting it, at least in the public square, as previously was the case. Religion increasingly becomes a private matter. So private that it might and will soon burst at the seams and pave the way for sealing an alliance with the most conservative or most fundamentalist elements in the uneasy cohesion, the uncertain coherence, of our social and political or economic and cultural goals for a sustainable world order of solidarity. In matters of religion, ours is an age of suspicion and of apocalyptic fear. Even Nietzsche's premonitions of Dionysiac fulfillment fell through the floor. The future sounds more and more like a threat rather than an adjuvant to any kind of hopeful expectation.

But, then, are we not liberated from the obsession of salvation? Are we not, especially, supposed not to take God for granted? How could God be justified by one thing and its opposite in a way that is denied to mere humans? Think of Voltaire and the Lisbon earthquake. Think of the tsunami and other Katrinas. Do we blame them on God's wrath? on God's superfluousness? By whose authority do such events occur? By none other than that of a language at once propitious to God and allergic to the idol; you can bend language your way some of the time, but not all of the time. Language is a continental divide between our past and our future. And that is why deconstruction, which is a matter of language, applies to the death of God itself before it does to God or the idol—not to the past metaphysics and its forgetfulness of Being so much as to the present and its forgetfulness of the Word. It applies not only to God but also to the world. Secularization, as we shall see, is the misbegotten Achilles' heel of Western thought in general. It is, more significantly, the unwanted offspring of meretricious theological theorizing turned sour.

Honestly put, it is because we pried the religious and the secular loose from each other and—Hegel notwithstanding, who blames it on the various guardians of the temple and, at that, was far from wrong—it is because we kept them apart that we killed God. A discrepancy between God and the world and an increasingly gaping hiatus between them: isn't that what Nietzsche is excoriating, given on the one hand what tools of grammar, what hoping against hope he can salvage from the wreckage of Christian Western rhetoric and, on the other hand, given the sudden outburst of a secret no Christian theorizing can withhold any longer and hide from the sight and hearing of the public square: "God is dead!" But is that a dead end? Unbeknownst to its specialists and other pallbearers, hasn't indeed the Bible, miraculously fallen in the public domain, taken away from its official interpreters and entrusted to whomever, having eyes to read, can read and in whose eyes, Scripture unfolding itself into new scripture, it interprets itself, deconstructing a future to which it would otherwise be fated as well as a past by which it would inevitably be obsessed? Luther: at once sinful and justified, a believer is likewise the perfectly free lord of all, subject to none, and the most dutiful servant, subject to all. Subversive? No less than the Bible, which defying—as well as standing up to—itself, from one challenge to "it is written" runs to another and still another challenge.

To wit: Neither Judaism nor Christianity is a religion of the Book (or merely a religion of salvation in expectation of a fenced-in paradise). Of the Word, yes. Of God's being this or

that, no. God speaks, and the thing happens—the world is beautiful and outside of it there is no salvation (Camus), and Adam
and Eve are spoken for one another. Immanent or transcendent,
the world hangs on a word, literally and figuratively, not on an
abstract God but, instead, on wording God through no other
words than of this world's koine, through which alone is "God
spoken here."

God is no God without the world, but the world is not God.
God is love, but love is not divine either: it's too good a thing
to be mostly enjoyed by characters, however divine, acting
by proxy. And because God is word, one and the same thing
amounts to saying either that love is God or that God is love
spread throughout the worlding of the word. But, either way,
throughout the Bible you're kept wondering what it's all about.
Doesn't God seem more concerned about the Garden of Eden
than about the world of which this garden is supposed to be em-
blematic? And, indeed, it does seem that God is more concerned
about the former, but only because God is, so to speak, concerned not with a haphazard order of things but with their real
word order, symbolic as well as literal. Take Cain: by murdering
his brother Abel he screens off this word order from the order of
the world, of the Sacred; he deafens the world to the primacy of
the word, of the Holy. Why does God prefer one offering over
another? Because even, and above all, love is a matter of words
(far beyond even the slogan "Make love, not war!" Unless you
make love with words, the neotenic sacred beast is still slumber-
ing in you.)

3. God is a matter of words. So also is deconstruction a matter of language. Concepts come and go. Language hangs on its
ability to transfer one tongue into another, transfer what's not
transferable, namely, its secret, what holds it together as well as
what is held together. Granted, the death of God is the secret of
ontotheism. What task then befalls deconstruction has to do with

the transfer of this secret, of the language, not the ontotheism of a concept summed up as (the death of) God—as seems to be suggested by shifting gears from power to weakness. What needs to be deconstructed is this phenomenon of the death of God, rather than the ontotheism of which it bears the secret. And then, even more ironic, what is at stake in the death of God is not a concept (of God or of no God), but at stake is theology, a language neither dreading the absence of God nor dreaded by the presence of God, those two parameters of God as traditionally conceived. Indeed, whether present or absent, God is wholly other. And it is a sense of this radical otherness, of its emancipating fragrance, that one feels, as already pointed out, upon coming to terms with Caputo's ultimacy or Vattimo's intimacy. They engage the twin dimensions of a human being eventuating in, or spoken for, being human, yet neither angel nor beast and (Pascal be thanked again) for reasons of the heart reason knows nothing of.

For a while the death of God posed as the horizon of theology. Some horizon! Fogged in from the start, it turns out to be even foggier than the debonair supernatural horizon it chased away. It taught us, at least some of us, one thing: you do theology not against the background of the death of God but in spite of it, i.e., by not domesticating it and not forgetting that no one uses language with impunity any more than one can see God and live.

After Auschwitz and Hiroshima, the question was, "How can you speak of God?" In contrast, 9/11 tears us apart and drives one world against another, and on both sides, in both camps, we do nothing but speak of God. Unable to justify ourselves, we try to justify God by further tearing the world apart as though it were not enough for it just to be beautiful by itself and for us to enjoy it, so precarious a world as it is, if only because it is contingent upon a word order even as God is upon a world created ex nihilo, i.e., once for all, out of no thing that comes before. And so also is the trinitarian conception of God, were it not for its contamination by a quest for some totalitarian universalism summed up in theodicy, which, however entertaining, is but a lateral excursion on the ontotheistic trip, a trip forgetful of the word even more than of Being—or of the corruption of power in the hands of power and its confusion with authority. Power is one thing, authority is another. Of power, you're on one side or the other. It divides. Authority is all encompassing: it rests on dissent as much as on consent. Delegated to so-called authorities, it is then no less but no more than delegated power and merely administrative, limited, as stipulated by John Cotton. Like anyone of that American period, with feet on the ground, Cotton knew that it is natural for administrations to perpetuate themselves. Above and beyond all else, they were accountable to the word (of God), not even to the powers that be. Not to sacralize power but to power secularized in view of hallowing the name of God, the word event of which this world is the worlding. The Holy Commonwealth consists neither in sacralizing its own decrees nor the religion on which it is weaned, let alone God, whose holiness it does not confuse with the Sacred—today elevated to the rank of the hermeneutic principle of the death of God.

No wonder, in spite of Gramsci's definition of religion as the most gigantic utopia ever to appear in history, as though orphaned by the death of God, religion is today identified with the Sacred. Worse still, it is merely an administration of it. I confess my surprise at the extent to which, in otherwise magnificent contributions to this book, both Caputo and Vattimo have been enticed by and have succumbed to the siren calls of the Sacred, an ersatz of God, an illusion of religion, a sociologists' dream of talking about God without talking about God or of the world's radical immanence by pulling the rug from under it. The profane, says Eliade, is that which is not sacred and, conversely, the Sacred is that which is not profane. It attaches to things or, for that matter, to beings. The Holy qualifies relations of the human to the divine, of this to that, and subverts all objectification of sacralized entities and what they stand for (as in the parable of the Good Samaritan). The Western dialectic of God and the world has developed on the pattern of the religious (the holy) and the secular and its subversion of the dichotomy of the sacred and the profane.

Worth repeating here, equally if not more cumbersome is in my view the telescoping of the sacred with anarchy. Caputo's "hieranarchy" has the unenviable virtue of combining a tongue twister with a conundrum. What is aimed at is a further deconstruction of teleology in view of what he calls an ateleolgy, an end without an ending, not unlike anarchy, which, at the other end of the spectrum, is the rebuttal of archy. So far so good. But is, for all that, the progressivism or the ideal of perfectibility conveyed by teleology nipped in the bud? Is not hieranarchy itself throughout pervaded with the call of perfection, however achieved? Replace teleology with progress and you have anarchy, sacred or otherwise, sharing the ideal of perfection hovering over so-called theocracy.

True, Caputo himself has a hard time swallowing such hieranarchy. This does not exonerate Vattimo of his own penchant—a weak spot—for the sacred that still lurks in his globally more positive assessment of the secular. But he too, if not more than Caputo, should remember that nothing is more hierarchically organized than the rigid dichotomy of the sacral universe of discourse against which he grows quite eloquent in other respects: he debunks an all-male priesthood and yet seems reluctant to accept the idea of the priesthood of all believers (and its implicit anarchy).

III   Worlding the Word

Let me conclude by rehearsing the following three propositions: 1. Beyond being and becoming, God as event of language; 2. The secular as worlding of the word; 3. Not because but in spite of its Christian coloration, the secular is what (a fortiori the Christian) religion and the religions have in common.

1. We are in dire need of further cleaning up our stables, especially if "after Christianity" we must not go back to business as usual. *Post mortem dei*, the event Caputo rightly keeps by turn evoking and invoking, hangs for its happening on being carried out not as a mere figure of speech but through a reconfiguration of language, even its transfiguration. Being born to the world as a human being is no event. Being human is, and that leaves no trace other than language, which is the reason that, as Augustine says, we're not human beings by nature but by grace. Being human depends on the human being's advent to language. An event is a language event in the occurrence of which, as with an academic cursus, the fulfillment is the commencement and, likewise, ultimacy coincides with intimacy. Or transcendence with immanence, such that, however, transcendence hangs on radical immanence (the world is not God) and, reciprocally, immanence on radical transcendence (God is God, though not without the world). Built is thus a dialectic the biblical tradition calls hallowing, whose two prongs (sorry if I keep flirting with one anachronism after another) are the religious and the secular, not the sacred and the profane. Why? Because rather than religion being the administration of the sacred, the religious consists in overcoming the religious and reciprocally the secular in overcoming the secular, as Amos and the prophets and Jesus remind us. Hallowing the Name or worlding the word is no sacralizing of any kind, but is even more consonant with secularizing not only religion but also the world itself so far as, on the one hand, the world is always the world of a religion, whether exclusive (theocracy) or pluralistic (anarchy) and, on the other hand, what these two options have in common is the logocratic hinge of

a language they seemingly articulate in opposite directions: In Christ there is neither Jew nor Greek, neither master nor slave, neither male nor female—neither "God" nor "man."

2. The Garden of Eden has no sacred precinct. There is no temple in the New Jerusalem. For good measure, add to this that, before Calvin was expelled from would-be theocratic Geneva, Joachim of Fiora's Age of the Spirit (in which those of the Father and of the Son eventuate) is as much theocratic as it is anarchic (so long as these terms do not run off their etymologies). In other words, the secular is treated no more only literally than the symbolic is treated only symbolically. Whether extremes meet or not, between them nothing is more symbolic than the literal (the sun still rises or sets, though the earth is no longer flat); nothing is likewise more literal than the symbolic (the Good Life need not shun the goods of life or, eucharistically speaking, real presence shun real bread *tout court*). Similarly, at least in the Christian perspective, the religious and the secular have always belonged together, each pointing to the other, as Vattimo is wont to remind us rightly—especially in the West (which is the reason it is often accused of materialism). Rather than merely changing worlds, Latin Christianity has, especially through its Anglo-Saxon metamorphoses, more and more emphatically sought to change the world. Perhaps even at the expense of the slogan "No salvation outside the Church," should there be none either outside the world. Doesn't even God—perhaps oblivious of rebuking Abraham—give his only Son, simply because "God so loved the world" (*Welt*), the secular (*Weltlich, Weltlichkeit*)?

3. I realize the ruinous impact of our sociologically inflated fascination with the sacred. Aggravated by this trend, and for lack of a renewed vision of its own legitimate acculturation, Christianity betrays its age-old involvement with the world and turns its back on the inalienable secular dimension of faith. De-

spite warnings about this secularity of its faith and the positive
balance of the process of secularization, it allows for the secular to be snatched away. Despite the fact that it had long since
turned away from the world, understood as being only worthy of
contempt, to its radical affirmation, secularism (at the expense of
secularity) will become the sole beneficiary of this process, further abetted by modernist scientism. Like blind fideism, secularism is not spared of dogmatism either. Only with the aftermath
of modernity will the secular begin to recover its erstwhile plas-
ticity in the couple it formed with the religious. Derrida himself
is eloquently sensitive to this.

Of course, though twin to the religious, historically it first
appears with the accoutrements of worldliness. But, soon trans-
figured, it will instantiate the worldhood of the world (as already
suggested by Augustine), whether by concretizing the religious
or acting, so to speak, as its unconscious. In this dyad of the religious and the secular, both result from, and are vindicated by,
the notion of a God who speaks, and whose word lies in worlding the word as well as in becoming flesh. Incarnation, no invention of the New Testament, has the same eschatological roots as
creation. Salvation is not the only aspect of incarnation. Jesus
comes proclaiming the kingdom: equally, if not more, important
is this other eschatological dimension. "Worlding the word"
tries to gather both aspects.

No, you cannot isolate a text from its context, its margins
(a book page heavily depends on its margins). Mainline theologians should lend an ear to marginal ones, though they are often
classified as heretics. The first and arch-heretic of them all was
Marcion. Comparing both testaments, he says history (read the
secular) is (at best) what both testaments have in common. In
the light of an inchoate Christian movement, Tertullian identified the secular with polytheistic paganism. But we are no less

mistaken today when we cut off the secular from the religious and let an atheistic posture of secularism unilaterally preempt the world of its genuine worldhood. Nevertheless, since Augustine the world is what, in the light of the dialectic of hallowing, Christianity has in common with the world religions. Caputo knows this. Vattimo too. Don't they tone it down? They grow eloquent in calling for overcoming religion through religions. What about the like effort at overcoming the secular through the secular? Why not? Metaphysics is what Christianity inherited from Greek antiquity and invested in its acculturation of faith and, yes, in the secularization thereof, even at the forbidding cost of the death of God. But will the scales ever fall off everyone's eyes? The secular is what Christianity has bequeathed to a world in a process of globalization, and, just for this reason, rather than being exhausted by the death of God, it faces a new challenge.

Notes

Introduction

1. See Gabriel Vahanian, *The Death of God: The Culture of Our Post-Christian Era* (New York: Braziller, 1961).

2. See Richard J. Rubenstein, *After Auschwitz: Essays in Contemporary Judaism* (New York: Macmillan, 1966).

3. See John Robinson, *Honest to God* (Philadelphia: Westminster Knox, 1972), and Harvey Cox, *The Secular City: Secularization and Urbanization in Theological Perspective* (New York: Macmillan, 1966).

4. See Thomas J. J. Altizer, *The Gospel of Christian Atheism* (Philadelphia: Westminster, 1966).

5. Sociologist of religion Richard Fenn describes this ideological crisis as follows: "The emergence of the radical death of God theology, therefore, is set within a cultural context of ideological crisis: in the absence of universals, of world-views and value-orientations, of sanctions for social arrangements, and of prototypes for individual motivations, the new theology acquires an empirical fit and significance far broader than its sources in academic theology would suggest." In "The Death of God: An Analysis of Ideological Crisis," *Review of Religious Research* 9, no. 3 (Spring 1968): 171.

6. Michael Hardt and Antonio Negri, *Empire* (Cambridge: Harvard University Press, 2000), p. 46.

7. Mark C. Taylor, *Erring: A Postmodern A/theology* (Chicago: University of Chicago Press, 1984), p. 6. In making this claim, Taylor is echoing a claim first made by Carl Raschke in *Deconstruction and Theology* (1982).

8. As the historian Hugh McLeod writes, "'Christianity' and 'Christendom' can be separated. There was Christianity for three centuries before Christendom. There are parts of the world, for instance China, where there has never been a Christendom, but where there are many millions of Christians." In Hugh Mcleod, "Introduction," in *The Decline of Christendom in Western Europe, 1750–2000*, ed. Hugh McLeod and Werner Ustorf (Cambridge: Cambridge University Press, 2003), p. 2.

9. Ibid., p. 1.

10. Elaine Pagels, *Beyond Belief: The Secret Gospel of Thomas* (New York: Random House, 2003), p. 168.

11. McCleod, "Introduction," p. 1.

12. Ibid., p. 2.

13. See Dietrich Bonhoeffer, *Letters and Papers from Prison*, ed. Eberhard Bethge (New York: Macmillan, 1972).

14. See especially William Hamilton, "Dietrich Bonhoeffer" in *Radical Theology and the Death of God*, ed. Thomas J.J. Altizer and William Hamilton (New York: Bobbs-Merrill, 1966), pp. 113–20.

15. Søren Kierkegaard, *Attack Upon Christendom* (Princeton: Princeton University Press, 1972).

16. Jack Miles, "Religion is Making a Comeback (Belief to Follow)," *New York Times Magazine* (December 7, 1997).

17. See Immanuel Kant, "What Is Enlightenment?" in *The Portable Enlightenment Reader*, ed. Isaac Kramnick (New York: Penguin, 1995).

18. See John D. Caputo, *Radical Hermeneutics: Repetition, Deconstruction, and the Hermeneutic Project* (Bloomington: Indiana University Press, 1987), and *More Radical Hermeneutics: On Not Knowing Who We Are* (Bloomington: Indiana University Press, 2000).

19. Richard Rorty, "Foreword," in Gianni Vattimo, *Nihilism and Emancipation*, ed. Santiago Zabala (New York: Columbia University Press, 2004), p. xi.

20. Vattimo, *Nihilism and Emancipation*, p. xxvi.

21. Ibid., p. 19.

22. Ibid., xxvi.

23. Caputo has acknowledged his indebtedness to Vattimo on this point. See the introduction to his forthcoming *The Weakness of God: A Theology of the Event* (Bloomington: Indiana University Press, 2006), n. 9.

24. See John D. Caputo, *The Prayers and Tears of Jacques Derrida: Religion Without Religion* (Bloomington: Indiana University Press, 1997).

25. For more about Caputo's theology of the event, see *The Weakness of God*.

26. Gianni Vattimo, *After Christianity*, trans. Luca D'Isanto (New York: Columbia University Press, 2002), p. 17.

27. See Gianni Vattimo, *Belief*, trans. Luca D'Isanto and David Webb (New York: Columbia University Press, 1999), p. 28.

28. John D. Caputo, *Demythologizing Heidegger* (Bloomington: Indiana University Press, 1993), pp. 7–8.

29. See John D. Caputo, *Against Ethics: Contributions to a Poetics of Obligation with Constant Reference to Deconstruction* (Bloomington: Indiana University Press, 1993).

30. John D. Caputo, *On Religion* (New York: Routledge, 2001), pp. 37–66. Further references will appear parenthetically in text.

31. See Vattimo, *After Christianity*, pp. 69–82.

32. Gianni Vattimo, *The Transparent Society*, trans. David Webb (Baltimore: Johns Hopkins University Press, 1992), p. 1. Further references will appear in text.

33. See Vattimo, *Belief*, pp. 80–84.

Toward a Nonreligious Christianity

Originally published in Giovanni Filoramo, Emilio Gentile, and Gianni Vattimo, *Cos'è la religione oggi?* (Pisa: ETS, 2005), pp. 43–61. Translated and edited by Jeffrey W. Robbins.

1. Erich Auerbach, *Mimesis: The Representation of Reality in Western Literature*, trans. Willard R. Trask (Princeton University Press, 2003).

2. Richard Rorty has explained very well this issue by showing that it is the linguistic turn that has led us away not only from epistemology but also from traditional metaphysics because we never understand anything except under a description, and there are no privileged descriptions. We should interpret the phrase *understanding an object* as a slightly misleading way of

describing our ability to connect old descriptions with new. "Being That Can Be Understood Is Language," in *Gadamer's Repercussions: Reconsidering Philosophical Hermeneutics*, ed. Bruce Krajewski (University of California Press: 2004), 21–29.

3. I have analyzed this problem in my *After Christianity*, trans. Luca D'Isanto (New York: Columbia University Press, 2002).

4. There are some very interesting books on the origin of interpretation available now as Kathy Eden, *Hermeneutics and the Rhetorical Tradition* (New Haven: Yale University Press, 1997); Gerald L. Bruns, *Hermeneutics: Ancient and Modern* (New Haven: Yale University Press, 1992); Gayle L. Ormiston, and Alan D. Schrift, eds., *Transforming the Hermeneutic Context: From Nietzsche to Nancy* (New York: State University of New York Press, 1990), and *The Hermeneutic Tradition: From Ast to Ricoeur* (New York: State University of New York Press, 1990).

5. Martin Heidegger, *The Phenomenology of Religious Life*, trans. Matthias Fritsch and Jennifer Anna Gosetti (Indiana University Press, 2004).

6. Benedetto Croce, "Why We Cannot Help Calling Ourselves Christians" (1942) in *My Philosophy*, trans. E.F. Carritt (New York: Collier, 1962).

7. Charles Baudelaire, *The Painter of Modern Life and Other Essays*, trans. Jonathan Mayne (London: Phaidon, 1964).

8. Editor's note: By charity, the author does not mean simply the act of almsgiving or of helping the poor. The actual word he uses is that of *caritas*, which has a broader meaning than that of charity alone. It refers to grace and love or the generosity of spirit and the act of self-giving upon which genuine charity is properly founded.

9. Giovanni Pascoli (1855–1912) was an Italian poet and classical scholar. He was the longtime chair of literature at the University of Bologna. He is best remembered for his experimental poetry, which incorporated his extensive knowledge of classical antiquity. He wrote in both Italian and Latin and also translated English poetry.

Spectral Hermeneutics

1. While points 4 and 5 are obviously of Derridean inspiration, the background for points 1–3 is found in Gilles Deleuze, *The Logic of Sense*, ed. Constantin V. Boundas, trans. Mark Lester with Charles Stivale (New

York: Columbia University Press, 1969); see especially pp. 149–50. See also Johann Baptist Metz, *Faith in History and Society*, trans. D. Smith (New York: Crossroads, 1980), pp. 109–15.

2. Slavoj Žižek, *The Fragile Absolute* (New York: Verso, 2000), pp. 118, 159.

3. Thus, instead of saying ethics, we might paraphrase what Deleuze says (*The Logic of Sense*, 149) as follows: "Either [theology] makes no sense at all, or this is what it means and has nothing else to say: not to be unworthy of what happens to us." Like Deleuze, theology, too, wants to "will the event," which means "primarily, to release its eternal truth, like the fire on which it is fed."

4. The theological character of the event is brought out by Alain Badiou who calls it a "laicized grace" or a "grace without God," which is an occurrence of a marvelous but mundane or immanent sort, not magic or supernaturalism. Think of a fortuitous visitation by something that we did not invite, the arrival of something unexpected, unforeseeable, unprogrammable, uncontrollable, and even unwarranted. We did not do anything to produce, earn, or deserve it; on the contrary, we must make ourselves worthy of it, after the fact, as it were. See Alain Badiou, *Ethics: An Essay on the Understanding of Evil*, trans. Peter Hallward (London: Verso, 2001), pp. 122–23. For Deleuze, this grace is waiting everywhere and in everything—it is just a question of realizing or actualizing it—while for Badiou the grace of the event is exceptional and it is a question, not exactly of making ourselves worthy of *whatever* happens to us, but of remaining faithful to the grace of an *exceptional* event, of allowing ourselves to be galvanized and organized and fired by the fire of the event, while laying aside the unnecessary and even cumbersome doctrine of the All. As Badiou puts it very nicely, for Deleuze, grace is all, everything is grace, which is the view of Georges Bernanos's Curé d'Ars, at the end of his famous *Diary of a Country Priest*. Everything is the will of God, whereas, for Badiou, grace is an exceptional moment, like the one that unhorsed Paul on the way to Damascus, making the story of Paul the story of his fidelity to this moment. These are two different theologies of grace. Indeed the debate between Deleuze and Badiou can be seen as that of a couple of hoary theologians arguing about grace behind seminary walls. See Alain Badiou, *Deleuze: The Clamor of Being*, trans. Louise Burchill (Minneapolis: University of Minnesota Press, 1999).

5. Deleuze is closest to Derrida, and I am closest to Deleuze, when Deleuze insists that the event is not what occurs but "something *in* that which occurs, something yet to come," which "signals" us and "waits for us and invite us in." *The Logic of Sense*, p. 148.

6. When Deleuze speaks of willing the event as willing what happens to us, which sounds like countersigning everything that happens as inevitable, he is trying to rehabilitate Nietzsche's doctrine of eternal recurrence. He would have done a lot better to follow Badiou's advice and drop the whole idea of *amor fati*, because it is only getting in the way of what he really means by willing the event. Deleuze avoids the fatalist implication only by saying that we should love not *whatever* happens, but rather the event that transpires *in* what happens, a distinction that completely transforms the Nietzschean theory to the point of near unrecognizability. See *The Logic of Sense*, p. 149,

7. "Nothing more can be said, and no more has ever been said: to become worthy of what happens to us, and thus to will and release the event, to become the offspring of one's own events, and thereby to be reborn, to have one more birth, and break with one's carnal birth—to become the offspring of one's events and not of one's actions, for the action is itself produced by the offspring of the event" (*The Logic of Sense*, pp. 149–50). Deleuze, in short, every bit as much as any evangelical Christian, wants to be "born again." And who does not? Who would not want a chance to make another start, to have one more birth, and this time around to glow with all "the splendor and magnificence of the event," with a divine splendor, having taken on a divine glow!

8. In *The Logic of Sense* the event is artfully cast as an irreducible irreality, in a certain dialogue with Husserl (pp. 96–99), or as an "absolute nature," in a surprising dialogue with Avicenna (p. 34). Either way, the event cannot be reduced to any of its mundane appearances and is allowed to circulate freely in a joyous indifference both to the existential sphere, where it is realized under the conditions of individuality, and to the logical sphere, where it is expressed under the conditions of universality.

9. That is the force of Derrida's distinction between the pure messianic that haunts the historical messianisms like a ghost. The same cause is promoted by Badiou's work of showing the Pauline proportions of the event, where "God is not partial" and the event is not restricted to a particular group specifically set apart by a privileged ethnicity, social status, or gender.

The event is available to each one in his or her singularity—there there is neither Greek nor Jew, male nor female, free man nor slave. The "universality" here is only superficially incompatible with the singularity; the singularity *is* the universality, indeed, the only possible form the universality can take, constituting what Derrida calls the "universality of singularity." For, by taking individuals in their singularity, we have subtracted not the regionalizing and particularizing characteristics of the individual, which is impossible and undesirable, but any arbitrary *privilege* attached thereto, any partiality of treatment, in order to inscribe around each one, each singularity (*tout autre*), a zone of absolute respect, just in virtue of this very singularity, which is very singular (*est tout autre*). The universality of singularity is a patch quilt universality, a rainbow coalition.

10. Jacques Derrida, *On the Name*, ed. Thomas Dutoit (Stanford: Stanford University Press, 1995).

11. For the most part, in Derrida's earlier writings theology tended to mean the very name of the transcendental signified, of everything that arrests the play of traces, even as Deleuze, in *The Logic of Sense*, could not think of things mean enough to say about theology, which seemed to him to be the very name of the Sedentary, the Reactionary, the sleepy drift of dogmatism that tries to close off the event (pp. 72–73, 103), to which a good deal of the history of theology bears witness. Only once did it hit Deleuze, in the essay on Klossowski the editors added in the appendix, that "it is our epoch"—let us say, these postmodern times in which we have discovered the potency of the event—"which has discovered theology." Deleuze was being as sassy as usual when he said this. He had in mind what he called a "structure," a "form which may be filled with beliefs," which he described thus: "Theology is the science of nonexistent entities, the manner in which these entities—divine or anti-divine, Christ or Anti-Christ—animate language and make for it this glorious body which is divided into disjunctions." (p. 281). I am taking Deleuze at his word and, without being drawn into everything that Deleuze finds in Klossowski, and I accept that text as recognition enough that theology provides a shelter for the event, a place to cultivate its force and nurture its fire.

12. In *Being and Time*, §7c, Heidegger says that potency is higher than actuality.

13. With Tillich, I displace the notion of God as a *summum ens* or an *ens omnipotens* who can intervene in the course of natural events, as super-

naturalism; but I also displace the notion of God as the Being of beings, or ground of Being as ontologism, and I locate the properly deconstructive or postmodern element of radical theology in God, or rather the event that transpires in the name of God, taken as the claim made upon us unconditionally but without force, physical or metaphysical, ontical or ontological. That might be a called a "death of God" theology but, for the reasons I give below, I take that to be a misleading description.

14. Badiou, *Ethics*, 47.

15. In a kind of postmodern analogy to Tillich's point that religion has to do with an ultimate concern, let us say here that it has to do with an irreducible or even unconditional desire, as opposed to our more proximate and quotidian desires. We cannot produce a final formulation of our desire, but that is not bad news, for it gives rise to an incessant and productive stream of provisional formulations of what we desire, which is what Tillich meant by symbolic. These formulations are cut to fit the needs of what Heidegger called the factical situation in which we find ourselves, which is why these formulations are "hermeneutical," albeit with a hermeneutics that requires radicalization. Deleuze himself touched upon one of the most famous of such formulations of our desire—the desire for a new birth—when he spoke of "becom[ing] the offspring of one's own events, and thereby to be reborn, to have one more birth, and to break with one's carnal birth" (*The Logic of Sense*, pp. 149–50). Whether he appreciates it or not, Deleuze here drifts appreciably close to Paul's theology of grace: we have put off the body of death, guilt, and transgression and made the transition to a new life, from the flesh to the Spirit, from the old creation to a new creation, from the old being to the new being, or, with a slightly postmodern twist, from the economy to the crowned anarchy of the gift, of grace.

16. To be sure, inasmuch as the "New Testament" is a vintage example of a "text," a pastiche woven from multiple authors and redactors with multiple theologies in different churches transcribed by not always neutral scribes, I am prepared to concede that this thesis is frequently enough contradicted by the opposing thesis, by a good deal of bravado about the mighty power of God.

17. It is also worth noting that the entire passage begins with a citation of Isaiah 29:14, in which the prophet has God say: "I will destroy the wisdom of the wise." If we recall that "destroy" (*apolo*) was rendered into Latin in the

vulgate by *destruere*, which was picked up by Luther in the Heidelberg dispu-
tations, who spoke of a *destructio* of pagan philosophy (Aristotle's metaphysics), which was then passed on to Heidegger, who spoke of a *Destruktion* of
the history of metaphysics, which was translated by Derrida as *déconstruction*,
then we might offer the following translation of this passage from Isaiah: "I
will deconstruct the metaphysics of presence of the philosophers, says the
Lord God." By which the sacred authors certainly meant, on my view, I will
release the event these philosophers mean to prevent. Let my events go!

18. On the orthodox telling, this death was the embodiment par excellence of divine love and divine freedom, an act of supremely free identification with the human condition, made in sacrificial payment for the sins of
the world. Like a lot of other writers today, I am not edified by the spectacle
of a bloody sacrifice made for any reason, by anybody to anybody, and I am
even less edified by the bloody sacrifice of the Divine Son to the Divine
Father. I find the very idea of blood sacrifice primitive and the idea of a
father requiring or being satisfied by such a sacrifice of his son to be morally repugnant. Of course, on my terms, this entire discourse is symbolic,
but symbols are important. One should avoid a symbolic description of the
scene of Jesus's execution rooted in an excess of patriarchal violence and a
violent masculine imaginary.

19. See Jacques Derrida, *Rogues: Two Essays on Reason*, trans. Pascale-
Anne Brault and Michael Naas (Stanford: Stanford University Press, 2005).
Derrida distinguishes the law from justice by saying that bad laws have
force but lack justice, while justice of itself has no force but lays claim to us
unconditionally. On this Derridean schema, God is more like justice than
the law. See Jacques Derrida, "The Force of Law: 'The Mystical Foundation of Authority,'" trans. Mary Quantaince, in Drucilla Cornell, Michel
Rosenfeld, and David Gray Carlson, eds., *Deconstruction and the Possibility of
Justice* (New York: Routledge, 1992), pp. 3–69.

20. Deleuze, *The Logic of Sense*, p. 148.

21. That is, of course, an almost irresistible way to imagine the event.
Still, it is possible to cooperate with the irresistible forces of imagination
without being deceived by them. That is what we call literature—the willing suspension of disbelief—or scripture, Sacred or not so sacred. But it is
in the end a mystification to treat these figures and images literally—even a
dangerous mystification—if the result is to get us in the habit of depending
upon a bail out by this divine superbeing at critical moments when things

threaten to go wrong. The name of God is the name of an unconditional claim, a call and an address, but it is not the name of a superhero, be he (*sic!*) cosmological or metereological, historical or physiological, coming over the hill in the nick of time to bail us out.

22. Mark C. Taylor, *Erring: A Postmodern A/theology* (Chicago: University of Chicago Press, 1885), p. 6.

23. This exclusivism is a tendency of monotheism itself, which is why it is necessary to offer a deconstructive reading of the "chosen people" of the sort that Levinas gives, according to whom being chosen is a structure of the ethical subject as such, not simply the Jews, where one is chosen, called upon, by the address of the other, not a sectarian God.

24. See note 13 above.

25. Gianni Vattimo, *Belief*, trans. Luca D'Isanto and David Webb (New York: Columbia University Press, 1999), p. 80.

26. I have almost found this phrase in Vattimo, who seeks "the most radical version of hermeneutical philosophy." Gianni Vattimo, *After Christianity*, trans. Luca D'Isanto (New York: Columbia University Press, 2002), p. 49. His telling of hermeneutics is more Heideggerian, mine more Derridean. He adapts Heidegger's history of Being by saying that in it Being "weakens" from "structure" to "event, " from metaphysics as delivering the *objective* structure of reality into a history of "interpretations" of Being. The strong thought of metaphysics is thinned out or attenuated into the realization that we have to do only with certain "sendings" of Being in which Being presents a certain face to us, which we "interpret."

27. Jeffrey W. Robbins, "Weak Theology," *Journal of Cultural and Religious Theory* 5, no. 2 (April 2004) (www.jcrt.org); and Ulrich Engel, O.P., "Religion and Violence: Plea for a Weak Theology *in tempore belli*," *New Blackfriars* 82 (2001): 558–60. Engel argues that, in view of the demands of religious tolerance, the great monotheisms must weaken their strong dogmatic traditions in favor of a weak and pacific theology.

28. I have also had in mind Walter Benjamin's idea of a "weak Messianic power," of a Messiah turned toward the past, the dead and forgotten, where we ourselves in the present occupy the messianic position, as the ones whom the dead were waiting for to redeem their unjust suffering. We are impotent to change the past—we cannot raise the dead from their graves—while the "messianic force" lies in the remembrance, the recollection, the thinking on that crosses over into devotion, *Andenken/Andacht*, like a prayer for

the dead whose death was violent or unjust. While we cannot alter their death, we can by recalling it find ourselves summoned to promote a more just future, so that we are responsible not only for the dead but for the future, for the children. See Walter Benjamin, "The Concept of History," no. 9, in *Walter Benjamin: Selected Writings: 1938–40*, ed. Michael Jennings (Cambridge: Belknap Press of Harvard University Press, 2003), 4:389–400. What Johann Baptist Metz—under the influence of Benjamin—called the "dangerous memories of suffering," of the unjust death of Jesus, of unjust suffering everywhere.

29. Vattimo, *After Christianity*, pp. 24, 72.

30. I don't quite understand Vattimo's one criticism of Altizer and the 1960s school—that they did not view secularization as a positive affirmation of divinity based on the Incarnation. Vattimo, *After Christianity*, p. 37.

31. Ibid., p. 23.

32. Richard Rorty and Gianni Vattimo, *The Future of Religion*, ed. Santiago Zabala (New York: Columbia University Press, 2005), p. 53.

33. Fundamentalist literalism is not only a form of intellectual suicide and a hermeneutical mistake; politically, it results in mutual intolerance and violence. The West is true to itself and true to the Gospel only insofar as it renounces imperialism and practices political hospitality, both within its own borders with regard to immigrants from the third world and in international relations. "Christianity" does not mean a particular sect but cosmopolitan political compassion and national and international hospitality.

34. Vattimo, *After Christianity*, p. 69.

35. Ibid., pp. 77–79.

36. Ibid., p. 93.

37. Jacques Derrida, *Given Time*, vol. 1: *Counterfeit Money*, trans. Peggy Kamuf (Chicago: University of Chicago Press, 1991), p. 101, n. 18.

38. Vattimo is making a consciously "Christian decision," he says, which separates him from Levinas and Derrida, who belong to "first stage" religion (of the Father). I don't see what improvement is made by saying that it would only be a "dogmatic hardening" of religion that would oppose Judaism and Christianity, as this opposition seems to me to go to the essence of the distinction between strong and weak theology: Christianity "weakens" by de-Judaizing. Vattimo, *After Christianity*, pp. 37–38.

39. Ibid., p. 37.

40. Vattimo, *Belief*, pp. 83–84.

41. Ibid., p. 84.

42. See John D. Caputo, *Radical Hermeneutics* (Bloomington: Indiana University Press, 1986), pp. 108–19 (especially 112–13).

A Prayer for Silence

1. See Gianni Vattimo, *After Christianity*, trans. Luca D'Isanto (New York: Columbia University Press, 2002), p. 17.

2. Gianni Vattimo, *Nihilism and Emancipation*, ed. Santiago Zabala, trans. William McCuaig (New York: Columbia University Press, 2004).

The Power of the Powerless

1. See Gregg Lambert, "Against Religion (Without 'Religion'): A New Rationalist Reply to John Caputo's *On Religion*," *Journal for Cultural and Religious Theory* 5, no. 2 (April 2004): 20–36. See also Caputo's response to Lambert, "Love Among the Deconstructibles: A Response to Gregg Lambert," *Journal for Cultural and Religious Theory* 5, no. 2 (April 2004): 37–57.

2. See Charles Winquist, "Postmodern Secular Theology," in *The Surface of the Deep* (Aurora, CO: Davies, 2003), pp. 199–212.

The Death of God

1. Which reminds me: the subtitle of my first book, *The Death of God*, was deliberately truncated by my editor, a noted literary critic, and changed from "a cultural analysis" to "the culture of our post-Christian era." Only later did I learn from a reputed French philosopher that *analysis*, the word expunged, is precisely the term by which ancient Greeks would have rendered what we were beginning to call deconstruction.

Index

doctrinal conformity, 94; fathers of
the church, 41; future of, 45, 95, 97;
image of, 6; metaphysical structure of,
97; politics of, 95;and secular culture,
75; and its teachings, 98; third world
churches, 95; in today's world, 101; *see
also* Weak
Christ, 7, 10, 34, 43–45, 75; death of,
90; of the gospels, 99; kiss of, 11
Christendom, 4, 34; collapse of Christendom, 3, 7, 8, 11; distinction between Christendom and Christianity,
3, 180; dream/ideal of Christendom, 6
Christianity; Christian, 18, 154; and
community, 5; consequences of,
98; core of, 91; and deconstruction,
127; and democracy, 98, 100; early
Christianity, 165; event of, 90–91, 100,
102; future of, 45, 100, 158; and global
community, 78; God of, 85; heritage
of, 100, historical relativity of, 127;
and religious triumphalism, 100; and
immanence, incarnation, love, 78; and
the Incarnation, 83, 100; as Jewish
science, 141; kenotic Christianity,
14; message of, 72; and metaphysics,
90–91, 178; and the modern world, 97,
100; and otherworldliness, 75; privileging of, 149; and reactionary views,
153–54, 159; as religion of love, 80; as
religion of the Son, 149; religionless
Christianity, 7; and secularization, 100;
and subjectivity, 32; triumphalism of,
100; truth of, 34, 77, 84, 98–99; and
weakening of the moral-metaphysical
assumptions, 44; and the West, 77–78,
170; *see also* Philosophy
Christianization, 5, 8

Christmas, 75
Civil rights, 71
Colonialism, 22
Commerce, 83–84, 105
Commodity, 21
Communism; in east Europe, 71
Community; and individualism, 156;
and tradition, 156
Constantine, 3, 6; Constantine's edict
of toleration, 4
Constitution, U.S., 77
Consumerism, 121
Contingency, 24, 84, 129
Cornell, Drucilla, 123
Cornwell, John, 101; *Breaking Faith:
The Pope, the People, and the Fate of
Catholicism*, 101
Cotton, John, 173
Covenant, 52–53
Cox, Harvey, 2, 92
Creation, 34, 49–50; mystery of, 99;
distinction between mystery of cre-
ation and creationism, 99
Creed, 6
Crisis, 2; existential spiritual crisis, 24
Croce, Benedetto, 36
Cross, 10, 62, 66, 73, 90; logos of, 62;
postmodern theology of, 66, 69
Crusades, 105
Cynicism, 120

Da Vinci Code, 99
Dalai Lama, 45, 102–3
Dante, 36
Darwin, Charles, 168
Death of God, 2, 3, 13–15, 19, 66–70,
80, 82, 89–92, 116–17, 144–50, 153,
164, 171, 172, 178; after the death of